Developing High-Frequency Trading Systems

Learn how to implement high-frequency trading from scratch with C++ or Java basics

Sebastien Donadio

Sourav Ghosh

Romain Rossier

BIRMINGHAM—MUMBAI

Developing High-Frequency Trading Systems

Copyright © 2022 Packt Publishing

Publishing Product Manager: Heramb Bhavsar
Content Development Editor: Shreya Moharir
Technical Editor: Rahul Limbachiya
Copy Editor: Safis Editing
Project Coordinator: Farheen Fathima
Proofreader: Safis Editing
Indexer: Tejal Daruwale Soni
Production Designer: Roshan Kawale
Marketing Coordinator: Priyanka Mhatre

First published: June 2022
Production reference: 1160622

Published by Packt Publishing Ltd.
Livery Place
35 Livery Street
Birmingham
B3 2PB, UK.

ISBN 978-1-80324-281-1

www.packt.com

Contributors

About the authors

Sebastien Donadio has two decades of experience in high-performance computing, software design, and financial computing. Currently an architect in the Bloomberg office of the CTO, he has a wide variety of professional experience, including serving as CTO of an FX/Crypto trading shop, head of engineering, quantitative analyst, and partner at a high-frequency trading hedge. Sebastien has taught various computer science and financial engineering courses over the past fifteen years at various academic institutions, including Columbia University, the University of Chicago, and NYU. Sebastien holds a PhD in high-performance, an MBA in finance, and an MSc in analytics from the University of Chicago. His main passion is technology, but he is also a scuba diving instructor and an experienced rock-climber.

Sourav Ghosh has worked in several proprietary high-frequency algorithmic trading firms over the last decade. He has built and deployed extremely low-latency, high-throughput automated trading systems for trading exchanges around the world, across multiple asset classes. He specializes in statistical arbitrage market-making and pairs trading strategies for the most liquid global futures contracts. He works as a vice president at a trading firm based in Sao Paulo, Brazil. He holds a master's in computer science from the University of Southern California. His areas of interest include computer architecture, FinTech, probability theory and stochastic processes, statistical learning and inference methods, and natural language processing.

Romain Rossier brings 19+ years of experience, mostly as a software architect in the financial industry, specializing in low latency, high-performance Java software design and development. He is currently the chief architect for the HCTech FX Proprietary Trading engine. He also built and led the software development team at HCTech, where he oversaw and developed the HFT platform architecture for FX, Futures, and Fixed Income. Prior to HCTech, Romain was director of the Currenex lab, where he led the team responsible for the development of the Currenex Intelligent Pricing System. Romain holds a Master of Science in Communication Systems from the Swiss Federal Institute of Technology in Lausanne.

About the reviewers

John Rizzo has applied his passion for technology and building complex computing systems in support of the financial markets throughout his career. Over the past 17 years, he has held a number of technology leadership roles, including CTO, director, and infrastructure architect at various hedge funds and other firms in the financial services industry. He started and sold a company that developed systems to help manage various aspects of the loan life cycle and the syndicated loan market. Today, he is focused on infrastructure security in Bloomberg's Office of the CTO.

Phil Vachon works on projects related to identity, authentication, and the application of data science to operational security challenges at Bloomberg. Prior to that, Phil co-founded a start-up focused on high-speed packet capture and analysis. He's also developed high-frequency trading systems, designed and implemented firmware for identity and security infrastructure devices, built synthetic aperture radar data processing tools, and worked on data plane traffic engineering for carrier routers. His main interests are developing threat models that are relevant to business problems, designing secure embedded systems, and working to improve individual privacy protections in our increasingly connected world.

Table of Contents

Preface

Part 1: Trading Strategies, Trading Systems, and Exchanges

1

Fundamentals of a High-Frequency Trading System

History of HFT	4	Tick-by-tick data and data distribution	12
The post-1930s era	5	Liquidity rebates	12
The modern era	6	Matching engine	13
		Market making	13
Why have HFT?	7	Scalping	15
What makes HFT so different		Statistical arbitrage	15
from regular trading?	7	Latency arbitrage	16
Effect of dark pools	9	Impact of news	17
		Momentum ignition	17
Who trades HFT?	10	Rebate strategies	18
What do I need to start an HFT?	10	Pinging	18
What are HFT strategies?	11	Illegal activities	19
Asset classes	12		
Liquidity	12	**Summary**	**20**

2

The Critical Components of a Trading System

Understanding the trading system	22	Gateways connecting to trading exchanges	25
Trading system architecture	24		

Making a trading system trade
with exchanges   27
Examining the API for communication   29

Order book management   30
Order book considerations   32

Strategy making decisions on
when to trade   34
The OMS   36
Critical components   36
Non-critical components   37
Command and control   37
Services   38

Summary   39

3

Understanding the Trading Exchange Dynamics

Architecting a trading
exchange for handling
orders at a large scale   42
History of trading exchanges   42
Understanding features of an exchange   43
Exchange architecture   44

General order book and
matching engine   46
Best price scenario   47
Partial fill scenario   48
No match scenario   49
Multiple orders with the same price   50

Summary   53

Part 2: How to Architect a High-Frequency Trading System

4

HFT System Foundations – From Hardware to OS

Understanding HFT computers   58
CPUs, from multi-processor to multi-core 59
Main memory or RAM   62
Shared memory   64
I/O devices   65

Using the OS for HFT systems   65
User space and kernel space   66
Process scheduling and CPU
resource management   67

Memory management   68
Paged memory and page tables   69
System calls   70
Threading   71
Interruption management   72

The role of compilers   73
Executable file formats   74
Static versus dynamic linking   74

Summary   75

5

Networking in Motion

Understanding networking in
HFT systems   78
Learning about network
conceptual models   78

Network communications
between
systems in HFT   80
Comprehending how switches work   82

Important protocol concepts   89
Using Ethernet for HFT
communication   90
Using IPv4 as a network layer   90
UDP and TCP for the transport layer   92

Designing financial protocols
for HFT exchanges   94

FIX protocol   95

Interior networks versus
exterior networks   101
Understanding the
packet life cycle   102
Comprehending the packet life in the
send/receive (TX/RX) path   104
Software layer receiving the packet   105

Monitoring the network   105
Packet capture and analysis   106

Valuing time distribution   108
Time-synchronization services   109

Summary   110

6

HFT Optimization – Architecture and Operating System

Performance mental model   112
Understanding context
switches ≣⏱   112
Types of context switches   113
Why are context switches good   114
Steps and operations involved in a
context
switch operation   115
Why are context switches bad for HFT?   116
Techniques to avoid or minimize
context switches   117

Building lock-free data
structures ≣⏱   118

When/why are locks needed
(non-HFT applications)   118
Types of synchronization mechanisms   119
Problems and inefficiencies
with using locks   119

Pre-fetching and
pre-allocating memory   127
Memory hierarchy   128
Pre-fetching based alternatives to
boost performance   131
Dynamic memory allocation   133
Pre-allocation-based alternatives to
dynamic memory allocation   134

Summary   135

7

HFT Optimization – Logging, Performance, and Networking

Comparing kernel space and user space ⏱	138
What is kernel and user space?	139
Investigating performance – kernel versus user space	140
Using kernel bypass	**141**
Understanding why kernel bypass is the alternative	142
Presenting kernel bypass latencies	142
Learning about memory-mapped files	**143**
Using cable fiber, hollow fiber, and microwave technologies 🥕	**146**

Evolution from cable fiber to hollow fiber to microwave	147
How hollow fiber works	147
How microwave works	148
Diving into logging and statistics	**150**
The need for logging in HFT	150
The need for online/live statistics computation in HFT	150
Measuring performance	**152**
Motivation for measuring performance	152
Linux tools for measuring performance	153
Custom techniques for measuring performance	156
Summary	**161**

Part 3: Implementation of a High-Frequency Trading System

8

C++ – The Quest for Microsecond Latency

C++ 14/17 memory model 🔧	**166**
What is a memory model?	166
The need for a memory model	167
The C++ 11 memory model and its rules	168
C++ memory model principles	172
Removing runtime decisions ⏱	**176**
Motivation for removing runtime decisions	177
Virtual functions	178
Performance penalties	179

Dynamic memory allocation ⏱	**184**
Runtime performance penalty	184
Using constexpr efficiently 🔧	186
Exceptions impeding performance 🔧	186
Templates reducing the runtime 🔧	**188**
What are templates?	188
Template specialization 🔧	189
Why use templates?	189

Disadvantages of templates	191	Types of static analysis	196
Performance of templates	192	Steps in static analysis	197
Standard Template Library (STL)	193	Benefits and drawbacks of static analysis	197
Static analysis	**195**	**Use case - Building an FX high-frequency trading system**	**200**
What is C++ static analysis?	195	**Summary**	**201**
The need for static analysis	195		

9

Java and JVM for Low-Latency Systems

Introducing the basics of Java	**204**	Real-time performance measures	220
Reducing the impact of the GC ⏱	**207**	**Java threading** ✦	**221**
What to do to keep GC events low and fast	208	Using a thread pool/queue with threads	222
Warming up the JVM ⏱	**213**	**High-performance task queue** ⏱	**227**
Tiered compilation in JVM	214	Queues	227
Optimizing the JVM for better startup performance	218	Circular buffer	227
		LMAX disruptor	228
Measuring the performance of a Java software	**219**	**Logging and DB access**	**230**
Why are Java microbenchmarks difficult to create?	219	External or internal thread?	231
		Summary	**232**

10

Python – Interpreted but Open to High Performance

Introducing Python	**234**	Using ctypes/CFFI to accelerate Python code	243
Making use of Python for analytics	234	SWIG	244
Why is Python slow?	236		
How do we use libraries in Python?	238	**Improving the speed of Python code in HFT**	**246**
Python and C++ for HFT	**239**	**Summary**	**248**
Using C++ in Python	240		
Using Python with C++	240		
Boost.Python library	241		

11

High-Frequency FPGA and Crypto

Reducing latencies with FPGA 🥕 250

Evolution of the fierce competition of speed in HFT	250
Introduction to FPGA	251
Diving into FPGA trading systems	254
Advantages of FPGA trading systems	256
Disadvantages of FPGA trading systems	257
Final words on FPGAs	258

Exploring HFT with cryptocurrencies 259

What is crypto?	259
How do crypto transactions work?	259

What is a blockchain?	260
What is cryptocurrency mining?	260
Similarities between traditional asset trading and cryptocurrency trading	260
Main differences between traditional asset trading and cryptocurrency trading	265
Trading with cryptocurrency exchange	267
HFT strategies in crypto	271
Building a high-frequency system for crypto trading	272
How to build a trading system in the cloud	275

Summary 280

Index

Other Books You May Enjoy

Preface

The world of trading markets is complex, but it can be made easier with technology. Sure, you know how to code, but where do you start? What programming language do you use? How do you solve the problem of latency? The *Developing High-Frequency Trading Systems* book answers all these questions.

This practical guide will help you navigate the fast-paced world of algorithmic trading and show you how to build a high-frequency trading system from complex technological components supported by accurate data.

Starting with an introduction to **high-frequency trading** (**HFT**), exchanges, and the critical components of a trading system, the book quickly moves on to the nitty-gritty of optimizing hardware and your **operating system** (**OS**) for low-latency trading, such as bypassing the kernel, memory management, and the danger of context switching. Monitoring your system's performance is vital, so you'll also get up to speed with logging and statistics.

As you move beyond the traditional high-frequency trading programming languages, such as C++ and Java, you'll learn how to use Python to achieve high-performance levels. And what book on trading would be complete without diving into cryptocurrency?

By the end of this book, you'll be ready to take on the markets with high-frequency trading systems.

Who this book is for

This book is for software engineers, quantitative developers or researchers, and DevOps engineers who want to understand the technical side of high-frequency trading systems and the optimizations needed to achieve ultra-low latency systems. Prior experience working with C++ and Java will help you grasp the topics covered in this book more easily.

What this book covers

Chapter 1, Fundamentals of a High-Frequency Trading System, gives an overview of the history of high-frequency trading. You will learn about the market participants, the fundamental HFT requirements (low latency connectivity and infrastructure), the trading time horizons in HFT versus non-HFT, and the holding periods/position management (HFT versus Ultra HFT). We will also detail HFT-specific strategies to make money.

Chapter 2, The Critical Components of a Trading System, explains in-depth how a trading system works. You will learn how the market data gets into the system, and the different functionalities needed to handle the data and send an order to the exchange.

Chapter 3, Understanding the Trading Exchange Dynamics, introduces how trading exchanges are a part of the microstructure of markets. We will start by giving the general infrastructure of an exchange, and we will talk about how the matching engine works and how the orders are matched and promoted to all the market participants.

Chapter 4, HFT System Foundations – From Hardware to OS, clarifies how the hardware and OS work together. You will have a clear understanding of the functions of the software interaction with the OS and the hardware. This chapter will go from the processor to the trading system, explaining all the layers between including the OS, networking, OS scheduler, and memory.

Chapter 5, Networking in Motion, expresses how networking benefits HFT. You will have a clear understanding of the functions of the network stack and its use when communicating between a trading system and an exchange.

Chapter 6, HFT Optimization – Architecture and Operating System, expounds on creating a HFT system from a regular trading system. This section will cover many modern techniques to achieve optimal low latency performance for HFT applications specifically. We will talk about the OS features and its scheduler, and we will do a deep dive into the kernel function of the OS.

Chapter 7, HFT Optimization – Logging, Performance, and Networking, covers a vital part of trading systems: logging and networking. You will understand how logging helps to monitor an HFT system, and we will learn how to make it efficient in a context of HFT. Finally, we will cover how to use networking to optimize communication with trading exchanges.

Chapter 8, C++ – The Quest for Microsecond Latency, defines the use of C++ in a context of an ultra-low latency system by optimizing cache, memory, and code execution. You will learn about modern C++ features and techniques to write ultra-low latency code efficiently.

Chapter 9, Java and JVM for Low-Latency Systems, details the use of Java in a context of an ultra-low latency system by optimizing garbage collection, communication, and data structure.

Chapter 10, Python – Interpreted but Open to High Performance, illustrates how to use Python in an HFT system. This chapter explains how to create and use HFT libraries in Python.

Chapter 11, High-Frequency FPGA and Crypto, depicts how to use **field programmable gate array** (**FPGA**) to create an even faster HFT system. It will introduce building an HFT system for crypto in the cloud.

To get the most out of this book

This book assumes that you are familiar with programming, hardware architecture, and OS. Because this book will discuss the optimizations required to reduce the tick-to-trade latency, it is essential to have the minimal knowledge of computer engineering.

Most of the HFT systems run with a Unix-based OS. We will recommend using a Linux OS to apply your knowledge of this book.

This book is a reservoir of knowledge from many computer engineering and finance domains. We recommend reading other *Packt* books such as the following:

- *Linux Kernel Programming* (https://www.packtpub.com/product/networking-and-servers/9781789953435)

- *Java Programming for Beginners* (https://www.packtpub.com/product/application-development/9781788296298)

- *C++ High Performance* (https://www.packtpub.com/product/programming/9781839216541)

We also recommend reading books such as *Compilers: Principles, Techniques, and Tools*, and *Computer Architecture: A Quantitative Approach*. These books will give you more in-depth knowledge of the optimization we are using for HFT.

Download the color images

We also provide a PDF file that has color images of the screenshots and diagrams used in this book. You can download it here: https://static.packt-cdn.com/downloads/9781803242811_ColorImages.pdf.

Conventions used

There are a number of text conventions used throughout this book.

`Code in text`: Indicates code words in text, database table names, folder names, filenames, file extensions, pathnames, dummy URLs, user input, and Twitter handles. Here is an example: "It offers one producer to one consumer (`OneToOneRingBuffer`) or many producers to one consumer (`ManyToOneRingBuffer`) solutions."

A block of code is set as follows:

```
/* Put header files here or function declarations like below */
extern int add_1(int n);
extern int add(int n, int m);
```

Any command-line input or output is written as follows:

```
>>> import math
>>> math.add_1(5)
6
```

Bold: Indicates a new term, an important word, or words that you see onscreen. For instance, words in menus or dialog boxes appear in **bold**. Here is an example: "The **Load Data** component (annotation **1**) will help get historical data."

> Tips or Important Notes
> Appear like this.

Get in touch

Feedback from our readers is always welcome.

General feedback: If you have questions about any aspect of this book, email us at customercare@packtpub.com and mention the book title in the subject of your message.

Errata: Although we have taken every care to ensure the accuracy of our content, mistakes do happen. If you have found a mistake in this book, we would be grateful if you would report this to us. Please visit www.packtpub.com/support/errata and fill in the form.

Piracy: If you come across any illegal copies of our works in any form on the internet, we would be grateful if you would provide us with the location address or website name. Please contact us at copyright@packt.com with a link to the material.

If you are interested in becoming an author: If there is a topic that you have expertise in and you are interested in either writing or contributing to a book, please visit authors.packtpub.com.

Share Your Thoughts

Once you've read *Developing High-Frequency Trading Systems*, we'd love to hear your thoughts! Scan the QR code below to go straight to the Amazon review page for this book and share your feedback.

https://packt.link/r/1-803-24281-7

Your review is important to us and the tech community and will help us make sure we're delivering excellent quality content.

Part 1: Trading Strategies, Trading Systems, and Exchanges

By the end of this introduction, you will have a quick overview of the history of **high-frequency trading (HFT)**. You will know about the market participants, the fundamental HFT requirements (low latency connectivity and infrastructure), the trading time horizons in HFT versus non-HFT, and the holding periods/position management (HFT versus ultra HFT). We will also talk about the places for HFT. This book is not about the business of trading or HFT; it is about how to implement an HFT system concretely by using Java, C++, and Python. You will know how a trading system works and which trading strategies you can run.

This part comprises the following chapters:

- *Chapter 1, Fundamentals of a High-Frequency Trading System*
- *Chapter 2, The Critical Components of a Trading System*
- *Chapter 3, Understanding the Trading Exchange Dynamics*

1

Fundamentals of a High-Frequency Trading System

Welcome to *Developing High-Frequency Trading Systems*!

High-Frequency Trading (**HFT**) is a form of automated trading. For the last twenty years, HFT has gained recognition in the media and in society. A book called *Flash Boys: A Wall Street Revolt*, written by Michael Lewis in 2014, topped the sales on the New York Times Best Seller list for three weeks. It relates to an investigation into the HFT industry and its impact on the trading world. Scholars, the financial world, and the non-financial world are fascinated by this form of trading. Meanwhile, this new era of trading has created a lot of fear while giving more and more control to machines.

The goal of this book is to review what HFT is and how to build such a system from a technical perspective. HFT is a multi-disciplinary matter involving thorough knowledge of computer architecture, operating systems, networking, and programming. By the end of this book, you will understand how to build a trading system from scratch by using the most advanced technical choices for optimizing speed and scalability. We chose to divide this book into three main parts.

In the first part, we'll go through how HFT tactics function and what kind of trading we may expect from HFT. Then we will go over the functions of an HFT system. We will conclude this part with a description of how a trading exchange works.

In the second part of this book, we will explain the theory of operating systems and hardware and the required knowledge to optimize a trading system, taking into account the hardware and operating system features.

The final part will explain in detail how to use C++, Java, Python, and FPGA to create an HFT system. We will also extend this knowledge to crypto trading, and we will review how to build a trading system in the cloud.

In this chapter, we will talk about how we got into HFT. We will review what kind of trading strategies work for HFT. We will explain in detail what makes HFT so different from regular trading.

Our objective in this chapter is to cover the following topics:

- History of HFT
- What HFT is
- Who the participants are
- What trading strategies work in HFT

History of HFT

Let's discuss the history of exchanges and financial markets prior to 1930.

When we talk about HFT, it is difficult to give a precise date for when it started. We need to come back to the primitive times when trade arose from human contact. Before the invention of modern-day cash, ancient people relied heavily on trading to trade products and services with one another in a gift economy. Long-distance trade extends back to almost 150,000 years ago, according to Peter Watson. Year after year, with more people, more goods, and more money, trading became one of the major activities of humankind. It is obvious that making money implies more business. One of the parameters was speed. If you make more transactions, you will make more money. Many stories describe the ambition of traders to get technologies such as better transportation to make deals more quickly or to get news more quickly to take advantage of other folks who do not have access to these new technical means.

We did not have to wait for too long before seeing cases of unfair trade involving those who have technical advantages over others. In 1790, a Georgia representative spoke to the US House of Representatives to expose high-speed traders. Indeed, Congress was debating the Secretary of the Treasury Alexander Hamilton's proposal that the US government absorb the previous debts accrued by the states during the Revolution (Funding Act of 1790). Traders who had learned the decision immediately bought or rented rapid boats. Their goal was to front-run messengers and buy the old debts since the passage of the Act would increase the market value. During the twentieth century, the idea of speed trading or HFT appeared.

The post-1930s era

Trading is the exchange of items for other items. It can be financial products, services, cash, digital assets, and more. One of the goals of trading is to make a profit from these transactions. The number of transactions will be correlated with the quantity of money generated by the exchange of assets. When we manage to increase the ratio between the number of transactions and the time, we can increase the profitability over time. Therefore, being capable of increasing the number of transactions is critical. Trading actors understood very quickly that they needed to shorten the trading time and started gathering in some specific places. They used to place their orders in these locations, which we call today the **trading exchange** (or **trading floor**). Major events participated in the expansion of fast-speed automated trading:

- **1969**: Instinet was one of the first automated system infrastructures. It speeded up the adhesion of high-speed transactions.

- **1971**: The **National Association of Securities Dealers Automated Quotations** (**NASDAQ**) was created in 1971 with electronic transactions.

  It was the world's first electronic stock market. Initially, it only used to send quotations.

- **1996**: Island ECN was the pioneering electronic communication network for US equities trading, while Archipelago facilitated electronic trading on the US trading exchange by creating **Archipelago Exchange** (**ArcaEx**).

- **2000s**: 10% of transactions are HFT transactions.

The financial sector gathered more and more technologists in the early 2000s. By getting this technological intake, the sector started evolving sharply. Automation, throughput, performance, and latency became words that were well known by trading firms. The HFT transactions reached more than 10% of the market. By 2009, 2% of trading firms accounted for 75% of the equity volume. Nowadays, only a few firms remain in HFT, such as Virtu, Jump, Citadel, IMC, and Tower.

The modern era

The post-1930s era focused on transparency and regulation in the equities markets (and the pit in commodities markets). The modern era gives prominence to electronic trading and improves transparency. In 2000, the US **Securities and Exchange Commission (SEC)** proposed the **Central Limit Order Book (CLOB)**. The CLOB is a transparent system matching orders between participants. Many more exchanges (such as Island and Arca) came to the trading scene. The number of trading firms, hedge funds, and electronic players kept increasing. They created their own technology stack to trade more quickly and stay competitive. After 10 years, only a few trading firms managed to remain competitive, becoming the 2% of the trading firms accountable for 75% of all equity volume.

The savoir faire for competing in HFT requires heavy investment: money, people, and time. It is a marriage of low-level system expertise and quants, as well as smart money (investors are more and more technology savvy). Engineers capable of creating performant code for designing ultra-low latency systems are very expensive. Only a few engineers had these skills. The performance for such a system required specialized hardware. Routers, servers, and network devices are also expensive. Therefore, the experience and the barrier of entry will prevent a lot of new incomers and will limit the competition. On top of the five firms we talked about previously, there are boutique shops that trade HFT strategies using an edge they found either in the market structure or some technical fact that other firms are not exploiting. The giant HFT firms are the companies responsible for moving most of the equity volume. Nowadays, HFT is estimated to account for at least 50% of the US equity (shares) trading volume. The market share of HFT has declined, as has profitability, since the peak year (2009).

After 2015, the growth of digital currencies cleared the way for new opportunities for high-frequency traders. Today, we can see an extensive growth of HFT strategies working with well-known crypto exchanges such as Coinbase, Binance, and hundreds of other crypto exchanges.

This modern era has anchored technology and automated trading for good. Trading models are data driven and model driven. The market data business definitely became a major part of trading. Exchanges and trading firms started making money by generating or collecting market data, the raw material of any algorithm trader.

Why have HFT?

HFT aims at getting many transactions per second. In this way, companies can react more quickly to a changing market. They can take advantage of more opportunities than they would have without this speed. Additionally, large institutions benefit from HFT by gaining a tiny but considerable advantage in exchange for delivering massive volumes of liquidity to markets. They place millions of orders that their systems are capable of placing. They help the market and, as a result, are able to boost earnings in their profitable trades and receive better spreads. Since the return is very low, they must complete many trades to benefit. On top of this revenue, they will gain rebates or discounted transaction fees, which are given by trading venues to make their markets more attractive to HFT firms.

What makes HFT so different from regular trading?

HFT trading should have the *shortest feasible data latency (time delays)* and the *highest level of automation* possible. HFT relates to algorithmic trading and automated trading. As a result, participants choose to trade in markets that have a high level of automation and integration in their trading platforms. Firms utilize computers programmed with precise algorithms to find trading opportunities and execute orders in algorithmic trading. To increase the speed of transactions, high-frequency traders use automated trading and fast connections (and cancellations or modifications). This is possible because of the technology that trading firms have in place but also because of the exchange technologies. The following exchanges have invested hundreds of millions of dollars in HFT technologies:

- **NASDAQ**, New York City, is the first electronic stock exchange in the world. All of its equities are traded over a computerized network. It revolutionized the financial markets in 1971 by removing the requirement for a physical trading floor and in-person trading. It is the world's second-biggest stock exchange by market capitalization. Half of NASDAQ's composite offering was made up of technology firms. With less than 20% of the overall composite, the consumer sector came in second, followed by healthcare.

- **New York Stock Exchange** (**NYSE**), New York City, is the world's largest exchange for the equity market. In 2013, **Intercontinental Exchange, Inc**. (**ICE**) bought NYSE.

- **London Stock Exchange** (**LSE**), London, UK, is the largest stock exchange in Europe and the principal stock exchange in the United Kingdom mainly with regard to trading in company stocks and bonds. It was created about 300 years ago.

- The **Tokyo Stock Exchange** (**TSE**), is Japan's largest stock exchange, with its headquarters in Tokyo. It was founded in 1878. The exchange has more than 3,500 listed businesses. The TSE, which is operated by the Japan Exchange Group, is home to the world's largest and most well-known Japanese corporations, including Toyota, Honda, and Mitsubishi.

- The **Chicago Mercantile Market** (**CME**), sometimes known as the Chicago Merc, is a regulated futures and options exchange in Chicago, Illinois. Agriculture, energy, stock indices, foreign exchange, interest rates, metals, real estate, and weather are among the industries in which the CME trades futures and, in most cases, options.

- **Direct Edge**, Jersey City. Its market share rapidly rose to tenth in the US stock market, and it typically transacted more than two billion shares daily. **Better Alternative Trading System** (**BATS**) Global Markets was a US-based exchange that traded a variety of assets, including stocks, options, and foreign exchange. CBOE Holdings purchased it in 2017 after it was created in 2005. BATS Global Market was one of the largest US exchanges prior to being bought, and it was well known for its services to broker-dealers, retail, and institutional investors.

- The **CBOE Options Exchange**, which was founded in 1973, is the world's largest options exchange, with contracts centered on individual stocks, indexes, and interest rates.

All the preceding exchanges are controlled on several levels:

- Trading limitations

- Trading system transparency (information shared among market participants on the specificities of the architecture, as well as the way of handling orders)

- The type of accepted financial instruments

- Constraints by security issuers

For most regulated exchanges, the order size is an issue. Large trades have an important effect on the market (they can create market impact). Traders use **Alternate Trading Systems (ATS)**, which have much less regulation in comparison to traditional exchanges (they don't have to be transparent). Dark pools are the most common sorts of ATS. The USA presently has around 30 dark pools, which represent a quarter of the US consolidated trading volume.

Dark pools are beneficial to HFTs because they can handle the speed and the level of automation demands while having reduced fees. This is not the case for any other type of trading, which makes HFT different from regular trading. In the following section, let's learn more about dark pools.

Effect of dark pools

For financial security, buy and sell orders are not displayed in dark pools (price and volume). Dark pools, in other words, are both opaque and anonymous since the order book is not advertised. Because it is not possible to see the size of the orders in this type of trading exchange, investors who place huge orders do not impact markets. Since the other participants do not see the size of the orders, the dark pools execute these large orders at a fixed price. It reduces the negative slippage given by trading exchanges.

Dark pools are obliged to notify deals once they have occurred, notwithstanding the lack of pre-trade transparency.

HFTs and dark pools have a complicated interaction. Dark pools rose in popularity partially as a result of investors seeking protection from HFTs' fraudulent activities on public exchanges, and HFTs finding it impossible to know the large orders in dark pools through pinging. Dark pools introduced a lack of transparency in the markets that allowed ill-equipped players (that is, on the sell side) to keep up with business practices that didn't match the state of the art at the time. And, of course, Haim Bodek wrote two books (*The Problem of HFT* and *The Market Structure Crisis*) about finding unordinary order types in dark pools.

On the other hand, a few dark pools encourage HFT traders to trade on their exchange. HFT strategies increase liquidity and the likelihood of having orders filled. Dark pools help HFTs to meet their speed and automation demands while still having reduced expenses. HFTs are responsible for the decrease in order sizes in dark pools. The dark pools have been hit by pinging trading strategies locating hidden large orders.

As a result, if these HFT tactics are present, the benefits of dark pools may be harmed. For example, in 2014, the Attorney General of New York filed a lawsuit against Barclays for its dark pool operations, alleging that it misrepresented the volume of Barclays's activity in dark pools. In 2016, Barclays paid a $35 million fine to the SEC and $70 million to the State of New York.

Dark pools can apply certain constraints to prevent HFTs from engaging in predatory behavior. The goal is to reduce pinging trading strategies. In 2017, Petrescu and Wedow imposed a minimum order size to minimize this type of strategy.

We could spend more time discussing the pros and cons of the impact of HFTs on dark pools, but we end up saying that the advantages of having more liquidity and faster execution are beneficial enough to have some dark pools being in favor of HFTs. It is fair for investors as long as they have a thorough understanding of how trading venues work so they can make educated judgments.

We have talked about the location of the major trading exchanges. Now we will introduce the HFT participants in the next section.

Who trades HFT?

The answer could be summarized in one word: *everyone*. From the buy side to the sell side, ECNs, and even the inter-dealer and inter-broker-dealer markets, they all use HFT. HFT is dominated by proprietary trading businesses and covers a wide range of products, including stocks, derivatives, index funds, **Exchange-Traded Funds** (**ETFs**), currencies, and fixed-income instruments. Proprietary trading businesses accounted for half of the current HFT players, multi-service broker-dealer proprietary trading desks accounted for less than half, and hedge funds accounted for the rest. Proprietary trading businesses such as KCG Holdings (created by the merger of Getco and Knight Capital) and the trading desks of major banks are among the major players in the field. There are some new types of venues (such as Dealerweb's OTR Exchange and IEX) that are looking to provide venues where dealers on the sell side feel safe to execute trades and HFTs are providing liquidity.

It is worth saying that HFTs have become major players in the market. They are also capturing retail flow. Citadel is controlling a large part of the retail flow.

What do I need to start an HFT?

Participants in HFTs must have the following:

- **Fast computers**: HFT focuses on single-core throughput in most cases, and parallelism is not used by the strategies necessarily.

- **Exchange proximity**: While some countries restrict the use of shared places to have trading systems and exchange, in the US, we use co-location. This is a place where all the HFTs participants have their production servers. They will pay to have their computers co-located with an exchange's computer servers in the same data centers in order to decrease latency and shorten the time it takes to complete a deal – even by microseconds. The cables linking trading systems from all market participants with the server are the same length to guarantee that nobody has an advantage over another market participant. The SEC has issued a wide request for feedback on co-location fees, as well as other concerns impacting the equity market structure. To ensure fairness among market participants, it is important that co-location fees are reasonably priced. The SEC invites the co-locations to report their fees.

- **Low latency**: In HFT, latency is the time it takes for data to reach a trader's computer, for the trader to make an order in response to the data, and for the order to be accepted by an exchange. The order may enter the market alongside many other orders issued by other traders at the most profitable time. There is a danger of competing against a large number of other people in this circumstance. The order may not be as profitable as it may have been in this scenario. High-frequency traders are able to make orders at unfathomably quick speeds because of technology advertised as *low-latency* or *ultra-low-latency*. It is important to use gear designed to reduce the latency of shuffling data from one place to another.

- **Computer algorithms**, which are at the heart of AT and HFT, and real-time data feeds, which could damage earnings.

In the previous sections, we learned where high-frequency traders make business. We also talked about the technological prerequisites to trade faster. Let's now focus on what HFT is in depth.

What are HFT strategies?

HFT strategies are a subset of algorithmic trading strategies. They are executed in the order of the microseconds (and sometimes nanoseconds). The strategies must be aware of this time limitation to be efficient HFT strategies. They deploy cutting-edge technology advancements to obtain information faster than the competition. The main game of this type of strategy is the tick-to-trade, which is the response time to send an order responding to incoming market data. As we will explain in the next chapter, it is important to host trading strategies on cutting-edge machines, and they must also run in a co-location.

We will be defining the domain of applications and some vocab to have when talking about HFT strategies.

Asset classes

HFT strategies can be applied to any asset classes, such as stocks, futures, bonds, options, and FX. We also have cryptocurrencies being traded using HFT strategies, even if the definition of speed is different (because of the settlement time).

Liquidity

The desire of players to interact with regard to a certain asset is known as liquidity.

We define depth as the number of price levels for a given asset. We will say that a book is deep when there are many levels (layers) for a given asset. We will define a book as big or broad if the volume per layer is high. If a book is deep or large, we will define a liquidity of a given asset liquid. The consequence of this statement is that it will be easier for a trader to buy or sell this asset whenever they want to. As a result, trading exchanges with a lot of liquidities are wanted by traders. Crypto trading exchanges have difficulty finding liquidities at the moment.

Tick-by-tick data and data distribution

HFT generates orders every microsecond. Since there are a lot of participants, it is likely to have huge amounts of data. Storage of this data will be key when we study HFT data to create models for trading strategies.

Thousands of ticks (security price changes from one order to another) are generated per trading day on liquid marketplaces, which make up high-frequency data. This material is randomly spaced in time by its very nature. HFT data exhibits fat tail distributions. That means that the trading strategies need to take into account that we can have big losses.

They distribution of the market data can be grouped into two categories:

- **Volatility clustering**: *Large changes follow large changes* whether in terms of signs or numbers, while minor changes follow smaller changes.
- **Long-range dependency** (long memory) refers to the pace at which statistical dependence between two sites decays as the time interval or spatial distance between them increases.

Liquidity rebates

To support the provision of stock liquidity, most exchanges have used a *maker-taker model*. In this arrangement, investors and traders who place limit orders often earn a modest rebate from the exchange when their orders are executed since they are considered to have contributed to stock liquidity, or *makers*.

Those who place market orders, on the other hand, are considered *takers* of liquidity and are charged a small fee by the exchange. While the rebates are normally fractions of a penny per share, over the millions of shares exchanged daily by high-frequency traders, they may add up to large amounts. Many HFT businesses use trading techniques that are geared to take advantage of as many liquidity rebates as feasible.

Matching engine

The software program that forms the heart of an exchange's trading system and matches buy and sell orders on a continuous basis, a service traditionally done by trading floor professionals, called the **matching engine** is critical for guaranteeing the efficient operation of an exchange since it matches buyers and sellers for all stocks. The matching engine is housed on the exchange's computers, and it is the main reason why HFT businesses strive to be as near to the exchange servers as possible. We will learn about it in *Chapter 3, Understanding the Trading Exchange Dynamics*.

Market making

Before going into details on what market making is, we need to explain the difference between market takers and market makers.

Market taker/maker

Figure 1.1 represents the limit order book on an exchange. When a trading strategy places an order close to the top of the book (the layer representing the best price for bid and for ask), we say that this order is an **aggressive order**. It means that this order is likely to be matched with another order. If the order is executed, it means that liquidity has been removed from the market; it is a **market taker**. We will say that a trader *crosses the spread* when they place a buy order at the price of the ask on the top of the book. If the order is less aggressive (or passive), this order will not remove liquidities from the market; it is a **market maker**.

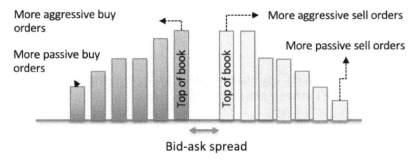

Figure 1.1 – Order book – passive/aggressive order

Let's look at the market-making strategies.

Market-making strategies

A trading corporation can provide market-making as a service on an exchange. Over time, a market maker assists in the matching of buyers and sellers. Rather than purchasing or selling securities based on their underlying assets, market makers maintain a continual offer to buy and sell securities and profit from the spread, which is the difference between the two offers.

To reduce the risk of keeping stocks for extended periods of time, every purchase should be matched with a sale and every sell should be matched with a buy. If a stock is trading at $100, a market maker can keep a buy offer at $99.50 and a sell offer at $100.50. If they are successful in finding both a buyer and a seller, it allows those who want to sell right now to do so even if no one else wants to purchase, and vice versa.

Market makers, in other words, supply liquidity—they make trading simpler. For the most traded stocks, this technique is not important; however, for smaller firms (less traded than the big ones), it can be critical to increase the trading volume to facilitate trading. Market making is one approach that many HFT businesses use. They out-compete everyone else by changing their quotations quickly and reducing the spread even further: they're willing to make less money each time since their market-making business can readily grow to massive quantities. However, an HFT firm's technology can be used for other purposes, such as arbitrage (making money on minor discrepancies between linked securities) or execution (breaking up huge institutions' trades to minimize market effect). I won't go into much more detail because the point is that HFT is capable of more than simply market-making. The only thing that matters is speed.

Market making can be done by the analysis of the order flow:

- A large volume of buy and sell can drive the market price of buying and selling on the basis of momentum.

- The flow of liquids (how big are the buy and sell orders: small, medium, or big).

- Exhaustion of momentum (when the order flow is drying off it may signal a price reversal).

Market-making is the most widely used trading strategy for high-frequency traders. We will talk about the other HFT strategies in the next sections.

Scalping

Scalping is a trading method that focuses on benefitting from tiny price movements and reselling for a quick profit. Scalping is a phrase used in day trading to describe a technique that focuses on generating large volumes from tiny profits. Scalping necessitates a tight exit plan since a single major loss might wipe out all of the modest wins the trader has worked so hard to achieve. For this technique to work, you'll need the necessary tools, such as a live feed, a direct-access broker, and the endurance to conduct a lot of trades.

The concept behind scalping is that most stocks will finish the first stage of a trend. But it's unclear where things will go from there. Some stocks stop rising after that early stage, while others continue to rise. The goal is to benefit from as many minor transactions as possible. The *let your gains run* mentality, on the other hand, aims to maximize good trading results by expanding the size of winning deals. By increasing the number of winners while compromising on the magnitude of the gains, this technique accomplishes outcomes. It's very uncommon for a trader with a long time period to produce good profits while winning just 50% of their transactions, or even less – the difference is that the wins are far larger than the losses.

Statistical arbitrage

The **Efficient Market Hypothesis** (**EMH**) claims financial markets are *informationally efficient*, which means that the prices of traded assets are accurate, and at any one moment represent all known information. Based on this hypothesis, the market should not fluctuate if there is not any fundamental news. However, this is not the case, and we can explain that with liquidity.

Throughout the day, many huge institutional trades have little to do with information and everything to do with liquidity. Investors who believe they are overexposed will aggressively hedge or sell their positions, impacting the price. Liquidity seekers are frequently ready to pay a premium to exit their positions, resulting in a profit for liquidity providers. Although this capacity to benefit from knowledge appears to violate efficient market theory, statistical arbitrage is based on it.

Statistical arbitrage seeks to profit from the correlation of price and liquidity by gaining from the perceived mispricing of assets based on the assets' anticipated value given by a statistical model.

Short-term price discrepancies in the same security sold on separate venues, or short-term price differences in related securities, are used in statistical arbitrage, often known as **stat arb**. Statistical arbitrage is based on the assumption that price differences in securities markets exist but go away quickly. Because the time period during which a price difference occurs might be as short as a fraction of a second, algorithmic trading is well suited to statistical arbitrage.

When trading the same security in several venues, for example, an algorithm tracks all of the locations where the security is exchanged. When a price difference arises, the algorithm buys in the lower market and sells in the higher market, resulting in a profit. Because the window of opportunity for such differences is small (less than 1 millisecond), algorithmic trading is ideally suited to this form of trade.

Statistical arbitrage becomes more challenging when investing in linked securities. An index and a single stock within that index, or a single stock and other stocks in the same sector, are examples of related securities. In linked securities, a statistical arbitrage approach entails gathering a large amount of historical data and estimating the usual connection between the two markets. The algorithm makes a buy or a sell whenever there is a variation from the norm.

Latency arbitrage

Modern equities markets are complicated, requiring highly technical systems to manage vast volumes of data. Because of its intricacy, data is invariably processed at varying speeds. Latency arbitrage takes advantage of market players' differing speeds. Latency arbitrage aims to take advantage of high-frequency traders' greater speed by leveraging high-speed fiber optics, superior bandwidth, co-located servers, and direct-price feeds from exchanges, among other things, to place trades ahead of other market players.

The hypothesis behind latency arbitrage is that in the US, the aggregated feed that determines the **National Best Bid and Offer** (**NBBO**) of all US stock exchanges is slower than the direct data feeds from stock exchanges available to high-frequency traders. An HFT program's algorithm can read transaction data more quickly than many other market players, seeing prices a fraction of a second ahead of the **Securities Information Processor** (**SIP**) feed, which is the consolidated US stock exchange price feed, thanks to its superior speed. This essentially provides information to the HFT software before it reaches the official market (the SIP feed), allowing high-frequency traders to observe where prices are heading ahead of other market players.

Impact of news

Information is at the heart of all trading, and it is used to make financial decisions. The utilization of news data by algorithmic trading systems to generate trading choices is referred to as information-driven strategies.

Algorithms have been developed to read and analyze news reports from major news organizations, as well as social media. Any news that has the potential to alter market prices causes the algorithm to purchase or sell.

High-frequency traders have gotten so accustomed to using information-driven methods that certain news agencies now package their press releases in a way that makes it simple for computers to analyze them. They employ predetermined keywords to characterize a favorable or bad occurrence, for example, so that an algorithm can act on keywords in a news release. Prior to their planned publication, news providers also place news reports on servers in crucial geographical regions (such as major financial centers). This reduces the amount of time it takes for data to move from one location to another. For this sort of service, news service providers charge an additional fee.

As seen by the hacking of the Associated Press Twitter feed, the use of social media for information-driven initiatives is growing. In 2013, a hacker tweeted that a bomb had gone off in the White House, injuring the president, causing an instantaneous plunge in equities markets throughout the world as algorithms analyzed the bad news from a trustworthy source and began selling in the market.

Next, let's learn about the momentum ignition trading technique.

Momentum ignition

You have the chance to trade financially if an order you send into the market may cause a price change and you know it can. The goal of momentum-ignition trading techniques is to achieve this. The objective is to get other algorithms and traders to start trading in a stock, causing a price change. In essence, a momentum ignition approach attempts to deceive other market players into believing that a large price movement is going to occur, causing them to trade. As a result, the price movement becomes a self-fulfilling prophecy: traders believe a price movement will occur, and their activities cause one to occur.

Sending enormous volumes of orders into the order book and then canceling them is a momentum-ignition approach. This creates the illusion of a huge shift in volume in the stock, which might prompt other traders to place orders, resulting in the start of a short-term price trend. Before attempting to ignite the market movement, the momentum ignition approach includes executing the real targeted trading position. This means that a deal is completed initially that does not significantly influence the market. This permits a trader using the momentum-ignition approach to enter the market before the price movement is initiated. The momentum ignition is set after the deal is completed by submitting a flurry of orders and canceling them in the hopes that other traders will follow suit and move the price.

The trader using the momentum-ignition technique then quits their initial position at a profit as the price begins to move.

Momentum-ignition methods require the use of specific order types, and traders may only utilize algorithms that can send and cancel huge numbers of orders in a short amount of time to execute them.

Rebate strategies

Market order traders must pay a fee to the exchange, whereas the limit order is reimbursed with rebates when they add liquidities. As a result, traders, particularly those engaged in HFT, submit limit orders to build markets, which in turn generates liquidity on the exchange. It is undoubtedly appealing to traders who place a large number of limit orders due to the pricing scheme's lower risk for the limit order.

There is also a charge structure called trader-maker pricing that is the polar opposite of market-taker pricing. In certain markets, it entails giving rebates to market order traders and collecting fees from limit order traders.

Pinging

Pinging is a strategy for learning about huge orders in trading exchanges and dark pools by placing tiny marketable orders (typically for 100 shares).

To lessen the market effect of large orders, buy-side businesses utilize this trading technique to split large orders into many small orders. This algorithm feeds these orders slowly into the exchange. In order to detect the presence of such large orders, HFT companies arrange bids and offers in 100-share lots for each listed stock.

These **ping** trades will alert HFT participants to the existence of a large order placed by the buy-side. HFTs will use this information to ensure risk-free profit from the buy-side.

Some significant market participants have compared pinging to *baiting* because its main objective is to entice institutions with huge orders to expose their hand.

Illegal activities

The **SEC**, the **Federal Bureau of Investigation (FBI)**, and other regulators have launched crackdowns on alleged HFT violations in recent years. The following sections are examples of possible offenses.

Front-running

Placing an order based on information that has not been publicly released is called front-running. This technique has been outlawed by SEC and the **Financial Industry Regulatory Authority (FINRA)**. Some have used the term *front-running* to describe a technique in which HFT firms utilize algorithmic trading technology to identify a large number of new orders for a given instrument. Before the large number of orders comes to the market, we place orders to benefit from this incoming large quantity. HFT corporations can earn almost instantly after purchasing assets by selling them to the original investors. Even if this way of trading is legal, regulators are concerned and may need to control this behavior moving forward.

Spoofing

Spoofing is not a legal trading strategy. It consists of a spoofing strategy sending orders that are not intended to be executed, just to have the other market participants react to these orders. They will probably send orders to get to this price level. Meanwhile, the initial orders are canceled and the spoofer takes advantage of the other orders remaining in the market.

The Dodd-Frank Wall Street Reform and Consumer Protection Act of 2010 specifically targeted the practice, and even before that, FINRA regulations barred orders whose goal is to mislead the market. The first criminal spoofing case disclosed by legislators in 2014 related to a Chicago trader accused of faking futures markets.

Layering

Layering is the same as spoofing except that the orders are placed at different price levels to give the appearance that there is a lot of interest in a certain security. The outcome of this strategy is the same as with regular spoofing. Because of the rapid advancement of technology, massive market manipulation may take place in fractions of a second. Layering, like generic spoofing, is typically illegal and forbidden under FINRA rules.

Even if these strategies are now outlawed, we need to keep in mind that some exchanges are less or not regulated. We will see in *Chapter 11*, *High Frequency FPGA and Crypto*, about cryptocurrencies that these strategies can still work.

Summary

In this chapter, we reviewed the origins of HFT. We went through what makes HFT so special in comparison to regular trading. We also layered the different types of strategies that any HFT trading system will be able to support. We talked about the history of trading systems. Our goal in this chapter was to give you a good understanding of what HFT is and what trading strategies we can use.

In the next chapter, we will talk about the main functionalities of a trading system. We will describe how to build a trading system.

2
The Critical Components of a Trading System

In the previous chapter, we learned how to create **high-frequency trading (HFT)** strategies. In this chapter, we are going to study how to convert these strategies into real-time software that will connect to an exchange to actually apply the theory that you've previously learned. We will describe the functioning of a trading system capable of trading assets.

In this chapter we will cover the following topics:

- Understanding the trading system
- Making a trading system trade with exchanges
- Order book management
- Strategy making decisions on when to trade

By the end of this chapter, you will be capable of designing a trading system, connecting a trading system to an exchange, and building a limit order book.

Understanding the trading system

Designing a trading system for HFT trading requires much more than knowledge of programming and trading. The following chapters of this book will describe these parts in depth, which will give you an edge in designing an HFT system. In this section, we are going to talk about the fundamentals of trading system design. One of the most critical parts of designing a system is having a detailed description of the requirements. The goal of a trading system is to support your trading ideas. Any trading strategies start by getting data and end up with making a decision based on this data. A trading system will oversee collecting market data (that is, price updates) and sending orders to the exchange. Additionally, it will collect answers from the exchange containing information on the orders. These market updates could be representing any state of the orders: canceled, rejected, filled, or partially filled. It will also compute metrics measuring the performance of your portfolio (such as profit and loss, risk metrics, or information about the different processes of the trading system).

When deciding whether to create this type of software, we need to keep the following points in mind:

- **Asset class**: Knowing which asset class will be employed in the trading system will change the data structure of this software. Each asset class is unique and has its own set of characteristics. Building a trading system for US equities won't be the same as building a system for **foreign exchange** (**FX**). Stocks in the United States are mostly traded on two exchanges, the **New York Stock Exchange** (**NYSE**) and NASDAQ. These two exchanges have roughly 7,000 firms (symbols) listed. FX contains six main currency pairs, six minor currency pairs, and six exotic currency pairs, as opposed to stocks. We can add additional currency pairs, but no more than 100 will be available. Unlike the US equity market, where we can have two main exchanges, in the FX market, there will be hundreds of exchanges. The number of symbols and the number of exchanges will change the architecture of a trading system.

- **Trading strategy type (high frequency, long-term position)**: The software architecture will be influenced by the trading strategy type. HFT tactics necessitate transmitting orders in a very short period of time. In the case of US stocks, a standard trading system will decide to send an order in microseconds. A **Chicago Mercantile Exchange (CME)** trading system has a latency in the order of nanoseconds. Based on this finding, technology will play a significant role in the software design process. If we only consider the programming language, Python is not well suited to speed, and we would rather choose C++ or Java. If we wish to take a long-term position, such as one that lasts many days, the speed with which a trader may obtain liquidity faster than others is irrelevant.

- **Number of users (or trading techniques)**: As the number of traders grows, so does the variety of trading tactics. This indicates that the number of orders will increase. Before submitting an order to an exchange, we must ensure that the orders we are about to send are valid; we must ensure that the overall position for a specific instrument has not been reached.

Trading strategies are being moderated by an increasing number of rules in the trading sector. We shall test the compliance of the orders that we wish to send in order to ensure that our trading strategy complies with the regulations. All of these tests will increase the amount of time it takes to calculate. If we have a lot of orders, we'll have to conduct all of these verifications in sequence for one instrument. If the program isn't fast enough, the orders will take longer to process. The more users you have, the more scalable the trading system must be.

These variables change the way you think about the trading system you're going to create. Let's discuss the design of a simple trading system in the following section.

Trading system architecture

The following schema represents the trading system architecture. On the left part of this diagram, we can see the venues. **Venues** are a more generic term for any platform matching buy and sell orders for the securities and/or derivatives of multiple parties. In other words, a venue can be a trading exchange, an **ECN**, an aggregator, or a bank. Trading systems communicate with venues to collect price updates from all the participants and send orders. To do so, a trading system needs a piece of software called **Gateways**, which will ensure the communication between the trading system and the venues. The **Book Builder** will build the limit order book from the data collected from Gateways. Finally, the **Strategy** will send the order to the venues through the **Order Manager**. The Order Manager is responsible for collecting all the orders coming from the strategies of the system and keeps track of the life cycle of the orders. All of these components are a part of the critical path of sending orders to the market.

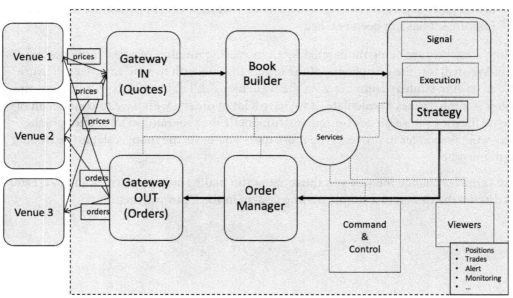

Figure 2.1 – Trading system architecture design

Additionally, we observe other less critical services, such as **command and control**, in charge of starting the components of the system. The viewers are critical in algorithmic trading because they will give you a status of all the components of the system, the orders and trades, and the metrics you consider important to monitor your trading strategies. Algorithmic trading automates trading. Therefore, it is important to keep track of the health of your trading system and trading strategies. It is particularly important to understand here that in HFT trading, a few microseconds can end up in colossal losses. Having viewers and user interfaces capable of efficiently reporting alerts is critical.

In the next section, we will talk more in-depth about the critical components of a trading system.

Gateways connecting to trading exchanges

Gateways are the components of a trading system communicating with the exchange and the trading system. They are essential because they are the greediest in terms of execution time. By design, they must get data from the network and provide this data to the rest of the system. This operation is demanding in terms of system resources and operating system. Price updates are collected by a trading system, which then transmits orders on your behalf. To do so, you must first code all the procedures you would do if you were trading without a trading system. If you want to make money by purchasing low and selling high, you must first decide what product you will trade. You should get the order from the other merchants after you have chosen these products.

The other traders will inform you of their willingness to trade a financial asset by identifying the size, price, and quantity. You can pick the trader with whom you will negotiate a transaction once you have received enough orders for the product you wish to trade. The price of this item will influence your selection. If you plan to resell this item in the future, you will need to acquire it for a cheap price. When you reach an agreement on a price, tell the other trader that you want to buy at the listed price. You will then own this product when the transaction is completed.

Data collection

Gateways collect price updates from the trading venues you have chosen (exchanges, ECNs, and dark pools). This component (shown as a Gateway in the following figure) is one of the most important in the trading system. This component's job is to get the book for the instruments from the exchange into the trading system. This component will be connected to the network and will be able to communicate with it via exchanges receiving and sending streams.

The position of the trade system's gates is depicted in the following diagram. They are the trading system's inputs and outputs:.

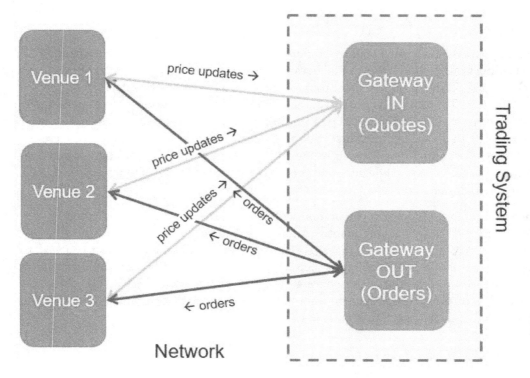

Figure 2.2 – Gateways in charge of collecting price updates and sending orders

The following points are depicted in the preceding diagram:

- Traders, exchanges, ECNs, and dark pools are represented by the venues.

- Different protocols might be used to connect the venues (they are represented using arrows).

- Wires, wireless networks, the internet, microwaves, and fibers are all options to transfer data. In terms of speed, data loss, and bandwidth, each of these network media has its own set of characteristics.

- The arrows for price updates and orders are bidirectional because we can have data sent to/received from the venues.

- To begin receiving pricing updates, the gateway will establish a network connection with the venue, verify itself, and subscribe to a certain instrument (we will explain this part in the next section).

- The order-processing gateway also receives and sends communications. When an order is placed, it is forwarded to the venue over the network.

- An acknowledgment of this order will be sent if the venue receives it. A message will be issued to the trading system after this order meets a matching order. If the venue does not receive an order, the acknowledgment will not be sent. It is up to the trading system to declare that an order has timed out. In this situation, a trader will need to intervene and check the problem that occurred in the system.

Making a trading system trade with exchanges

A trading system contains a number of functional components that are responsible for trading and risk management, as well as monitoring the trading process on one or more exchanges. A trading strategy becomes a part of the trading system once it is coded. As input, you'll need price data, and as output, your orders. This will give out trading signals. We'll need gateways to finish this flow because they're the most important components.

The functional components of a trading system, the gateway's interface, and the trading system's interaction with the outside world are depicted in the following diagram:

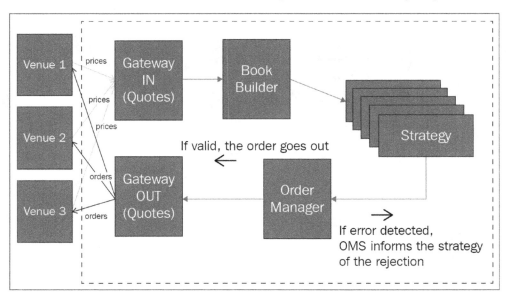

Figure 2.3 – The functional components of a trading system

The gateways gather and send orders based on pricing and market reactions. Their primary function is to establish a link and translate data received from the outside world into the data structure needed by the trading system.

The following points are depicted in the preceding diagram:

- This trading plan will be on your machine when you apply your trading strategy. The trade will take place on a different computer.

- Because these two devices are located at different locations, they must connect over a network.

- The methods of communication employed by the system might vary depending on its location.

- A single wire will be utilized if the trading system is collocated (the machines are in the same facility), which will minimize network latency.

- The internet might be another mode of communication if we adopt a cloud solution. The communication will be substantially slower than with a direct connection in this instance.

Examine the following figure, which displays the communication that occurs between the gateways:

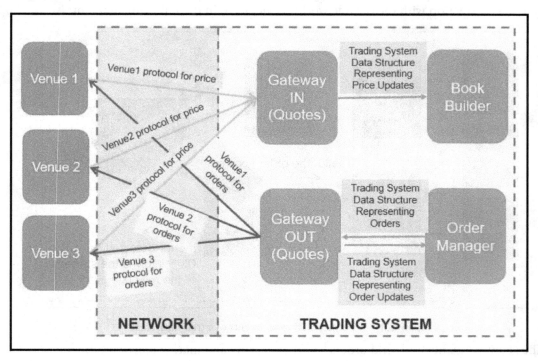

Figure 2.4 – Communication between exchange and trading system

We understand the following points from the preceding diagram:

- When we examine the communication handled by the gateways more closely, we can see that the venues may use various protocols.

- To transform protocols into trading system data structures, gateways will need to be able to process a variety of protocols.

We learned about how a trading system connects to trading exchanges. We will now talk about how communication can happen and which protocol we are using for receiving market updates and sending orders.

Examining the API for communication

The rules of communication between machines are defined by network protocols. They specify how these devices will be identified on the network and how they will communicate with one another. The **User Datagram Protocol** (**UDP**) and **Transmission Control Protocol** (**TCP**) over **Internet Protocol** (**IP**) protocols are used in trading finance. Furthermore, we employ a software protocol that specifies how to send an order and obtain a price update. At the software level, the communication API will establish communication rules. The communication API is provided by the entity with which you wish to transact. This document contains all of the messages you will need to get price updates and place orders.

Examples of trading API documents can be found at `https://en.wikipedia.org/wiki/List_of_electronic_trading_protocols`. Before we go into the trading API, let's go over some networking fundamentals.

The fundamentals of networking

The network is responsible for allowing computers to connect with one another. To share data, networks require a physical layer. For a network to achieve a certain level of speed, dependability, or even security, selecting the appropriate medium (communication layer) is crucial. We use the following terms in trade finance:

- **Wire**: Electrical currents with a narrow bandwidth.

- **Fiber**: More bandwidth.

- **Microwave**: It's simple to set up and has a lot of bandwidth, but it's susceptible to storms.

Depending on the sort of trading technique you choose, the media will change. In the **Open Systems Interconnection** (**OSI**) model (developed in *Chapter 5, Networking in Motion*), selecting the appropriate medium is part of the first layer of the network. The physical layer is the name given to this layer. There are six more layers on top of this one that describe the sort of communication.

Like most of the communication, finance is also using IP. This is part of the ISO model's network layer. This IP establishes the rules for network packet routing. The transport layer is the final layer we'll discuss. TCP and UDP are the two most well-known protocols in banking. These two procedures are diametrically opposed. TCP is a protocol that allows two machines to communicate with each other. All messages sent initially will be delivered first. UDP lacks a means for determining whether network packets were received by the network. All of the exchanges will use either TCP or UDP as their protocol.

In *Chapter 5, Networking in Motion*, we will go deeper into the study of these protocols. Let's learn about order book management in the following section.

Order book management

The primary goal of data handling is to copy the limit order book from the venues into your trading system. The book builder will be in charge of gathering the pricing and categorizing them for your tactics in order to integrate all of the many books you obtain.

The pricing changes are transformed by the gateway and then passed to the book builder, as shown in the following diagram. The book builder will use the books that the gateways have received from the venues, as well as gather and sort any pricing changes:

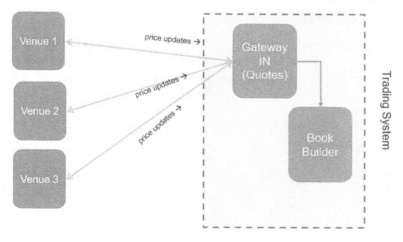

Figure 2.5 – Book builder getting price updates from Gateway IN

In the following diagram, we use an example of an **order book** for a given financial product. The order book will contain two parts, one for the bids and one for the offers. For each part, we will store the orders represented by the venue, the volume, and the price. Every venue will send its own order books. The goal of the book builder is to create a book taking into account the three books coming from each venue. The data represented in this diagram is artificial:

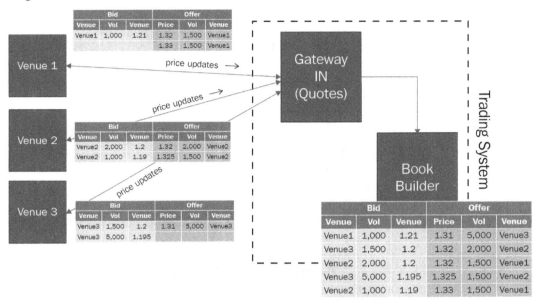

Figure 2.6 – Trading system building the book out of three different venues

The following is depicted in the diagram:

- You can see that there is an order for each row in these books.

- For example, a trader on Venue 1's offer list is ready to purchase 1,000 shares for $1.21. On the other hand, there's a list of people who are eager to sell.

- The offer (or ask) price will almost always be greater than the bid price. Indeed, it would be far too simple to profit if you could purchase for less than you could sell.

- The book builder's job is to collect the three books from the three places that the gates have collected. The book builder organizes and sorts the three books.

We have learned how the trading system gets price updates and how to build a limit order book. We will now explain in detail the different functionalities of the order book.

Order book considerations

A limit order book collects all price updates (orders) and arranges them in a way that makes the trading strategy's work easier. Exchanges utilize the order book to keep track of bids and offers. When trading, we receive the book from the exchange in order to figure out an indication of the asset prices, which prices are the best, or just to get a sense of the market. We'll have to utilize the network to convey changes to the exchange book because the exchange is on another platform/server. We have two options for doing so:

- The first way entails sending the entire book. Sending the full book is consuming in terms of time. Indeed, if we have large trading exchanges (such as NYSE or NASDAQ), there are millions of orders sent within one second. If each time the exchange receives a new order, the full book is sent, the network will be saturated and it will take too long to send price updates.

- The second way will send a full snapshot of the book as described previously. Then, the exchange will send incremental updates. The book is a critical part of the trading system since it will provide the trading strategy with the information to decide when to send an order or not. An order book contains bids and orders that are presently on the exchange. When a price update is sent to our trading system, the other market participants receive the same update concurrently. All the other market participants can also decide to run after this price update. When the exchange receives many orders (explained in detail in *Chapter 3, Understanding the Trading Exchange Dynamics*), the orders received first will be executed first. That's why the book plays a large part in the latency and all the operations of the book must be optimized.

For the life cycle of the orders, we will need to handle the following operations:

- **Insertion**: An insertion is a book entry that adds a new order to the book. This should be a quick operation. Since we must sort the bids and the offers for any received price updates, the method and data structure we choose for this operation are crucial. To insert a new order, we'll need to use a data structure with an $O(1)$ or $O(log\ n)$ complexity.

- An **amendment/modification** will use the order ID to seek the order in the book. This operation should have the same level of difficulty as the insertion.

- **Cancelation**: Using the order ID, a cancelation allows an order to be withdrawn from the book.

The data structure chosen and the method connected with it have a significant impact on performance. If you're creating an HFT system, you'll need to make the appropriate decisions. The order book that we are implementing in HFT is called an **order-based book**. Since this is a critical component in the system, it is very important to consider the complexity of the execution of this book.

An efficient data structure to model the order book must ensure the following:

- **Constant look-up, fast quantity update**: An order book stores a lot of orders for one given instrument. Large exchanges can get millions of orders per second. Because we will have a growing number of orders in this book, it is important to keep a constant look-up time for order IDs. We will have to look up order IDs millions of times per second to update these orders. Additionally, we will need to retrieve orders with the best price rapidly. Looking up orders by price cannot be linear in terms of complexity. Therefore, we will use fast indexing (having a logarithmic time to find an order for a specific price).

- **Iteration in order of prices**: When buying or selling large quantities, we may need to find many orders to reach a given volume. In this situation, we will start with the best price, then we will go to the second-best price, and we will keep on going like this. In this situation, it is also critical for the execution speed to reach the next best price with very low complexity.

- **Retrieving best bid and ask in constant time**: Since we will mainly work with the best prices, we need to have a data structure capable of returning the best orders for bids and offers.

We will need to take into account the following considerations:

- Organize order identifiers to order information in a huge associative array (for C++, it could be a `std::unordered` map or `std::vector`).

- The order metadata includes references to the order book and price-level it belongs to, therefore, after checking up the order, the order book and price-level data structures are only a single dereference away. When using an **Order Execute** or **Order Reduce** action, having a reference to the price allows for an $O(1)$ decrease. You may preserve pointers to the next and previous orders in the queue if you wish to keep track of time priority as well.

- Because the majority of changes occur near the inside of the book, employing a vector for each book's price levels will result in the quickest average price lookup. Because the desired price is usually just a few levels from the interior and a linear search is simpler on the branch predictor, optimizer, and cache, searching linearly from the end of the vector is, on average, quicker than a binary search. Of course, pathological orders can exist outside of the book, and an attacker might, theoretically, transmit a large number of updates at the end of the book to slow down your implementation. In reality, however, this usually yields a cache-friendly, almost $O(1)$ implementation for insert, lookup, update, and delete (with an $O(N)$ memcpy in the worst-case scenario).

- This has $O(1)$ best-case behavior for insertion, lookup, deletion, and update, with extremely low constants. Unfortunately, because of the cache, TLB, and compiler-friendliness, you may achieve $O(N)$ worst-case behavior with a low probability and still have extremely excellent constants. It's also very quick, almost ideally so, when it comes to **Best Bid and Offer** (**BBO**) updates, which is what you're normally after.

By explaining how a book should be implemented in HFT, we can already see why we need to develop an in-depth knowledge of computer operating systems and programming. In the following section, we will cover in depth the use of these components to achieve the best performance.

Strategy making decisions on when to trade

The trading strategy is the system's brain. This is where we will put our algorithm that represents our trading concept into action. Let's take a look at the diagram:

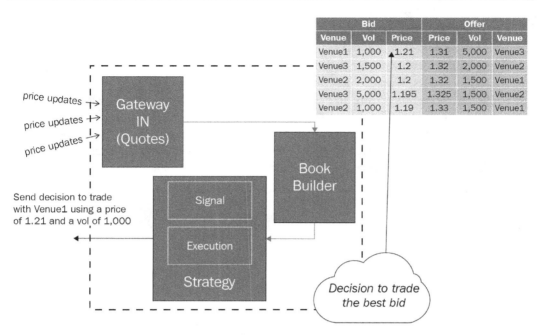

	Bid			Offer		
Venue	Vol	Price	Price	Vol	Venue
Venue1	1,000	1.21	1.31	5,000	Venue3
Venue3	1,500	1.2	1.32	2,000	Venue2
Venue2	2,000	1.2	1.32	1,500	Venue1
Venue3	5,000	1.195	1.325	1,500	Venue2
Venue2	1,000	1.19	1.33	1,500	Venue1

Figure 2.7 – Trading strategy receiving data from the book builder to make a decision on when to trade

The diagram shows that the trading strategy is divided into two main components, signal and execution:

- The signal component of this strategy only focuses on generating signals. However, having the intention (a signal) does not guarantee you will get the liquidity you are interested in. For instance, in HFT, it is highly likely your orders will be rejected because of the speed of your trading.

- The execution part of the strategy will take care of handling the response from the market. This part decides what to do for any responses from the market. For instance, what should happen when the order is rejected? You should continue trying to get equivalent liquidity and another price.

In this section, we learned about the trading strategy; we will now learn all about the **order management system (OMS)** being the last critical piece of the trading system.

The OMS

The OMS gathers orders submitted from the strategy. The order life cycle is tracked by the OMS (creation, execution, amendment, cancelation, and rejection). The OMS collects trading strategy orders. If an order is invalid or malformed, the OMS may reject it (too large a quantity, wrong direction, erroneous prices, excessive outstanding position, or order type not handled by the exchange). The order does not leave the trading system when an error is identified in the OMS. The rejection occurs sooner. As a result, the trading strategy can react more quickly than if the order is rejected by the exchange. Let's have a look at the following figure, which depicts the OMS's key features:

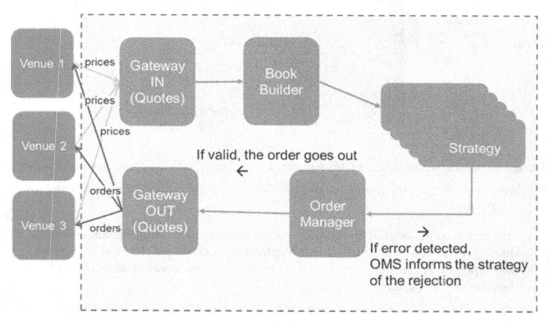

Figure 2.8 – Order manager collecting all the orders in a trading system

Let's now discuss the critical components of a trading system.

Critical components

A trading system's key components include gateways, a book builder, strategies, and an OMS. They bring together all of the capabilities you'll need to get started in trading. We calculate a trading system's performance in terms of speed by aggregating the processing times of all important components. When a price update enters the trading system, we start a timer, and when the order generated by this price update leaves the system, we terminate the timer. This period is known as the **tick-to-trade** or **tick-to-order** period.

The OMS gathers orders submitted from the strategy. The order life cycle is tracked by the OMS (creation, execution, amendment, cancelation, and rejection). The OMS collects trading strategy orders. If an order is invalid or malformed, the OMS may reject it (too large a quantity, wrong direction, erroneous prices, excessive outstanding position, or order type not handled by the exchange). The order does not leave the trading system when an error is identified in the OMS. The rejection occurs sooner. As a result, the trading strategy can react more quickly than if the order is rejected by the exchange.

Non-critical components

Non-critical components are those that aren't directly related to the choice to submit an order. They change settings, collect data, and report this data. When designing a strategy, for example, you'll have a set of parameters that you'll need to alter in real time. You'll need a component that can transmit data to the trading strategy component. We'll use a component called **command and control** for that.

Command and control

The link between traders and the trading system is known as command and control. It might be a command-line system or a user interface that receives orders from traders and routes them to the necessary components. Take a look at the following diagram:

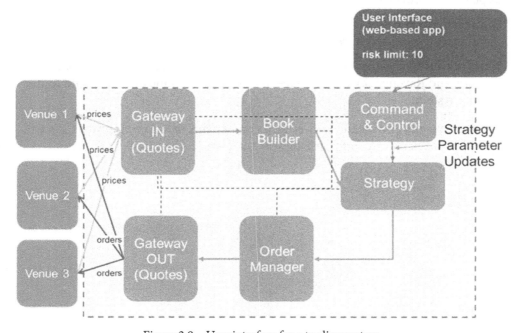

Figure 2.9 – User interface for a trading system

We covered the command and control service responsible for interacting with all the trading system components. We will now see the remaining functions of a trading system.

Services

Additional components may be added to the trading system. We will talk about the following components (it is not an exhaustive list):

- **Position server**: This keeps track of all the trades. It updates the positions for all the traded financial assets. For instance, if a trade is made for 100,000 EUR/USD at a price of $1.2, the notional position will be $120,000. If a trading system component needs the position amount for EUR/USD, it will subscribe to the position server for getting position updates. The order manager or the trading strategy may want to know this information before allowing an order to go out. If we want to limit the position to $200,000 for a given asset, another order to get 100,000 EUR/USD will be rejected.

- **Logging system**: This gathers all the logs from the components and will write a file or modify a database. A logging system helps with debugging, figuring out the causes of issues, and also just reports.

- **Viewers (read-only user interface view)**: These display the views for trading (such as positions, orders, trades, and task monitoring).

- **Control viewers (interactive user interface)**: These provide a way to modify parameters and start/stop components of the trading system.

- **News server**: This gathers news from many news companies (such as Bloomberg, Reuters, and Ravenpack) and provides this news in real time or on demand to the trading system.

This section covers the critical and non-critical components of a trading system. We will now conclude this chapter by summarizing what we have learned.

Summary

We learned how to create a trading system in this chapter. The trading system we created includes all of the necessary components for you to design a trading system and start trading.

It takes years to learn how to construct a trading system. Because of the difference between the asset classes, it is likely that you will become an expert in one asset class rather than another. We created the bare minimum of features that a trading system should have. We must learn how to link this component to a trading system in order for it to be completely functioning.

In the following chapters, we will explain in detail how trading systems should be implemented and especially related to the operating system and the hardware. In the next chapter, we have more pieces of knowledge to learn about the trading exchange.

3
Understanding the Trading Exchange Dynamics

In the previous chapter, we learned how to create **High-Frequency Trading** (**HFT**) systems. We focused intensely on the critical components of a trading system. We also reviewed in detail how to create an order book, which is basically a replication of what an exchange collects from all the trading participants. In this chapter, we are going to study how an exchange works.

We will describe the functional components of an exchange and we will focus in depth on the matching engine. Understanding how the matching engine of an exchange works is one of the most important tasks you will have to do when creating HFT strategies.

This chapter will cover the following topics:

- Understanding trading exchanges
- Understanding matching engines
- Architecting a trading exchange

In *Chapter 2, The Critical Components of a Trading System*, we gained a decent idea of how to design a trading system. We went over how to design a book, create trading signals, and receive a market response in great detail. In this chapter, we will explain in depth how an exchange works.

Architecting a trading exchange for handling orders at a large scale

Existing owners can deal with potential purchasers on stock exchanges. Exchanges are not primary markets: they can be secondary, tertiary markets. Companies that trade on stock exchanges don't buy and sell their own assets every day. They may buy back stock or issue new stocks when necessary. In a stock exchange, we purchase stocks from another shareholder. When we sell stocks, we sell them to another investor.

History of trading exchanges

In the 16th and 17th centuries, the first stock exchanges arose in Europe, mostly in port towns or commerce centers such as Antwerp, Amsterdam, and London. However, because a small number of corporations did not issue equity, these early stock markets were more analogous to bond exchanges. Most early corporations were deemed semi-public enterprises since governments had to allow them to conduct business.

The **New York Stock Exchange** (**NYSE**), enabling equity trading, first appeared in America in the late 18th century. The **Philadelphia Stock Exchange** (**PHLX**) is credited as America's first stock exchange. With the signing of the New York Stock Exchange Act in 1792, the NYSE was born.

With the introduction of contemporary stock markets, a new era of regulation and professionalization began, ensuring that buyers and sellers of stocks could trust that their transactions would be completed at acceptable prices and within a reasonable time frame. Today, there are several stock markets in the United States and across the world, many of which are electronically linked. As a result, markets have become more efficient and liquid. Stocks are, of course, the most well-known traded asset classes; however, foreign exchange, fixed income, future, options, crypto, and many other types of asset classes are also traded.

A stock exchange's share prices can be determined by a variety of methods. Conducting an auction, in which buyers and sellers make bids and offers to purchase or sell, is the most common approach. An offer (or ask) is the price at which someone wishes to purchase something, whereas a bid is the price at which they wish to sell something. When the bid and ask are equal, a transaction is made.

Understanding features of an exchange

A **stock exchange** (**exchange**) has a lot of diverse features. An exchange is a marketplace that brings together various market players to streamline transactions, decrease risks, and help in price discovery. There are several components in an exchange. The following are the primary systems, in general:

- **Listings**: These are the corporations that are traded by market participants on the exchange. They are essentially private enterprises that go through the initial public offering procedure to become public. Valuation, liquidity, and compliance expenses are all important factors to consider when choosing an exchange to list on.

- **Matching engine**: This would be similar to the old pit, where brokers stood about yelling instructions to each other. It's now fully automated as a matching engine algorithm, which takes care of the transactions. In the market, the engine publishes the order book (pending trades) and matches them properly. The speed at which these deals are matched and completed varies and is measured in nanoseconds. The way the trading engine determines the prices varies slightly between exchanges. In the *General order book and matching engine* section, we will explain it more in depth.

- **Post-trade**: Payment and settlement, as well as trade reconciliation, are all part of this process to guarantee that all orders are correctly matched and completed. Essentially, this is the tedious (but necessary) backend job.

- **Market data**: The exchange handles large amounts of data. It is sold to a variety of market participants. Trade prices, trading volumes, firm announcements/filings, and so on are all examples of this. Co-location (as we defined in *Chapter 1, Fundamentals of a High-Frequency Trading System*) has also become widespread because of HFT. As a result, the speed at which this data may be accessed is also marketed.

- **Market participants**: Clearing and trading members are the market participants. Each has its own set of qualifications, with clearing members having stricter restrictions.

Members also place collateral with the exchange to protect themselves in the event of a member's collapse. Because deals involve two parties, the exchange will step in to perform the trade with the second party if one side defaults. As a result, collateral is necessary for the exchange to assert a claim against the defaulting party while also maintaining market stability. Brokers and proprietary trading houses are the most common trading members. Clearing members are major participants who assist in the *clearing* of deals.

- **Regulation**: Depending on the asset class, the regulations differ. Different exchanges will have different regulations, depending on the jurisdiction. This is done to prevent money laundering and market tampering such as insider trading and market manipulation.

  Exchanges can also monitor company announcements to ensure that all required disclosures are made, promoting a transparent marketplace. In addition to managing market participants, the exchange must also deal with internal compliance and government authorities.

We have learned what features an exchange must have; now we will discuss in detail the architecture of an exchange.

Exchange architecture

Trading platforms are responsible for executing orders received from buy-side portfolio managers, managing and monitoring orders during the execution process, and offering electronic access to a number of venues. On the sell side, support is required for processing customer orders and maintaining trading positions.

An exchange architecture provides buy/sell trading capabilities and must meet the following business requirements:

- Support front, middle, and back office trading capabilities as well as basic and complicated rule-based and algorithmic trade techniques.

- Support backtesting and live execution of the preceding strategies throughout the development lifecycle.

- Display trading and blotter UIs (desktop applications, web-based/mobile apps).

- Support a **trading as a service** (**TaaS**) business model that might be delivered as a utility using open APIs. We talked about the integration with the trading system and the exchange using API working with the FIX protocol in the previous chapter.

- Support global integration with a wide range of external parties.

- Support a wide range of financial products.

- Should be highly scalable.

We are presenting the main functionality of an exchange in the following figure (we represented three queues for three companies: Tesla, Microsoft, and Apple):

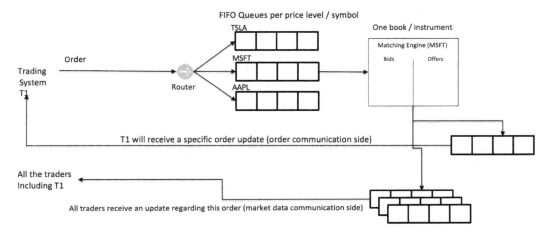

Figure 3.1 – Trading exchange architecture

In this figure, we can see a **Trading System T1** connected to the exchange. As we explained in *Chapter 2, The Critical Components of a Trading System*, the trading system initiates two connections with the exchange: price updates and orders. When an order is sent to the exchange, it will follow these steps:

1. Depending on the asset class and the instrument, it will be routed to queues. Each queue is created for one given price and one given symbol.

2. The matching engine handles the orders one at a time.

3. If there is a change in the order book (handled by the matching engine), the change will be communicated to the trader and also given to all the market participants (every update will be sent to the clearing/post trades if a trade occurs).

It is easy to observe that the communication between traders and exchanges must be fast-paced to be able to reach the speed for HFT. Therefore, the choice of protocol to convey a message is critical. A string-based protocol such as the FIX protocol is not sufficient. Most of the exchanges where it is possible to trade within microseconds use binary protocols. Trading systems are designed to provide data very quickly to trading strategies. For an exchange, the goal is to provide data to the matching engine. We are going to describe in depth what the matching engine algorithm is in the next section.

General order book and matching engine

Millions of investors and traders make up the total market, all of whom may have various opinions on the worth of a particular stock and, as a result, the price at which they are willing to purchase or sell it. Over the course of a trading day, the thousands of transactions that occur when these investors and traders transform their intentions into actions by buying and/or selling a stock generate minute-by-minute gyrations in it.

A stock exchange provides a platform for this type of trading by connecting buyers and sellers of equities. A stockbroker is required for the typical person to have access to these markets. This stockbroker serves as a go-between for the buyer and the seller.

Initially, matching buyers and sellers of stocks on an exchange was done manually, but computerized trading systems are now being used more frequently. The open outcry system, in which dealers utilized verbal and hand-signal communication to purchase and sell large blocks of stocks in the trading pit or on the exchange floor, was the manual form of trading. It has been replaced by electronic trading platforms. These technologies can match buyers and sellers significantly more efficiently and quickly than people, leading to major advantages, including cheaper trading costs and speedier trade execution.

The intention of creating a transaction between buyers and sellers is kept in what we call an order book. This order book is the same as the one we previously described for a trading system. It contains bids and offers from all the market participants. The process, which is going to match buyers and sellers, is handled by the matching engine. This algorithm matches buy and sell orders to execute securities deals. Matching engines have different algorithms to describe how orders are matched and filled in what sequence, which varies depending on where the trade is routed.

The matching engine algorithm is depicted in *Figure 3.2*. The inputs are the **Order** (1) coming from the trader and the **Order book** (2) (which contains the orders already placed on the exchange). This algorithm will return the list of the **Trades** (3) and the list of **Resting orders** (4). Every order coming to the system will be processed one by one.

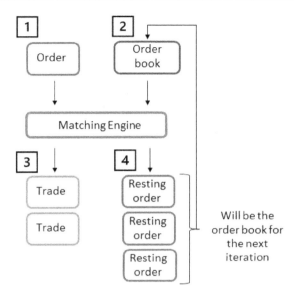

Figure 3.2 – Matching engine algorithm with inputs and outputs

When using HFT strategies, nanoseconds are important to be profitable. In this book, we will learn in detail how to optimize a trading system to get to the best performance possible. Meanwhile, an understanding of the exchange is required. As we previously described, an exchange is a server accepting connections from trading systems and running the matching engine algorithm on the order book being the structure collecting all the orders. Since all exchanges have their own matching algorithm, it is important to know the basic scenarios you will encounter when trading.

In all the following scenarios, we will explain what occurs in the exchange for an **Order** getting into the exchange in relation to the **Order book**. We will first learn about the most basic case, which is matching for the best price.

Best price scenario

By default, a matching engine will always try to find the best price available (**2**) for a given order (**1**).

The matching engine algorithm finds the best price available as it is written in *Figure 3.3*. In this figure, we can see order **#1** getting into the exchange. This order will match with order **#3**, since the price of the order is better for the buyer. Indeed, the buyer wants to buy an asset for **$100**. The exchange has this asset for **$99** and for **$100**. The matching engine will match with the available best price, which is **$99**:

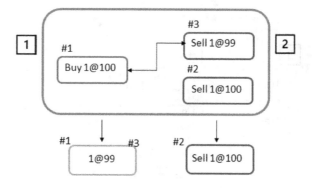

Figure 3.3 – Best price scenario

The result of the algorithm in this context will be to have a trade at **$99** between orders **#1** and **#3**. Order **#2** will remain.

In this example, the quantity was 100. We need to learn what will happen when the quantities of two matching orders are different.

Partial fill scenario

In the previous example, we had two orders matching with the same quantity. In the example in *Figure 3.4*, we have order **#1** with a quantity of **4** and order **#3** with a quantity of **1**. In this situation, to fill order **#1**, we will need to have three more shares. This trading exchange doesn't have in its order book the amount to satisfy this transaction. Therefore, orders **#3** and **#2** will be filled and the remaining quantity of **1** coming from order **#1** will remain on the exchange. That's why the output of the algorithm for this case is two filled orders and one order left.

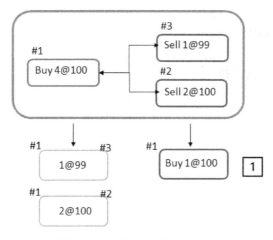

Figure 3.4 – Partial fill scenario

In the two previous examples, we had matching liquidities. Indeed, for the price that was asked, we had a liquidity to match this price. We now need to study what would happen when the liquidity cannot be matched with another one.

No match scenario

In the scenario represented in *Figure 3.5*, we have order **#1** getting into the system and the order book has two orders, **#2** and **#3**. Since the price to buy is **$98**, which is way lower than the price where the participants are ready to sell, **$99**, the matching engine will not match any orders. Order **#1** will stay on the exchange:

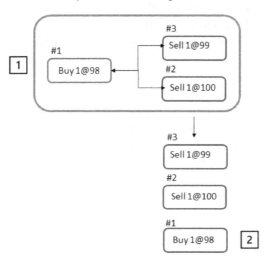

Figure 3.5 – No match scenario

In the previous scenario, we have different price levels in the book. We need to study what would happen if the price of the liquidities is the same.

Multiple orders with the same price

In the scenario represented in *Figure 3.6*, we have two orders with the same price and the incoming order with the same price. The way that the orders will be filled depends on the configuration of the matching engine:

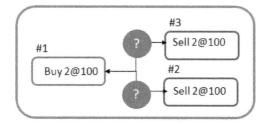

Figure 3.6 – Multiple orders with the same price in the order book

The matching engine's algorithm is crucial in determining what kind of behavior we want to encourage in the exchange. The two most popular implementations of these algorithms will be discussed in the sections that follow.

Let's talk about the different types of algorithms.

FIFO

Time/price priority, also known as **First In First Out** (**FIFO**), is the most widely used algorithm. We know, from the **exchange architecture** represented in *Figure 3.1*, that orders are stored in a queue for a given price level. Once the orders get into the matching engine, they will be stamped with the time that they entered the system. Therefore, no orders will have the same timestamp. With this observation, when we apply the FIFO algorithm, we will match the incoming order with the one that has the lower timestamp. In this situation, order **#3** has been on the exchange for a period longer than order **#2**. Consequently, order **#3** will be matched first with the incoming order **#1**. Any modifications to the orders will result in their position being lost in the order of execution. Depending on the exchanging, changing the quantity of a given order will cause this order to lose its priority. But for all the exchanges, if we have a price change, the order will lose priority because it will need to change the FIFO queue.

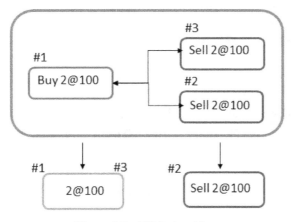

Figure 3.7 – FIFO algorithm

Even if the FIFO algorithm is the one that is used the most, many other algorithms can be used. The last algorithm we will discuss is the pure pro-rata algorithm.

Pure pro-rata

Orders are filled using a pro-rata algorithm that considers pricing, order lot size, and time. A market participant's entering order is shared evenly among matching counterorders proportionally to their quantity.

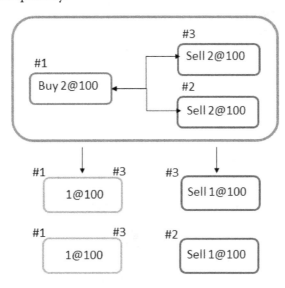

Figure 3.8 – Pure pro-rata

Figure 3.8 shows that a buy order with a price of **$100** will be executed with two orders with the same price, regardless of their timestamps. The exchange will use this algorithm to encourage participants to place orders, even if these participants are slower than the fastest participants.

Other forms of pro-rata matching

To encourage trading, the pro-rata algorithm is frequently used with other algorithms. It is generally used to incentivize particular behaviors among market participants.

Pro-rata with top-order is a method linked with pro-rata. In this situation, the oldest counter order is completed in full first, followed by a pro-rata distribution of the other counter orders, as indicated in the following diagram:

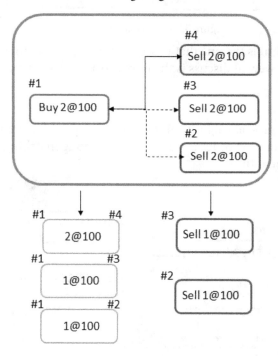

Figure 3.9 – Pro-rata algorithm variant

Figure 3.9 explains the pro-rata algorithm variant. In *Figure 3.8*, all the orders in the book were filled with the same quantity. In this variant, we give more weight when filling the orders to the older ones in the book. With this method, the exchange will still encourage participants to trade even if they are not fast enough, but the faster participants will be rewarded more by getting more traded quantities.

Any exotic configuration can be added to this algorithm. For instance, if we want to encourage bigger orders, a weight could be introduced by filling the orders with a larger quantity.

Let's end our coverage of the different scenarios that a matching engine can encounter. We will now wrap up this part by summarizing what we discussed.

Summary

As previously described, one nanosecond can create an edge in HFT. Knowing the microstructure of the market by learning how an exchange works (in terms of priority queues and the matching engine) will help you understand how to design your trading strategy. You now know that amending the price of an order will result in the loss of priority of the amended order in the queue. We also learned that depending on the exchange, changing the quantity of an order can get the same result. This chapter showed you how to design a trading exchange. We developed an in-depth understanding of how a matching engine works. In the next chapter, we will explain how hardware and operating systems operate in the context of HFT systems and trading exchanges.

Part 2:
How to Architect a High-Frequency Trading System

This part aims to give you the basics of a **high-frequency trading** (**HFT**) system. The book provides a step-by-step guide to optimizing the code and the **operating system** (**OS**) to create ultra-low latency software. It will describe the main optimizations to get the trading system, the OS, and the hardware to work together.

This part comprises the following chapters:

- *Chapter 4, HFT System Foundations – From Hardware to OS*
- *Chapter 5, Networking in Motion*
- *Chapter 6, HFT Optimization – Architecture and Operating System*
- *Chapter 7, HFT Optimization – Logging, Performance, and Networking*

4

HFT System Foundations – From Hardware to OS

In the previous chapter, we learned how an exchange works. We reviewed the functional components of an exchange and the matching engine. This chapter will explain the basic hardware and **operating system (OS)** of an HFT system.

This chapter will cover the following topics:

- Understanding HFT computers
- Using the OS for HFT
- The role of compilers

We will learn in later chapters that *high frequency* is relative to the types of trading strategies and the assets you're trading, as well as the capabilities of the exchanges you're trading on. Achieving a tick-to-trade latency of 100 microseconds requires careful programming and a good understanding of the underlying hardware. You need to write code best to take advantage of the CPU and its memory architecture and minimize the overhead of I/O operations. This chapter focuses on getting the baseline (in terms of the hardware and OS that we should have) in order to have an automated trading system that will achieve good performance. Later chapters will help us refine this, applying different optimization techniques to improve latencies in the trading system, getting us down to even below 10-microsecond latencies.

Suppose you want to get an in-depth explanation of how a modern computer system architecture works. In that case, the classic book *Computer Architecture: A Quantitative Approach* by John Hennessy and David Patterson explains that in detail and develops statistical models to help understand performance trade-offs. In this chapter, we will focus on the pieces that an HFT system needs to function. The following section will introduce the hardware of the machines used by such a system.

Understanding HFT computers

It's easy to imagine you might need some specialized computer hardware for any low-latency trading strategy. This is not the case – most hardware is normal *off-the-shelf* hardware. How you configure the hardware is more important for most cases. *Figure 4.1* shows a primary CPU, representing how a developer of an HFT system thinks about the CPU's architecture.

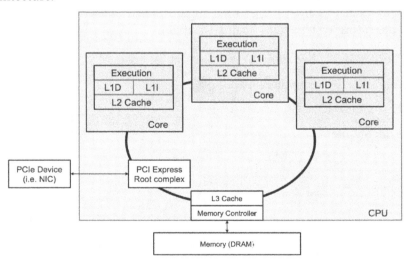

Figure 4.1 – Primary CPU

As we discussed in previous chapters, the purpose of a server in an HFT system is to handle baseline trading functions: receiving market data, executing algorithmic models, and sending orders to an exchange. This system has a network interface to send and receive data to and from a business or communicate with other trading systems inside the firm. *Chapter 5, Networking in Motion*, focuses on this aspect. Once a packet comes off the wire, the **central processing unit** (**CPU**) does the heaviest lifting. Packets will arrive in host memory from the network interface; then, the CPU will pull pieces of the packets into caches so that the CPU execution cores can decode and act on the contents of the packets.

To achieve low latency, you need to consider how your software executes in the CPU and how data flows from the various hardware components to be processed by your trading system and algorithms. In the following sections, we will look at how a CPU works and some CPU microarchitecture details that impact the performance of your software.

CPUs, from multi-processor to multi-core

A CPU is a collection of one or more processor cores that fetch and execute program instructions. These instructions can act on data stored in memory or interface with a connected device. These devices, often called **input/output** (**I/O**) devices, connect to the CPU over some expansion bus, such as **PCI Express** (**PCIe**). In the past, you needed to have multiple physical chips in a single computer to achieve multi-processing. Over the past decade, to deal with the scaling limits imposed by Moore's law, most CPUs shipped have multiple cores on a single silicon die. As silicon features (such as transistors) have become smaller, yield (the number of fully functional chips) during manufacturing has become a concern, and so there is a move back toward multiple chips (sometimes called **chiplets**) in a single package.

The CPU core is very good at performing many small logical operations. For example, the CPU can perform basic arithmetic operations (add, subtract, multiply, and divide) and logical operations (AND, OR, NOT, XOR, and bit shifting). More specialized operations, such as CRC32, steps of the **Advanced Encryption Standard** (**AES**) algorithm, and a carry-less multiplication (for example, PCLMUQDQ), are also implemented directly by some CPU cores. The CPU can also act on information loaded from memory or read from an input device. The CPU can also change its execution path based on the information it has calculated or read elsewhere. These control flow instructions are the building blocks for high-level language constructs, such as conditional statements or loops.

When market data arrives on a network interface, the CPU handles it. This means parsing the data sent over the network, managing this market data across the different functional parts of the trading systems, and possibly sending an order triggered by this market data to the exchange. In *Chapter 2, The Critical Components of a Trading System*, we described the essential elements. We discussed that the gateways, order book, and trading strategies were all components working together to trigger an order. With a single CPU execution core, each of these actions would have to happen in sequence, meaning only a single packet could be processed at one time. This means that packets could queue up and wait for the previous packet to finish being processed; this increases the time a message could wait before the trading system can provide this new data to a trading strategy. To reduce latency, we want many processing units working in parallel, handing off the processed market data as quickly as possible to move on to the following message that has arrived. Parallel computing systems have been around since the dawn of computing, though these were used in highly specialized scientific computing applications in the early days. In the 1990s, multi-socket servers became prevalent with two or more CPUs on the same board. Since single-CPU cores could not scale in performance due to Moore's law's limitations, CPU vendors started to add multiple processing cores on a single chip. A modern server can have multiple CPU sockets, each with multiple CPU cores present, achieving a considerable amount of parallelism in a single machine.

Figure 4.2 depicts a modern multi-socket system architecture. Memory or I/O devices are attached directly to a particular CPU socket. These are referred to as being local to the CPU. Other CPUs can be connected in a single system using an interconnect, such as Intel's Ultra Path Interconnect or AMD's Infinity Fabric. Suppose one CPU attempts to access memory or an I/O device attached to a different CPU. In that case, this is referred to as accessing a remote resource. When we compare the time it takes for one CPU to access its local resources with that of a remote CPU over an interconnect, we find that the interconnect is much slower than just accessing local memory. We call this access time *non-uniform* and call these architectures **non-uniform memory access** (**NUMA**). The term **cache-coherent NUMA** or **ccNUMA** refers to the fact that a CPU core is guaranteed to have the correct view of memory even if another CPU core has modified the data. NUMA architectures can scale to large numbers of cores. It's possible to think of each CPU as being a separate computer system, all interconnected with each other over a fabric.

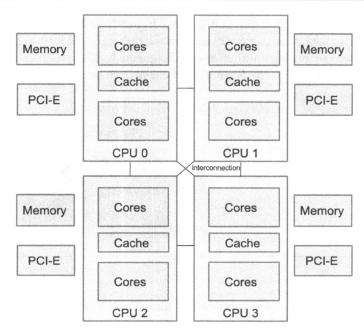

Figure 4.2 – A four-way NUMA architecture. Note how the CPUs form a fully connected graph in this configuration

Figure 4,2 also represents a few more components. PCIe is a bus connecting other devices, such as the **Network Interface Card** (**NIC**). When there is more than one CPU present in a NUMA architecture, additional CPUs are capable of sharing data by requesting it over the interconnect bus.

A note about hyper-threading and simultaneous multithreading

Simultaneous multithreading, known on Intel CPUs as hyper-threading, is a trick where the CPU keeps track of multiple parallel execution states (two such states, in the case of hyper-threading). When one execution state needs to wait for a high-latency event (such as fetching data from a higher-level cache or RAM), the CPU switches over to the other execution state while waiting for the fetch to complete; this is a kind of automatic threading that is managed by the CPU itself and makes each physical core appear as multiple *virtual* cores.

There is a temptation to double the number of physical cores using hyper-threading, but this introduces hard-to-control latency that looks like a context switch.

Figure 4.3 depicts the use of hyper-threading in one **hyperthreaded core**. We can observe that the hardware can fake a concurrent execution if a task needs to wait to access a memory segment while running another one simultaneously. If a system call (or an interruption) demands access to the **Kernel**, all the tasks will be on hold.

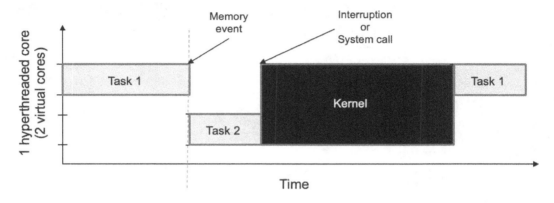

Figure 4.3 – Hyper-threading

The major problem of hyper-threading is that it removes the control of task switching (at the software level), which can create higher jitter and higher latency.

Main memory or RAM

Often called **Random Access Memory (RAM)**, main memory is a large, non-persistent store for program instructions and data. RAM is the first stop for any data read from an I/O device, such as a network card or a storage device. Modern RAM can return data bursts at high throughput but at the expense of latency when data at an address is requested and the data becomes available.

In a typical NUMA architecture, each CPU has some local RAM. Many configurations will have an equal amount of RAM connected to each NUMA node, but this is not a firm requirement. The latency of access to RAM, especially on a remote NUMA node, can be pretty high. So, we need other ways to hide this latency or buffer data, close to the CPU executing some code. This is where caches come into play.

Caches

Modern processors, with many cores, have caches local to each core and caches shared by all cores on a single socket. These caches are designed to take advantage of the fact that programs typically operate on data in the same memory region within a particular time window. This spatial and temporal locality of data access presents an opportunity for the CPU to hide the latency of access to RAM.

Figure 4.4 shows a typical cache hierarchy for a modern multi-core CPU. The **L1** cache is split into two parts: a data cache and an instruction cache. The **L2** and **L3** caches will mix instructions and data freely, as does the main memory.

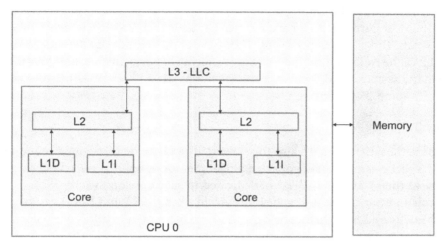

Figure 4.4 – Cache system

We will now talk about the structure of the caching system.

Cache structure

Rather than reading a single word or byte from the main memory at a time, each cache entry typically stores a particular number of words, referred to as a **cache line**. The entire line is read and cached at the same time. When a cache line is read in, another line needs to be *evicted* to make room for the new cache line. Which line is evicted is often determined on a least-recently-used basis, but other schemes exist. Different levels of cache have different cache line sizes – this is a property of the CPU design itself. There are a variety of details on how to align data structures to cache line sizes to increase the odds of a cache hit, mainly when many related data structures are accessed.

L1 cache

The L1 cache (Level 1) is the quickest memory available in a computer system and it is placed close to the execution units of the CPU. The L1 cache has the data that the CPU has most recently accessed and loaded into registers. The CPU vendor determines the L1 cache size.

The L1 cache is divided into the data cache and the instruction cache. The instruction cache stores information on the operation that the CPU must complete, whereas the data cache stores the data on which the process will be performed.

L2 cache

The L2 cache (Level 2) is slower than the L1 cache but larger. Modern L2 memory caches are measured in megabytes(MB), whereas L1 caches are measured in kilobytes(KB). The size of the L2 store varies depending on the CPU. However, it is usually between 256 KB and 8 MB. Most current CPUs have a larger L2 cache than 256 KB, which is now considered small. Today's most powerful CPUs have an L2 memory cache of more than 8 MB. The L2 cache trails behind the L1 cache in terms of performance, but it is still far quicker than the system RAM. The L1 cache is generally 100 times faster than RAM, while the L2 cache is about 25 times faster.

L3 cache

The L3 cache is the largest, but it's also the slowest. The L3 cache is included in modern CPUs. The L3 cache is more analogous to a global memory pool that the whole chip may utilize, whereas the L1 and L2 caches are dedicated to each core on the chip. The L3 cache is what we call a *victim cache*: any cache line evicted from the L1 and L2 caches local to a core will be delivered to L3 before being sent to the main memory. It is a usually fully associative cache placed in the refill path of a CPU cache that stores all the blocks evicted from that level of cache. All cores share the L3 cache on a modern CPU.

Shared memory

Most computer systems today, especially those with multiple sockets, create the illusion of a single design with one pool of main memory. We refer to these as **shared memory systems**, where programs running on any CPU can access any memory attached to another CPU as though it were local to the CPU running the code.

Today, there are two types of shared memory models: **uniform memory access (UMA)** and **non-uniform memory access (NUMA)**. UMA uses a single memory controller, and all CPUs communicate with the system memory through this single memory controller. In most cases, the memory controller is a separate chip that all CPUs connect to directly. In NUMA architectures, there are memory controllers, with memory being physically connected to a particular socket. The main benefit of a NUMA architecture over UMA is that a NUMA system can scale more quickly to a more significant number of CPUs, because interconnecting NUMA nodes is less complex than connecting several CPUs to a single pool of system memory.

In the case of UMA, as more microprocessors are added, the shared bus becomes congested and becomes a performance bottleneck. This severely limits the ability of a UMA system to scale the number of available CPUs, and it increases the amount of time each CPU core has to wait for requests to main memory to be serviced.

All modern multi-socket servers on the market today are NUMA architectures. Each CPU socket has its pool of memory physically connected to it. Since each CPU has multiple layers of cache present, it's a possibility that the CPU will have cached an old version of data contained in another CPU's memory (or even that another remote CPU will have modified memory local to this CPU). To solve these cases, we need cache coherency protocols. These protocols enable a CPU to determine whether it uniquely owns, shares, or has a locally modified version of a particular memory region, and share information with other CPUs if they try to access the exact memory location. Ideally, an application is written to rarely require the use of these protocols, especially where latency and throughput matter, since the cost of synchronizing this ownership is high.

SMP and NUMA systems are commonly employed for HFT systems, in which processing could be distributed among several processors working in a single memory location. This must be considered when designing data structures and systems to pass messages between trading system components.

I/O devices

There are many different types of I/O devices connected to a computer, such as hard drives, printers, keyboards, mice, network cards, and many others. The primary device we should consider in HFT is the network card described in *Chapter 5*, *Networking in Motion*. Most I/O devices are connected to a CPU using **Peripheral Component Interconnect Express** (**PCIe**). PCIe devices are directly related to a particular CPU in a NUMA infrastructure. When building a trading system, you need to consider which CPU your networking code (such as market data gateway), is keeping local to the CPU that the network device is connected to minimize latency.

A device that we always try to limit the usage of is the hard disk. Accessing the data on a hard disk is very costly and will rarely be used in HFT systems. However, when we backtest a trading strategy, the information is stored on disks. We will need to have data stored in a specific way to ensure fast access. We will not address this part in this book since it is not specific to HFT systems.

Using the OS for HFT systems

Any HFT software runs on top of an OS. The OS is an abstraction on top of the hardware, hiding the details of how to launch executables, manage memory, and access devices. One of the techniques used to reduce latency is to break this abstraction where appropriate and interact directly with the hardware. These applications interface between the users (programmers) and hardware.

The OS has several main functionalities, including the following:

- Abstracting access to hardware resources
- Process scheduling
- Memory management
- A means of storing and accessing data
- A means of communicating with other computers
- Interruption management

For HFT systems, the main critical functionality is process scheduling. We will describe in detail what the process of scheduling tasks is in the following sections.

User space and kernel space

The heart of the OS is its kernel. The kernel is a highly privileged chunk of code that sits between applications and the hardware. The kernel typically provides many services, ranging from managing protocol stacks for networking and communication to providing abstractions on top of hardware devices in the form of device drivers. A kernel is highly privileged and can control how a system works, including reading and writing from arbitrary physical memory addresses, creating and destroying processes, and even altering data before making it available to applications running on the system. The kernel must be carefully protected, and only trusted code should run in the kernel context, referred to as kernel space.

User space is where applications run. A user space process is a separate virtual memory space with multiple threads. User space processes tend to be much less privileged and require exceptional support from the kernel to access devices, allocate physical memory, or alter the machine state. A trading system runs in user space, but one of the challenges of building a low-latency trading system is to minimize the number of abstractions between the hardware and your trading system. After all, the more code that has to be executed to convert data between different formats, switch context to the kernel or other processes to deliver messages, or handle unnecessary changes in the state of hardware, the more time is wasted not running critical trading system code.

One important concept is the separation of address spaces. As we'll see, this is in part related to how memory is allocated by the OS and understood by the CPU, but this is also a security and stability feature. One process should not be able to impact the kernel or another process without explicit permission to do so. Without shared memory or similar communication techniques, there are few ways that processes in user space can directly interact with each other. This applies equally to the kernel, as there are very few ways a process can directly interact with the kernel. The kernel is designed to protect access to its sensitive resources and data structures carefully.

Process scheduling and CPU resource management

Any software is first compiled and sits on durable long-term storage (some solid-state drive or hard disk). When we want to launch a trading system (or any software), we invoke one or more executables stored on a disk. This results in the OS creating one or more processes.

The OS will load the software into the main memory, create a virtual memory space, and invoke a thread to execute the code that was just loaded. This combination of the software running, the virtual memory space, and one or more threads is called a **process**. Once loaded, the OS will eventually *schedule* the process' main thread. The **scheduler** is in charge of determining where and when threads associated with a process will be executed. The scheduler can manage the execution of threads across multiple execution cores, which can be scheduled in parallel across multiple physical CPU sockets. The scheduler is an abstraction on top of this multitude of CPU cores, as in a modern computer system described in the previous section.

When we have more processes than execution cores available, the scheduler can restrict how long a thread executes before it steps in to swap with another waiting thread. This is called multitasking. The action of changing the process running from one to another is called a **context switch**.

A context switch is an expensive operation. The OS saves the execution environment of the process being switched out and restores the environment of the process being resumed. As discussed earlier, trading systems leverage multiple cores to achieve real-time parallelism. The more physical execution cores there are available, the more threads there are running in parallel, typically mapping one thread to one execution core.

There are two traditional approaches to process scheduling used in modern OSs:

- **Preemptive multitasking**: Linux and most OSs implement a preemptive multitasking approach. Preemptive multitasking aims to ensure that one process cannot monopolize the system. Each process is given a specific amount of time to run. This amount of time is called a **timeslice**. The scheduler will stop the process from running after that timeslice has expired. In addition to preventing processes from consuming too much time, this approach allows the scheduler to make global processing decisions. Many preemptive multitasking schedulers try to be NUMA topology-aware and execute a thread close to its resources, but this is generally difficult to achieve.

- **Cooperative multitasking**: This differs primarily because it will allow a process to run until the process voluntarily decides to stop running. We call the act of a process willingly choosing to stop running *yielding*. This approach is typical for real-time OSs since engineers would not want latency-sensitive code disrupted by the scheduler or other running tasks. You could imagine that this would be disastrous in a real-time control system for some critical safety process, or if you delayed an order reaching the market until long after someone else took that liquidity. OSs such as Linux have a form of cooperative multitasking available, which can be useful for latency-sensitive code if used with care. Usually, this is to support real-time applications using Linux.

Almost all task scheduler implementations provide several mechanisms to tune the scheduler's behavior. This can include guidance on a per-process basis, such as prioritization, NUMA and execution unit affinity, hints about memory usage, rules on I/O priority, and so on. Linux allows multiple scheduling rules to be applied to running processes, enabling some groups of tasks to use real-time scheduling rules. Many of these settings are helpful when designing low-latency systems but they need to be used with care; incorrect prioritization could lead to priority inversions or other deadlock scenarios.

A scheduler will always use the same fairness for all the resources and processes in its default configuration. This gives the assurance of granting each request, from a set of requests, within a predetermined bound time, even though the scheduling request primitives are unfair or random. In *Chapter 6, HFT Optimization – Architecture and Operating System*, we will explain how to make this process scheduling specialized for HFT systems by limiting the number of context switches.

Memory management

To be executed, the software needs to have its instructions and data available in memory. The OS instructs the CPU on which memory belongs to which process.

The OS must track what memory regions have been allocated, map memory to each process, and specify how much memory to allocate to a given process.

The address space that the memory management unit accesses is called the **physical address space**. This is the physical memory that is available on your computer. The CPU will allocate portions of this space to the executing processes. These subdivided spaces are referred to as the **virtual address space**. The memory management unit's job is to map that space from physical to logical in real time, so that the CPU can quickly figure out which physical address a virtual address corresponds to.

Paged memory and page tables

Modern OSs do not know the objects or data that a process is accessing or storing. Instead, the OS focuses on fundamental system-level units of memory. The most basic team of memory the OS manages is a *page*. Pages are uniformly sized regions of physical memory with exact alignment, the size of which is usually determined architecturally by the CPU. A page can be *mapped* to a particular virtual address using hardware built into the CPU called the **memory management unit** (**MMU**). By remapping disparate physical pages to a contiguous, virtual range of talks, application developers don't have to think about how the hardware manages memory or where pages exist in physical memory. Each process executed by the OS will have its page mappings, referred to as a page table.

Figure 4.5 represents processes using pages. Any physical page can exist in multiple sets of page mappings. This means that various threads, perhaps running on different CPU cores, can access the same memory page within their address space.

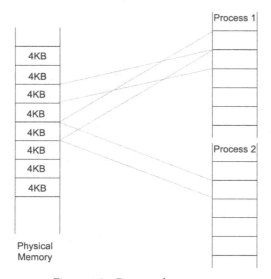

Figure 4.5 – Pages and processes

Translating physical and virtual addresses back and forth is done automatically by hardware in the CPU. For this reason, the performance of the translation would be improved if the information we are translating was in a speedy location close to the CPU. Indeed, a location used to store this information, the page table, will often be in dedicated registers in the CPU, but this is only possible when the page table is tiny. A special-purpose high-speed cache in the CPU called the **translation lookaside buffer** (**TLB**) is used for any practical page tables. Since page tables are an in-memory data structure, if the address space for a process is too large to fit inside the TLB, most CPUs have hardware that will pull the relevant page tables into the TLB from other CPUs' caches or even main memory.

Paging can hurt the performance of a process. When there is a cache miss in the TLB, the OS must load data from elsewhere in memory. In HFT systems, we sometimes minimize the impact of the TLB cache miss by increasing the page size. Virtual memory pages larger than the standard base page size of 4 KB are referred to as **huge pages**. For frequent access patterns on big datasets, huge pages can increase memory speed. Huge pages come with a cost – the TLB that tracks huge pages can sometimes be orders of magnitude smaller than that which manages standard pages, meaning more frequent trips to memory could be needed if you have many huge pages mapped. Thus, huge pages must be used with care.

System calls

A system call means a user space application requests a service from the OS' kernel. A system call is a way for applications to communicate with the OS. A system call is a request from software to the kernel of an OS to perform some sensitive action such as manipulating the hardware state. Some critical system calls on modern OSs are requested to handle process creation and termination, manage files on disk, manage I/O devices, and communicate with the outside world.

When a system call is requested, the kernel will carry out the operation if the request is allowed. For many system calls, if the call is completed successfully, the application receives some response from the kernel. Once the system call is complete, the scheduler can schedule the requesting task to resume if it has time left in its timeslice, or if there isn't a higher priority task waiting for CPU time. The kernel provides the results to the application and then transfers data from kernel space to user space in memory after the procedure is completed.

Some particular system calls, such as getting the system date and time, may take a few nanoseconds to complete. A more extended system call, such as connecting to a network device or interacting with files on disk, may take several seconds. Most OSs launch a separate kernel thread for each system call to minimize bottlenecks. Multi-threaded OSs can handle several system calls at the same time. An HFT system will heavily use this notion of concurrent execution, such as using threads.

Modern versions of Linux provide the **virtual dynamic shared object** (**vDSO**) exporting some special kernel space functions to user space, especially those related to retrieving current system time. The power of vDSO is that these functions, under the control of the kernel and thus aware of the hardware specifics, execute directly in the user space process. Unlike open and read system calls that require an entire trip into the kernel (and thus a complete context switch), functions such as `clock_gettime` (in the case of `CLOCK_MONOTONIC` at least) have a very low overhead to call because the call is in vDSO.

Threading

The most fundamental division of work in any process is a thread. By doing work across many threads, parallelism may be achieved. All threads inside a single process share a common virtual memory space. Each process, a grouping of one or more threads, has its own unique memory space. The main activity of a trading system is to share data across the different functionalities (potentially processes) to decide to send an order. The use of threads or a process will be considered when optimizing the communication between concurrent functionalities. This also impacts how you structure data being passed between threads and processes. Data passed between threads can take advantage of concurrency in memory allocation, allowing you to pass data by simply giving another thread a pointer to the message in a data structure. Passing data between processes either requires a shared memory pool mapped by both processes or serializing messages into some queue, as discussed in *Chapter 6, HFT Optimization – Architecture and Operating System*.

On top of being capable of sharing memory, threads have a faster response time than processes. If a process is separated into numerous threads, the output of one thread may be returned promptly as it completes its execution. Their context switch time is also shorter than the one for processes.

Because system calls are required in any HFT system, it is essential to offset the cost. We will see how to benefit from threads and processes in *Chapter 6, HFT Optimization – Architecture and Operating System*.

Interruption management

Interrupt requests are how peripherals alert the CPU when something has happened. The CPU will then halt one of the processing cores and switch the context to the interrupt handler assigned to that device. Limiting the number of interruptions that can create context switches; we will also return to this in *Chapter 6, HFT Optimization – Architecture and Operating System.*

Figure 4.6 depicts the impact of using an interruption (or a system call) in a CPU's time executing a task in a single-core model. We can observe that the scheduler will switch between the currently running task and the interrupt context in the kernel. The kernel spends more time on servicing interrupt requests, and then there's less CPU time available to run user tasks.

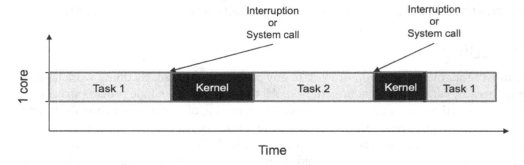

Figure 4.6 – Interruption or system call impact on task scheduling

Figure 4.7 shows the benefit of two CPU cores, having two tasks that do not need to share time. This example shows that if we pin a task to a given core, we will reduce the number of context switches and reduce the impact of kernel interruptions. This example also assumes that interrupt requests are serviced by only one core. Thus, only **Task 1** will be disrupted to service hardware.

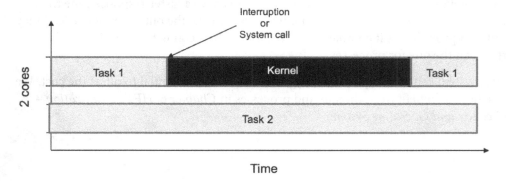

Figure 4.7 – Advantage of two CPU cores

Chapter 6, HFT Optimization – Architecture and Operating System, details this task scheduling pinning a task to a given core.

In the first two sections, we learned about the hardware, the OS, and their involvement in HFT systems. We will now tackle the last piece: the compilation and libraries, which are also essential to HFT systems.

The role of compilers

Compilers translate human-readable code written in a programming language (the source language) into another language, usually a machine-specific language, though this can be a virtual machine. They translate code from a high-level language to a lower-level one. They can generate intermediate code, assembly languages, object code, or machine code. They also play an essential role in speeding up software runtime. Compilers keep getting smarter by improving the abstraction of what developers wanted to express with efficient execution in hardware. New programming paradigms were added to improve software engineering. In the 1990s, Python and Java made object-oriented programming available to everyone. We recommend that the reader check out the book *Compilers: Principles, Techniques, and Tools*, also known as the *Dragon Book*, written by Aho, Lam, Sethi, and Ullman. This book will explain in depth how compilers are designed.

In HFT systems, the compilers can help optimize the part of the code where we spend most of the time: loops. *Advanced Compiler Design and Implementation*, written by Steven Muchnick, describes the loop optimization that compilers can do. We must keep in mind that the critical part of HFT systems is the space-time tradeoff (increasing memory usage and cache utilization while decreasing execution time). We can talk about a few examples of optimization using this paradigm:

- Loop unrolling is an example of this tradeoff. Because there are fewer iterations when a loop is unrolled, the overhead of exit checks is reduced. Furthermore, there are fewer branch instructions, which may have an overhead depending on the architecture. There are no exit tests in the case of a fully unrolled loop. Unrolling a loop can lead to further optimizations that a compiler can do (for example, in the preceding fully unrolled version, all the array offsets are constants, which is something the compiler may be able to exploit).

- Function inlining can replace the function call by the assembly code of this function itself on the callee side, giving opportunities for more assembly code optimizations.

- Table and calculation. The compilers can help create data structures to avoid recalculation. They will hold values of values already calculated.

The primary function of the compiler is to generate an executable that's runnable by the OS. We will now discuss the executable file formats.

Executable file formats

The compiler and linker convert a high-level program into an executable file format appropriate for the target OS. The OS parses the executable file to figure out how to load and run the program. On Windows, this is a **portable executable** (**PE**) file, whereas on Linux, this is an **executable and linkable format** (**ELF**) file. Each OS has a loader. The loader determines which chunks of the program on the disk are loaded into memory. The loader allocates the virtual address range that the executable will be using. Then, it will start the execution from the entry point (in the example of the C language, the `_start` function), which then calls the programmer-defined `main` function. In terms of memory, it is essential to remember that the OS protects processes from one another by using virtual memory, as we described when discussing virtual memory and paging. Every executable runs isolated in its own virtual address space.

Static versus dynamic linking

Many executable programs on modern systems depend on external code libraries, often provided by third parties, such as an OS vendor. To deal with these external dependencies, there are two ways that a program can integrate this code. The first is by statically linking in all the code, building a standalone binary. The second is by dynamically linking in the external code, requiring the OS to inspect the executable file to figure out which libraries are needed to run the program, loading them separately.

The linker will arrange the application code and dependencies into a single binary object with static linking. Since this binary object has all the dependencies included, there is no opportunity for a program to take advantage of the same library being reused by multiple programs, thus requiring all the code to be loaded separately at runtime. For example, on Linux, many programs utilize the `glibc` library. If these programs were statically linked, they would waste a lot of memory storing the same dependent library repeatedly. Static linking has a significant advantage: the compiler and linker can work together to optimize all function calls, even with objects pulled in from an external library.

Dynamic linking allows the linker to create a smaller binary file where the dependent libraries' locations would have been replaced with a stub. The dynamic linker will load that library, often on application startup, by loading the appropriate shared object from the disk. Only when the dependency is needed will it be loaded into memory. If multiple running processes use the same library, the library's code's memory can be shared across multiple processes. However, this efficiency comes at a cost: library functions are referenced indirectly when called through the **procedure linkage table** (**PLT**). This indirection can lead to added overhead, especially if a short function within the library is called frequently. Typical HFT systems will use static linking where possible to avoid this overhead.

Summary

In this chapter, we developed a conceptual model of how computers work and how to think about the overall performance impact of the various components. Each of the multiple pieces of hardware and software must work in a manner ideal for a trading system. That often requires an understanding of how the hardware and software interact so that the negative impact of inefficient algorithms or interactions can be circumvented or optimized.

Then we are using the fundamentals developed in this chapter as a foundation. The following chapters will build on optimizing the OS, kernel, and application for HFT systems. This will include reducing the impact of context switching, techniques for safely accessing shared data structures, and other means of mitigating inefficient components of the underlying hardware and software.

The next chapter will focus on networking. We will explain the role of a network card for HFT systems and how communication with the exchange needs to be optimized to reduce latency.

5
Networking in Motion

In the previous chapter, we talked in depth about the hardware and the operating system. Any trading system must collect data from the exchange and make decisions based on this data. To do so, communication will be essential in the performance of the **high-frequency training** (**HFT**) system. In this chapter, we will review how trading systems communicate in depth, how to use networks in HFT systems, and how to monitor network latency.

In this chapter, we will cover the following topics:

- Understanding networking in HFT systems
- Network communications between systems in HFT
- Important protocol concepts
- Designing financial protocols for HFT exchanges
- Interior networks versus exterior networks
- Understanding the packet life cycle
- Monitoring the network
- Valuing time distribution

The following section will describe networking basics; we will go through the fundamentals that we will optimize later on.

Understanding networking in HFT systems

Trading systems receive market data and send orders from/to exchanges. The numerous processes spread out across different machines within a trading system need to communicate with one another—for instance, a process keeping track of a position of an instrument across the design will need to send information to all components regarding the position of a given asset. Networking defines how devices are interconnected with each other. Networking is required to transfer data from a machine to another one (by extension, to an exchange).

The network is the underpinning of all HFT systems and needs to be considered as carefully as the design decisions for software systems.

The device ensuring communication in any system is called the **Network Interface Card** (**NIC**). It allows communication between the computer where software runs and the outside world. When we understand how a trading system works, we must examine the layered model used to describe the networking stack within the operating system required for computers to talk with each other.

Learning about network conceptual models

The **Open Systems Interconnection** (**OSI**) model is arguably the most common depiction of how computers speak to each other in modern networked environments. The OSI model is a conceptual framework used to describe the functions of a networking system. The following screenshot depicts the complete seven layers of the OSI model and the related operations typically found at each layer:

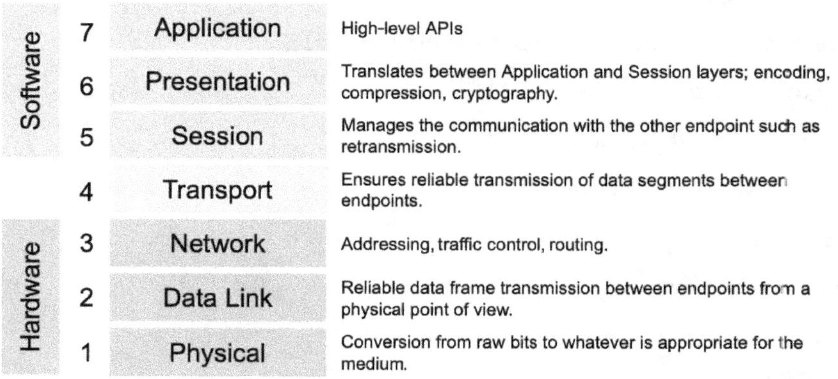

Software	7	Application	High-level APIs
Software	6	Presentation	Translates between Application and Session layers; encoding, compression, cryptography.
Software	5	Session	Manages the communication with the other endpoint such as retransmission.
	4	Transport	Ensures reliable transmission of data segments between endpoints.
Hardware	3	Network	Addressing, traffic control, routing.
Hardware	2	Data Link	Reliable data frame transmission between endpoints from a physical point of view.
Hardware	1	Physical	Conversion from raw bits to whatever is appropriate for the medium.

Figure 5.1 – The seven-layer OSI model

This model is divided into seven independent layers, which all have specific functions and communicate with their adjacent layers only and don't communicate with all the other layers. The layers are described in more detail here:

- **The session, presentation, and application layers**: These three layers can be regrouped (to simplify) because these are the layers that we will use at the software level. In HFTs, we focus on the following four layers because they give advanced optimization opportunities.

- **Transport layer**: This manages the delivery and also contains errors in data packets. Sequencing, packet size, and transfer of data between systems are the responsibility of the network layer. In finance, we mainly use two protocols: the **Transmission Control Protocol (TCP)** and the **User Datagram Protocol (UDP)**.

- **Network layer**: This receives frames from the data link layer and delivers them to the intended destinations using logical addresses. We will use the addressing protocol called **Internet Protocol (IP)**. Unlike **IP version 6 (IPv6)**, **IP version 4 (IPv4)** is a light and user-friendly protocol and is the most widely used protocol in the financial sector.

- **Data link layer**: This layer corrects errors that may have occurred at the physical layer by detecting errors with techniques such as **parity checks** or **cyclic redundancy checks (CRCs)**.

- **Physical layer**: This is the media that two machines use to communicate, including optical fiber, copper cable, and satellite. All these media have different characteristics (latency, bandwidth, and attenuations). Based on the type of application we want to build we will leverage one versus the other. This physical layer is considered the lowest layer of the OSI model. It is concerned with delivering raw unstructured data bits across the network, either electrically or optically, from the sender's physical layer to the receiver's physical layer. Network hubs, cabling, repeaters, network adapters, and modems are examples of *physical* resources found at the physical layer.

As you can see from how the layers are grouped in *Figure 5.2*, we often refer to several of them simultaneously. For example, we may refer to *layers 5-7* as the **software layer** and *layers 1-3* as the **hardware layer**, with *layer 4* getting mixed between the two. This is so common that a simplified model that consolidates the software, transport, and hardware layers is frequently used and looks like this:

Application	OSI Layers 5-7
TCP/IP	OSI Layers 3-4
Physical	OSI Layers 1-2

Figure 5.2 – Simplified OSI model

Now that we have discussed the high-level layered path that a packet must take when moving through the networking stacks on two communicating computers, we will discuss how to design a network for HFTs.

Network communications between systems in HFT

When designers build a network for HFT systems, they focus on the different modes of communication. Because microseconds matter, they must consider the benefits of using a microwave network or a Cisco switch over another switch.

The innovation in networking has the potential to make enormous differences in trading.

The following diagram represents an abstract model of a network. When two devices communicate, they need a medium to have the data transferred. They communicate through a physical connection connected to a network device such as a switch. The switch is in charge of moving the packet from one part of the network to the other, where we can find the recipient of the data the sender sends:

Figure 5.3 – Abstract model of a network

Every network component is essential for network latency. These are all sources of latency:

- The NIC converts the signal from a computer to a network and vice versa. The time for the NIC to process data is negligible but is not zero. The NIC is chosen for low-latency data paths and other capabilities, such as the following:

  - **Bus**: A bus transfers data from one component of a computer to another one. We can find three main types of buses: **Peripheral Component Interconnect** (**PCI**), **PCI eXtended** (**PCI-X**), and **PCI Express** (**PCIe**). They all have different speeds. In 2017-2018, the industry started using PCIe 5.0, working with a rate of 63 **gigabytes per second** (**GB/s**). Even though PCIe 6 was announced in 2019, PCIe 5.0 is the fastest bus for NIC.

- **Number of ports**: A NIC card can have different numbers of ports: one, two, four, or six. It can allow a machine to access multiple networks at the same time. However, it is also possible to have multiple NICs on the same machine.

- **Port type**: NICs can have different types of connections. A **Registered Jack-45** (**RJ-45**) port is one type of port. It uses a twisted-pair cable named **Category 5** (**Cat5**) or **Category 6** (**Cat6**). The other common cable type we can have is the coaxial one, which connects to a **Bayonet Neill-Concelman** (**BNC**) port. The last one is an optical port that works with a fiber-optic cable.

- **Network speed**: The standard supported network speed is single-lane 100 **gigabits per second** (**Gbps**), 25 Gbps, and 10 Gbps signaling. Anything else (that is, 400 Gbps, 50 Gbps, 40 Gbps, and so on) comprises multiple parallel lanes. Ethernet with 10 Gbps and 25 Gbps is used in data centers and financial applications every day.

- **Application-specific integrated circuit** (**ASIC**): Integrates the functionality to interface with the host PC over PCIe and the network itself.

- **Hub**: A hub is a device with several ports connecting a **local area network** (**LAN**) network together. When a packet gets into the system by a port, it is replicated throughout the LAN, allowing all recipients to see all packets. A hub serves as a central connecting point for all devices in a network. This technology has been almost obsolete. Metamako/Exablaze revived this technology, and it is a latency-saving method for applications in HFTs.

- **Switch**: A switch works at the data link layer (layer 2) and sometimes the network layer (layer 3); therefore, it can support any packet protocols. Its main role is to filter and forward packets across the LAN.

- **Router**: A router joins—at a minimum—two networks and facilitates packet delivery from hosts on one network to those on the other. In an HFT system, the router is found at the gates (gateways in *Chapter 2, The Critical Components of a Trading System*) of the trading system. The router finds the best way to forward a packet from one host to another.

The primary components (such as routers, NICs, and switches) will introduce latency in the HFT system.

Comprehending how switches work

Switches are the primary support of communication within an HFT network. Observe the following diagram:

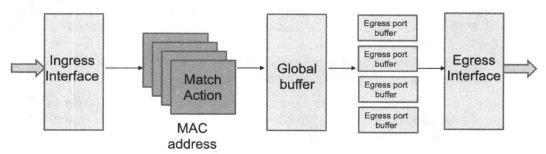

Figure 5.4 – Abstract model of a switch

Figure 5.4 represents the abstract model of a switch. *Ingress* and *egress* are words used in the industry to denote the **input and output (I/O)** of any network device. The switch works at the network layer 2. Its primary function is to transfer a packet from its input to its output, which you can see in the preceding diagram as **Ingress Interface** and **Egress Interface**, by applying forwarding rules. A switch handles two sorts of operations, as outlined here:

- **Configuring packet forwarding**: For a naive switch, the model is just to observe **media access control** (**MAC**) addresses on a port and switch traffic to that port. More sophisticated switches (that is, ones that support layer 3/4) will allow actions on other match patterns (that is, IP address or port).

- **Forward/filter decisions**: Switches read configuration tables to forward packets accordingly and remove packets when necessary.

The switch is set up once at startup time, and then tables are generated on the fly as new forwarding entries are required, such as when routing tables are updated.

The *parser* is the first to deal with new packets (the packet body is buffered independently and is unavailable for matching). The parser defines the switch's protocols, identifying and extracting information from the header.

Following that, the extracted header fields are sent to the match-action tables (component matching header fields to perform an action). Ingress and egress are separated in the match-action tables. Ingress match-action decides the egress port(s) and the queue into which the packet is routed, while both may alter the packet header. The packet may be forwarded, duplicated, discarded, or triggered by a control flow based on ingress processing. The egress match-action modifies the packet header on a per-instance basis (for example, for multicast copies). To track frame-to-frame state, action tables (counters, policers, and so on) can be linked to a flow.

Metadata, regarded similarly to packet header fields, can be carried by packets between stages. All metadata instances are the ingress port, the transmit destination and queue, and data moved from table to table without modifying the packet's parsed representation.

Beyond the network structure, the key part of the networking metrics is speed. We will define some metrics for speed in the following section.

Bandwidth, throughput, and packet rate/size

The **bandwidth** is the theoretical number of packets exchanged between two hosts. The pace at which communications reach their intended destination is referred to as **throughput**. The key distinction between the two is that the throughput measures real packet delivery rather than theoretical packet delivery. You can see how many packets arrive at their destination by looking at the average data throughput. **Packets** must effectively reach their destination to provide a high-performance service. It is very important to not lose any packets. If, for instance, we want to build an order book by incremental update, losing a packet means having an incoherent book.

When assessing and measuring the performance of networks, packet size and packet rate are two crucial criteria to take into account. The network performance varies depending on the settings of these parameters. The throughput value rises in proportion to packet size, then falls until it reaches the saturated value. Increasing the packet size increases the quantity of data sent, thus boosting throughput.

The following screenshot illustrates the network throughput (in **kilobits per second**, or **Kbps**) versus the packet rate (number of packets per second in bytes):

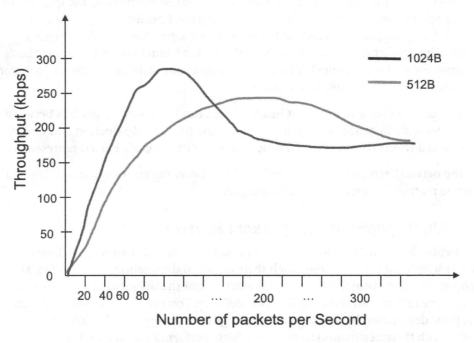

Figure 5.5 – Throughputs versus packet rate for different packet sizes

Each of the two lines shown in *Figure 5.5* corresponds to a different packet size (512 bytes and 1,024 bytes). The network throughput improves when the packet rate increases because raising the packet rate means increasing the amount of data, which raises the throughput. In addition, the chart shows that as the number of packets increases, the throughput declines until it approaches the saturation point. The increase in throughput for bigger packets is faster than for smaller ones, and the peak value of throughput for 1,024-byte packets is reached at 50 packets.

When the maximum throughput of an interface is reached, multiple ingress interfaces trying to submit outbound packets to the same egress interface can lead to buffering.

Switch queuing

A switch's main function is to route packets to the proper recipients. When there is too much incoming data, the time to process data can take longer than the arrival time of this data into the switch. To not lose any data, it is essential to have a buffer. This buffer will store data waiting to be processed. The primary role of a switch is to receive a packet on the input port. It looks up the destination to get an output port and then puts the packet in the output port queue. A large data stream going toward an output port can saturate the output port queue. If too much data sits in the queue, this will result in significant latency. Data can be lost if the buffer is full (packet drops). If market data packets drop, it becomes impossible to build the order book, which interrupts trading. The following diagram depicts the queue for a switch:

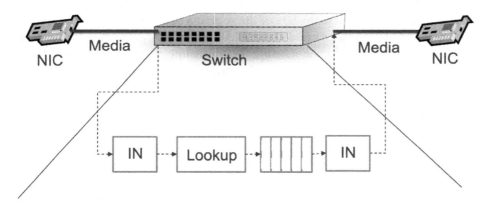

Figure 5.6 – Switch queuing

One of the significant problems is **head-of-line** (**HOL**) blocking. This problem occurs when many packets are held up in a queue by a packet about to leave the queue, which can increase latency or reordering of the packets. Indeed, if many packets are blocked in one queue, the switch will keep processing other packets going toward another output; this will result in packets being received not in order.

We saw how queuing can impact packet delivery; now, we will talk about the two main switching modes.

Switching modes – Store-and-forward versus cut-through

The switch must receive and review various bytes depending on the switching mechanism before processing the packet and forwarding the packet to the correct egress port. There are two switching modes, as detailed here:

- Cut-through switching mode has two forms, as follows:

  - Fragment-free switching

  - Fast-forward switching

- Store-and-forward switching mode

Both switching types make forwarding decisions based on the destination MAC address of the Ethernet frames. They parse the bits of the source MAC address in the Ethernet header; they record MAC addresses and create MAC tables. The amount of frame data that the switch must receive and review before the frame may be transmitted out the egress port varies between switching types, as illustrated in the following screenshot:

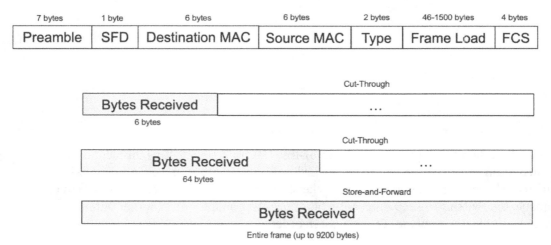

Figure 5.7 – Switching modes based on frame bytes received

Figure 5.7 shows the three modes and represents how much information should be received. Here, we will learn about them in detail, as follows:

- **Store-and-forward mode**: Before forwarding the frame, the switch must receive the frame entirely. The decision to forward this frame is based on a destination MAC address lookup. To confirm the integrity and accuracy of the data, the switch uses the **frame-check-sequence** (**FCS**) field of the frame. The frame is invalid and discarded if the CRC values do not match. Before the frame is transmitted, the destination and source MAC addresses are checked to see if they match.

  By default, any frame size between 64 bytes and 1,518 bytes is accepted and the other size will be discarded, resulting in a higher delay than the other three methods.

- **Cut-through switching mode**: This mode allows an Ethernet switch to make a forwarding choice when it receives the first few bytes of a frame. This mode has two types, as outlined here:

  - **Fragment-free switching**: This mode requires switches to parse the first 64 bytes of a frame before forwarding it.

  - **Fast-forward switching**: A cut-through switch forwards the frame when it receives the frame's destination MAC address, which implies just the first 6 bytes are required.

We saw the two main switching modes; we will now describe the different layers where switches can perform packet forwarding.

Layer 1 switching

A physical layer switch, also known as a **layer 1** switch, is part of the OSI model's physical layer. A layer 1 switch may be an electronic and programmable patch panel. It does nothing more than establishing a physical connection between ports. The link is made by software instructions, allowing test topologies to be configured automatically or remotely. A layer 1 switch does not read, alter, or use packet/frame headers to route data. These switches are entirely invisible to data and have very low latency. In testing settings, transparent connections between ports are critical because they allow the tests to be as accurate as though a patch cable connected the devices. Arista/Cisco is an example of a layer 1 switch.

Layer 2 switching (or multiport bridge)

A layer 2 switch has two functionalities, as outlined here:

- Transferring data on layer 1 (physical layer)
- Checking errors for any frames that are received and sent

This type of switch needs the MAC address to forward frames to the correct recipients. All the MAC addresses received will be kept in a forwarding table. This table allows the switch to forward data in a very efficient way. Unlike higher-level switches (higher than 3) that can transfer packets based on IP addresses, a layer 2 switch cannot use IP addresses and has no prioritization mechanism.

Layer 3 switching

A layer 3 switch is a device that acts as the following:

- A router with smart IP routing by analyzing and routing packets based on the source and destination addresses
- A switch linking devices on the same subnet

We will now talk about the system that is capable of routing data from many private IP addresses using a public address.

Network address translation

The process of converting private IP addresses into public addresses is known as **network address translation** (**NAT**). Most routers employ NAT to allow many devices to share a single IP address. When a machine communicates with the exchange, it looks for directions to the exchange. This request is sent as a packet from a machine to the router, forwarding it to the business. The router must first transform the source IP address from a private local address to a public one. The receiving server will not know where to send the information back if the packet contains a private address. The information will be returned to the laptop using the router's public address rather than the laptop's private address, thanks to NAT.

NAT is a resource-intensive operation for any device that uses it. This is because NAT requires reading and writing to the header and payload information of every IP packet to accomplish address translation, which is a time-consuming process. It increases the consumption of the **central processing unit** (**CPU**) and memory, which might reduce throughput and increase packet delay. As a result, while installing NAT in a live network, knowing the performance impact of NAT on a network device (specifically, a router) becomes critical, especially for HFT. Most modern switches can perform at least static NAT in an ASIC, but an increasing number can also do dynamic NAT with a little performance penalty.

We studied in detail how to transmit packets. We will now describe the protocols setting the rules for packet forwarding.

Important protocol concepts

When two devices need to communicate, once they have a way to transfer a signal from the sender to the recipient, we need to have protocols setting the communications rules. A protocol is like a language that two components agree to use in the system to communicate; it sets the rule of communication. The following diagram represents a network infrastructure of exchanges and trading systems:

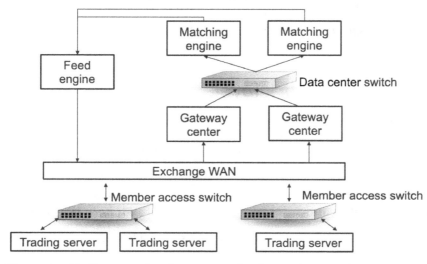

Figure 5.8 – Trading network infrastructure of trading exchange and trading servers

In *Chapter 2, The Critical Components of a Trading System*, and *Chapter 3, Understanding the Trading Exchange Dynamics*, we saw that the trading exchange, market data-feed handlers, and market participants are the three main components of a conventional trading system.

Through gateway servers, the matching receives orders from market participants. The feed handlers get their data from the stock exchange and deliver it to interested market players with minimal delay. To transport market data, we use the **FIX Adapted for STreaming (FAST)** protocol (described later in the *FAST protocol* section).

We will now talk about the Ethernet protocol for HFTs.

Using Ethernet for HFT communication

Ethernet is the most used protocol to link devices in a wired LAN or **wide area network (WAN)**. This protocol sets the communication rules between devices.

Ethernet specifies how network devices structure and send data so that it may be recognized, received, and processed by other devices on the same LAN or company network. This protocol is highly reliable (resistant to noise), fast and secure, and was designed by the **Institute of Electrical and Electronics Engineers (IEEE)** *802.3* working group in 1983. The technology kept improving to get a better speed.

The different norms—*802.3X* and *802.11X*—defined another type of support, such as 100BASE-T, which has been named **Fast Ethernet** that we are still using today.

Using IPv4 as a network layer

The IP protocol operates at the OSI model's network layer while TCP and UDP models operate at the internet layer. As a result, this protocol is in charge of recognizing hosts based on their logical addresses and routing data between them through the underlying network.

An IP addressing system offers a technique for uniquely identifying hosts. IP utilizes best-effort delivery, which means that it cannot promise that packets will be sent to the intended host, but it will try its hardest to do so. The logical address in IPv4 is 32 bits.

We can use three different addressing modes when using the IPv4 protocol, as detailed next.

Unicast mode

Only one designated host receives data in this manner. The 32-bit IP address of the target host is stored in the **Destination Address** field. In this case, the client transmits data to the desired server, as illustrated in the following diagram:

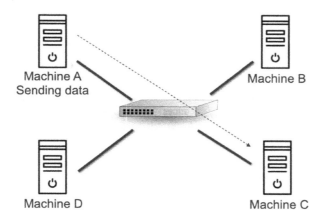

Figure 5.9 – Unicast mode

As seen in the preceding diagram, **Machine A** sends information to **Machine C**.

Broadcast mode

The packet is addressed to all hosts in a network segment in this mode. A specific broadcast address, 255.255.255.255, is included in the **Destination Address** field. When this packet is seen on the network, a host is obligated to process it. In this case, the client transmits a packet received by all of the servers. Broadcast is rarely used in HFT systems because it gives you almost no control over which machines will receive traffic and could create unnecessary overhead. You can see an illustration of broadcast mode in the following diagram:

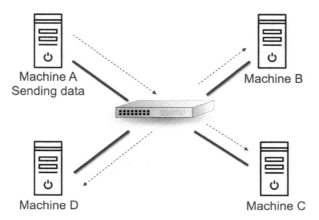

Figure 5.10 – Broadcast mode

As seen in the preceding diagram, **Machine A** sends information to all the machines.

Multicast mode

This mode is a hybrid of the previous two in that the packet is transmitted to neither a single host nor all of the hosts on the segment. The **Destination Address** field in this packet has a unique address that starts with 224. x.x.x and can be served by several hosts. Hosts will subscribe to particular multicast feeds. A machine communicates to the upstream service using the **Internet Group Management Protocol (IGMP)** that it wishes to subscribe to a specific feed. Many switches have the logic that monitors IGMP traffic from hosts and *snoops* on subscriptions for feeds. This enables the switch to determine which hosts it should replicate multicast traffic to. Switches that don't implement IGMP snooping treat multicast traffic like broadcast traffic. You can see an illustration of multicast mode in the following diagram:

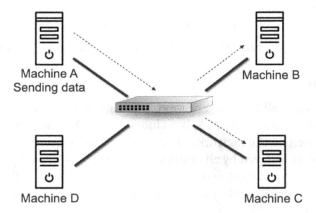

Figure 5.11 – Multicast mode: Machine A sending information to Machine B and C

In this section, we reviewed the network layer and its components. We will now talk about the transport layer and the UDP and TCP protocols.

UDP and TCP for the transport layer

TCP/IP or UDP over Ethernet is the most common communication protocol used by stock exchanges and other market players. Non-essential data, such as market data feeds, is often transmitted using UDP to reduce latency and overhead. One of the most important protocols in the TCP and UDP protocol family is IP. Critical data such as orders is carried out using the TCP/IP protocol.

TCP specifies how a computer is connected to another machine and how we can transmit data between them. This protocol is reliable and provides an **end-to-end** (**E2E**) byte stream over the network.

A datagram-oriented protocol (UDP) is used for broadcast and multicast types of network transmission. UDP is different from TCP as it does not ensure packet delivery.

The main differences are outlined here:

- TCP is a connection-oriented protocol, and UDP is a connectionless protocol.
- Because UDP doesn't have any mechanism to check errors, UDP is faster than TCP.
- TCP needs a handshake to start communicating while UDP does not.
- TCP checks errors and has error recovery, while UDP checks for errors and discards packets when there is a problem.

UDP doesn't have TCP's session, ordering, and delivery guarantee features. UDP is used where latency matters because data is delivered on a datagram basis. Market data often uses it for one of two reasons, as outlined here:

- Datagram-oriented delivery can be lower-latency (but recovery is more complicated if something gets lost).
- Multicast inherently does not support connection-oriented protocols (since the traffic is a many-to-many communication type).

This is often addressed through sequence numbers in the application-layer protocol and providing an out-of-band mechanism to request retransmission of missing sequence numbers. Today, there is a trend to use **UDP for Orders** (**UFO**), which allows us to send orders faster.

Designing financial protocols for HFT exchanges

Let's come back to the following diagram, introduced in *Chapter 2, The Critical Components of a Trading System*. It is important to understand how communication works between a trading system and an exchange:

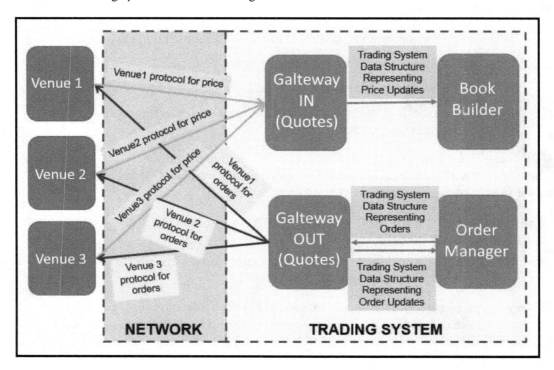

Figure 5.12 – Communication between exchange and trading system

Two entities must speak the same language to communicate with one another. To accomplish that, they use a protocol used in networking. This protocol is utilized in trading for any exchanges (sometimes called venues). Depending on the venue, there may be a variety of protocols. The connection is possible if the protocol between a given venue and your trading system is the same. Depending on the number of venues, one venue will frequently use a given protocol, and another venue will use a different one. The trading system will need to be built on understanding the other protocols. Even though their protocols differ among venues, the processes they take to create a connection and begin trading are similar, as outlined here:

1. They establish a logon that specifies who the trade initiator is, who the recipient is, and how the connection will continue to exist.

2. They next enquire about what they expect from the various companies, such as trading or receiving price updates by subscription.

3. They then get orders as well as pricing changes.

4. They then send heartbeats to sustain a connection.

5. Finally, they say their goodbyes.

We will now introduce the **Financial Information eXchange** (**FIX**) protocol in the following section.

FIX protocol

Because it is the most used protocol in trading, the **Financial Information eXchange** (**FIX**) protocol is the one we'll be discussing in this chapter. It was founded in 1992 to handle securities between Fidelity Investments and Salomon Brothers on an international real-time exchange. **Foreign exchange** (**FX**), **fixed income** (**FI**), derivatives, and clearing were included. This is a string-based protocol, which implies that people can read it. It's platform-agnostic, open, and comes in a variety of flavors.

There are two different kinds of messages, as outlined here:

- Administrative notifications that do not include any financial information

- Messages sent by the program to get pricing changes and orders

The content of these messages is a list of **key-value pairs**, similar to a dictionary or a map. Predefined tags serve as the keys; each tag is a number that corresponds to a particular characteristic. Values, which might be numerical or textual values, are associated with these tags. Consider the following scenario:

- If we wish to send an order for $1.23, let's imagine the price tag has the number 44. As a result, 44=1.23 will be in the order message.

- Character 1 separates all of the pairs. This indicates that if we add the quantity 100,000 using tag 38 corresponding to the quantity in the FIX message definition in our previous example, we'll get 44=1.23|38=100000. The | symbol symbolizes character 1.

- 8=FIX.X.Y is the prefix used in all messages. This prefix denotes the FIX version numbers. Version numbers are represented by X and Y.

10=nn is equal to the *checksum*. The checksum is the total of the message's binary values. This aids in the detection of infection.

Here is a FIX message example:

```
8=FIX.4.42|9=76|35=A|34=1|49=TRADER1|52=20220117-
12:11:44.224|56=VENUE1|98=0|108=30|141=Y|10=134
```

The necessary fields in the preceding FIX message are listed here:

- A tag containing the number 8 and the value FIX.4.42. This is the same as the FIX version number.
- 8 (BeginString), 9 (BodyLength).
- 35 (MsgType), 49 (SnderCompID), and 56 (SnderCompID) are version numbers greater than FIX4.42.
- The tag 35 specifies the message type.
- The character count from tag 35 to tag 10 is represented by the body-length tag, which is 9.
- The checksum is stored in field 10. The value is derived by multiplying the decimal value of the **American Standard Code for Information Interchange** (**ASCII**) representation of all bytes up to the checksum field (which is the final field) by 256.

Now that we know what the FIX protocol is, we will see in detail how this protocol is used in trading.

Protocols for FIX communication

To be able to trade, a trading system requires two connections: one to receive price updates and another to place orders. The FIX protocol complies with this criterion by utilizing different messages for each of the following connections.

We will discuss the price changes connection first and then describe the order connection.

Price changes

When building a trading system, the first feed to get is price updates. Price updates are the orders from the other market participants. The trading system will initiate a connection with the exchange to get a connection established and subscribe to the price updates. We will define the trading system as the initiator and the exchange as the receiver or acceptor, as depicted in *Figure 5.13*.

Trading systems require prices for the instruments that traders choose to trade. To do so, the trading system establishes a connection with the exchange to subscribe to liquidity updates. The connection between the initiator, which is the trading system, and the acceptor, which is the exchange, is depicted here:

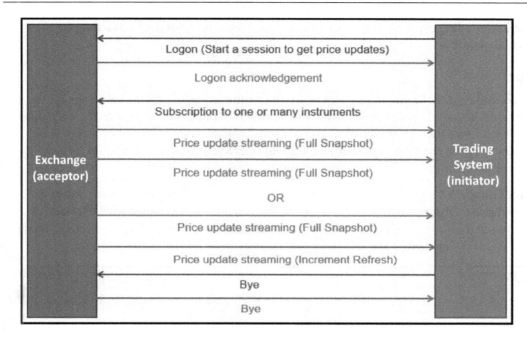

Figure 5.13 – Trading system asking for price updates

The FIX messages that are sent between the acceptor and the initiator are depicted in the following screenshot:

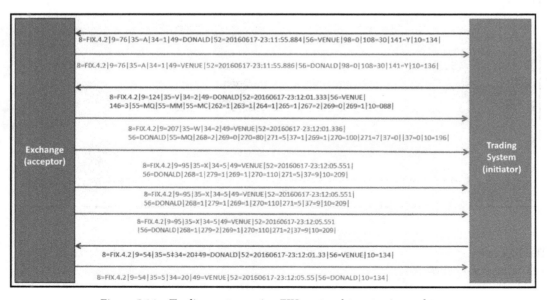

Figure 5.14 – Trading system using FIX protocol to get price updates

When the trading system receives these price updates, it updates the books and places orders depending on the signal.

Orders

The second feed that a trading system needs is communication with the exchange for the order side. The trading system (initiator) will establish communication with the exchange (receiver). Once the communication is established, the initiator will send orders to the exchange. When the exchange needs to send updates about an order, it will use this channel to communicate.

By initiating a trading session with the exchange, the trading system will send orders to the exchange. Order communications will be delivered to the exchange while this active trading session is open. The exchange will use FIX messages to transmit the status of these orders. This is depicted in the following diagram:

Figure 5.15 – Trading system sending an order to the exchange

The FIX messages that are sent between the initiator and the acceptor are depicted in the following screenshot:

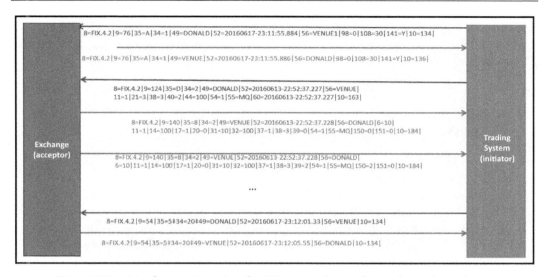

Figure 5.16 – A trading system using the FIX protocol to send an order to the exchange

Because the FIX protocol is string-based, parsers can take some time to process the stream. The FAST protocol has been developed to be faster than the FIX protocol.

FAST protocol

The FAST protocol is the high-speed version of the FIX protocol. Market data is transmitted from exchanges or feed handlers to market participants via the FAST protocol, which operates on top of UDP. FAST messages feature a variety of fields and operators for transporting meta- and payload data. FAST has been designed to use as little bandwidth as possible. Hence, it makes use of a variety of compression techniques, as outlined here:

- The first essential approach is delta updates, which offer just changes—such as the current stock price and the previous one—rather than continually transferring all stocks and their accompanying data.

- The second approach uses variable-length encoding for each data word to compress the raw data. While these strategies allow for keeping up with the increased data speeds given by feed handlers, they significantly increase processing complexity.

The compressed FAST data stream must be decoded and analyzed in real time to convert it into processable data. If the processing system cannot keep up with the data flow, critical information is lost.

Furthermore, decompressing the data stream increases the amount of bandwidth that must be handled successfully. As a result, two distinct criteria must be met to design a high-performance trading accelerator, as follows:

- First, the various protocols' decoding must be done with the shortest possible delay.

- Second, it must sustain data processing at a given data rate. A deeper look at the FAST protocol is necessary to examine the data rates of modern trading systems.

The UDP protocol is used to send FAST messages. Multiple FAST messages are packed in a single UDP frame to decrease UDP overhead. FAST communications do not provide any size information or a framing definition. Instead, each letter is specified by a template that must be understood before decoding the stream. Most feed handlers design their FAST protocol by offering distinct template requirements. Care must be taken because a single decoding error will drop the entire UDP frame. Templates define a set of fields, sequences, and groups. These groups specify a set of fields.

FAST belongs to a family of protocols developed to improve the bandwidth and the speed of communication named **Simple Binary Encoding** (SBE). We will now talk about protocols that are way more efficient than string-based protocols for communication.

ITCH/OUCH protocol

ITCH and OUCH are considered binary protocols. OUCH is usually over TCP, and ITCH is multicast or TCP. ITCH is mainly for market data, while OUCH is made for the orders. Nasdaq created these protocols in 2000 after a patent infringement lawsuit impacted FAST. ITCH-based exchange feeds are widely used in the industry. Because many different exchanges than Nasdaq use it, it has different versions. The **Chicago Board Options Exchange** (CBOE) is also another major exchange that heavily uses a variant of ITCH (such as the CBOE protocol).

Let's study another one—the **Chicago Mercantile Exchange** (CME) market data protocol.

CME market data protocol

CME also created its SBE protocol optimized for HFT.

Additionally to the prior protocols, many other proprietary binary protocols are famous for low-latency venues. All these protocols are considered exterior protocols that are responsible for connecting/interacting with exchanges. We will now talk about the difference between exchange protocols made for exterior networks and protocols made for internal networks.

Interior networks versus exterior networks

When looking at *Figure 5.8*, we can observe two different levels of the network. There is the level of network talking to the outside world using the prior protocols, and there is the networking within the company network (interior network). The following diagram illustrates the main difference between the exterior and internal networks in trading and exchange networks:

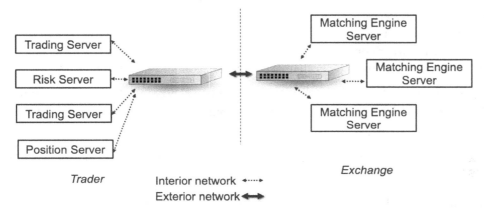

Figure 5.17 – Interior network and exterior network

A trading server communicating with the risk server uses the interior network, while the trading system on the left side of the preceding diagram will be connected with the exchange through the external network.

The internal network will be for the following activities:

- Internal market data distribution
- Signal sharing
- Order entry

It is essential in this network to minimize hops between hosts (servers). The best system will be a system where there is a segue into systems that exist purely on the NIC (in other words, a **field-programmable gate array** (**FPGA**), which we will discuss in *Chapter 11, High-Frequency FPGA and Crypto*. The choice of switches and routers is decisive for the network latency.

The external network will be for the exchange native protocol for order entry and market updates.

We are now aware of which network can be considered interior and exterior. We also know which hardware a packet will use to go from one place to another. In the next section, we will describe the structure of a packet and dig further into the life cycle of a packet and what happens as a packet moves from one point to the other.

Understanding the packet life cycle

In the *Learning about network conceptual models* section, we explained that to optimize the communication between the exchange and trading systems, we will use copper or optical wire. This wire is connected to the NIC. This wire will transport the packets containing market data from the exchange and orders going to the exchange.

We first need to discuss which message we are passing on this wire. This section will use the FIX protocol we defined in this chapter. Let's consider the following example of a FIX message:

```
8=FIX.4.2|9=95|35=X|34=5|49=NYSE|52=20160617-23:12:05.551|56=TR
ADSYS|268=1|279=1|269=1|270=110|271=5|37=9|10=209|.
```

This FIX message will be the payload of the packet shown in *Figure 5.18*.

The packet has two main parts. The headers contain information for each layer of the OSI model and a payload containing the FIX message, as shown here:

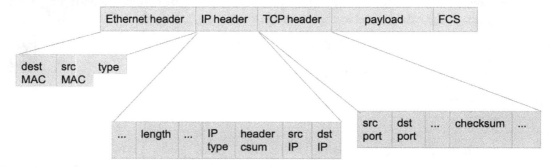

Figure 5.18 – Packet headers

The Ethernet layer will represent the data link layer (as shown in *Figure 5.19*), the IP header for the network layer, and the TCP header for the transport layer. The FCS is an error-detecting code added to this packet. As we described earlier, each layer of a packet (or a frame) contains information for each layer. We will specify in *Figure 5.20* how this packet is processed in the machine, but first, observe the following diagram:

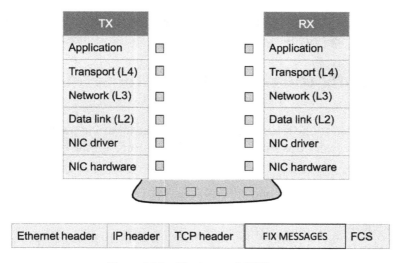

Figure 5.19 – Headers and OSI layers

In the following diagram, you can follow the life of a packet carrying a market data update getting through the system to reach the trading system (one of the applications running on this architecture):

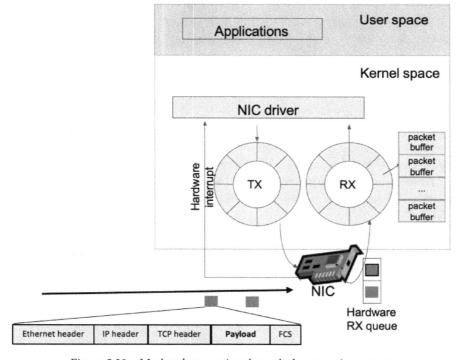

Figure 5.20 – Market data moving through the operating system

We will talk in detail about all the necessary steps to get the packet from the wire to the application—our trading system. We will first talk about the send/receive path.

Comprehending the packet life in the send/receive (TX/RX) path

The exchange connected to the trading system sends a packet to the trading system. The copper wire will transfer this packet to the machine. Here are the steps that the packet will follow:

1. The NIC receives the packet and verifies if the MAC address (**unique identifier (UID)** assigned to a NIC) address corresponds to its MAC address. If that is the case, this NIC will process this packet.

2. Then the NIC validates that the FCS is correct (checksum operation).

3. When these two verifications are completed, the NIC will use a **direct memory access (DMA)** operation to copy the packet to the buffer in charge of receiving data (**receive (RX)** buffer).

4. In *Figure 5.20*, the RX buffer is a circular buffer (or ring buffer), which is a data structure using a fixed-size buffer, connected E2E (mainly used to avoid using locks). DMU speeds up memory operations by allowing an I/O device to transmit or receive data directly to or from the main memory, bypassing the CPU.

5. The NIC then triggers an interrupt for the CPU to take care of this packet. Interrupt handlers are typically broken up into two halves—a top half and a bottom half. The top half handles any work that needs to be done urgently, and the bottom half deals with all other processing. The top half will manage activities such as acknowledging the interrupt and moving data from the network to a buffer for subsequent processing by the bottom half. The processor will switch from the user space to the kernel space, look up the **interrupt descriptor table (IDT)**, and calls the corresponding **interrupt service routine (ISR)**. Then, it will switch back to the user space. These operations are done at the NIC driver level.

6. The CPU will then initiate the bottom half when free (the **soft interrupt request (soft-IRQ)**). We will switch from the user space to the kernel space. The driver allocates a **socket buffer** or **SK-buff** (also called **SKB**). The SKB is an in-memory data structure containing the packet headers (metadata). It includes pointers to the packet headers and, obviously, the payload. For all packets in the buffer (RX buffer), the NIC driver dynamically allocates an SKB, updates the SKB with the packet headers, removes the Ethernet header, and then passes the SKB to the network stack. The socket is the endpoint to send and receive data on the software level.

7. We will now address the network layer. We know that the network layer contains the IP address. This layer will verify the IP address and the checksum and remove the network header. When verifying the IP address, the address will be compared against the route lookup. If some packets are fragmented, this layer would be in charge of recombining all the fragmented packets. Once this is done, we are taking care of the next layer.

8. The transport layer is specific to the TCP (or UDP) protocol. This layer handles the TCP state machine. It will enqueue the packet data to the socket read queue. Then, at the end, it will signal that a message can be read in the reading socket.

We will conclude this section by talking about the software layer in charge of writing and reading network data.

Software layer receiving the packet

Once the payload is written in the reading socket named read queue, the only missing step is to have the application (trading system) read the payload. We know that the operating system schedules the application to read data from the socket when possible (fairness rules). Once the trading system (the application) reads the payload (which is in this example the FIX message in the *Understanding the packet life cycle* section), it will start parsing the different tags and values of the message.

When we review all the steps that a trading system must do just to read market data, HFT is predominantly concerned with the amount of time required for an operation to complete in microseconds or nanoseconds. Therefore, we will see how to improve this path.

Since the network is critical in terms of speed, we need to be able to monitor it. In the next section, we will talk about monitoring techniques.

Monitoring the network

The network is critical for HFTs. Saving microseconds from the critical path to send orders in the network is key. When the network is built and the system is running, it is essential to analyze network traffic. In HFT, security is not a real issue since the network is located in a co-location most of the time. The part of the monitoring that we will give more weightage to is analyzing the amount of data loss, latency, and interruption. We need to ensure that the network is up and running and delivers the best possible performance.

Packet capture and analysis

Capturing Ethernet frames for examination or analysis is referred to as packet capture. The word can also refer to the files produced by packet-capture programs, commonly saved in the .pcap format. Capturing packets is a typical network troubleshooting tool, and it's also used to look for security vulnerabilities in network traffic. Packet captures give crucial forensic information that enhances investigations following a problem with the number of orders rejected, which could seem like a network latency problem.

What is packet capture and how does it work?

A packet can be caught in a variety of ways. Packet captures can be performed via networking equipment such as a router or switch with specific hardware known as a **test access point** (**TAP**) (which we will describe in the following section). The final aim determines the method utilized. Regardless of the mechanism used, packet capture works by creating copies of some or all packets traveling through a given place in the network.

The simplest method to get started is to capture packets from your system, but there are a few limitations. Network interfaces handle only traffic destined for them by default. You can put the interface in promiscuous mode or monitor mode for a more comprehensive view of network activity. Remember that this method only captures a portion of the network. For example, on a wired network, you'll only observe activity on the local switch port to which your computer is attached.

Port mirroring, port monitoring, and **switched port analyzer** (**SPAN**) are capabilities on routers and switches that allow us to duplicate network traffic and transmit it to a specific port. Much network equipment has a packet-capture feature that may be used to diagnose problems directly from the hardware's **command-line interface** (**CLI**) or the **user interface** (**UI**).

A dedicated **network TAP** can be ideal for doing a packet capture on a particularly big or busy network. TAPs are an expensive way to collect packets, but there is no performance impact because they are dedicated hardware. To make the TAP effective, it is necessary to capture both directions (**transmit** (**TX**) and RX). We need to tap both the RX and TX side to build a complete picture.

Ethernet TAPs – passive versus active TAP trade-offs

A network TAP is the most precise technique to reproduce traffic for monitoring and analysis. There are a variety of network TAPs, each with its own set of advantages for network uptime and analytical dependability. This method can be passive and active network TAPs. The distinctions between passive and active TAPs might be perplexing.

Passive network TAP

A device with no physical separation between its network ports is referred to as a passive network TAP, as shown in the following diagram. This implies that traffic can continue to flow across network ports, maintaining the connection even if the device loses power:

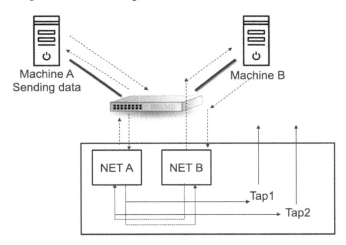

Figure 5.21 – Passive network TAP

This is true for network TAPs with **10/100-meter** (**10/100M**) copper interfaces and fiber TAPs. Fiber TAPs work by dividing the incoming light into two or more pathways and do not require electricity. When utilized, 10M or 100M copper TAPs require electricity, although they are entirely passive due to a lack of physical separation between network ports. In their situation, the link remains operational during a power loss with no failover time or link restoration delay.

Active network TAP

Because of the electrical components utilized inside the TAP, active TAPs have a physical separation between network ports, unlike passive TAPs. As a result, they require a fail-safe mechanism to ensure that the network remains operational even if the TAP loses power. The system works by keeping a set of relays open when the gadget is turned on. These relays switch to a direct traffic flow through the TAP when the power goes out, ensuring that the network operates. You can see an illustration of this in the following diagram:

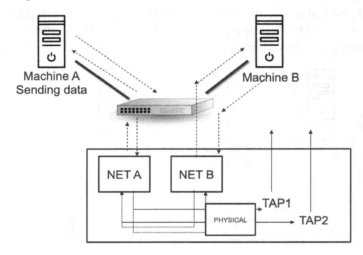

Figure 5.22 – Passive network TAP

These two TAPs will help capture market data to analyze latency and troubleshoot issues in the network. Getting this data will not be sufficient if the time of this data is not accurate. It is essential in HFT to measure time accurately. In the next section, we will explain how to do so.

Valuing time distribution

As you certainly understood with this book, HFT fights with time. This is the most critical resource we have to be sure to get our trading models right. Because we send orders that can be executed or not depending on the arrival time, we need to be confident when we build trading strategies that the time we will use to make them fits the time that the exchange is using. We will need to use time-synchronization services to accomplish this measurement accuracy.

Time-synchronization services

Before starting this section, we need to talk about getting precision time. Anywhere in the world, we can have precise time without engineering timing distribution. We use the **Global Positioning System** (**GPS**) or the **Global Navigation Satellite System** (**GNSS**), as they use atomic clocks.

The **Network Time Protocol** (**NTP**) service is one of the most widely used to synchronize the uptime of our computers with a time server. This service has a few layers called strata, as described in more detail here:

- **Stratum 0**: The highest layer, this uses GNSS satellites
- **Stratum 1**: The layer that gets the time servers, having a one-on-one direct connection with the stratum 0 clock. You can accomplish a microsecond-level synchronization with this layer.
- **Stratum 2**: The layer that connects to multiple servers of stratum 1.

There are up to 15 layers that help get different types of accuracy. The returned timestamp is as large as a 64-bit timestamp and can accurately be in the order of picoseconds. There will be a day in the near future when a 128-bit timestamp will be in place, and we might even get an accuracy of femtoseconds.

The **Precision Time Protocol** (**PTP**) is a network-based time synchronization standard that strives for nanosecond—or, perhaps, picosecond—precision. PTP equipment employs hardware timestamping rather than software, and it is designed for one unique purpose: keeping devices synchronized. PTP networks provide far higher time resolutions than NTP networks. PTP devices, unlike NTP devices, will timestamp the amount of time synchronization messages spend in each device, allowing for device latency.

These two synchronization mechanisms use **pulse-per-second** (**PPS**) signals from satellites, giving high accuracy. These signals have an accuracy going from 12 picoseconds to a few microseconds per second.

Why does timing matter so much in HFT?

When inserting timestamps in orders, HFTs require accurate **Coordinated Universal Time** (**UTC**) to follow orders in the market. Most HFTs run many computer systems on dedicated LANs, with each LAN utilizing a single PTP grandmaster clock and each computer on the LAN synced to that grandmaster. A grandmaster takes its time from an external source, and it is necessary to have a grandmaster per physical location. These parallel, high-speed computer systems must be coordinated for the algorithms to handle market buy-side and sell-side data. In network analysis of log files and all trading activity, timestamps and computer synchronization are also utilized.

Understanding and analyzing LAN latency is critical to HFT performance. HFTs would struggle to optimize both hardware and software if time synchronization were not exact to the microseconds. For non-co-located traders, real-time market data travels via cables, switches, and routers, with a delay ranging from 1 millisecond to 5 milliseconds. When compared to traders who are not co-located, co-located HFTs cut latency to below 5 microseconds, allowing them a substantial amount of time to process market data.

It is critical to measure market behavior and algorithm signals accurately, therefore the accuracy of measurement must be very high.

Summary

During this chapter, we talked about the importance of communication and networking. We learned about the network components of HFTs. We talked in depth about the Ethernet protocols adapted to fast communication. We described the design of financial protocols, and we finished by talking about the value of time distribution. You are now equipped with the knowledge to understand networking in HFT.

In the next chapter, we will finally start talking about how to optimize all the pieces of the puzzle we talked about during this chapter and the previous chapters.

6

HFT Optimization – Architecture and Operating System

In the previous chapter, we were presented with an outline of how a computer works with a focus on the main components that relate to **HFT**. In this chapter, we will discuss some of the commonly employed computer science and architecture optimization techniques specifically as they relate to HFT applications. We will provide some context with the details of how certain specific operations work in terms of what goes on under the hood, why they are inefficient, slow, and problematic for HFT software, and what techniques are used to get around it.

Some of the operations and constructs we will discuss are context switching between threads, locks to concurrently access shared data structures, and memory management/optimization motivations and techniques.

HFT is primarily an arms race where each HFT competitor is trying to execute trades as quickly as possible. So, getting to grips with the computer science fundamentals for the topics we cover in this chapter will help the reader understand how to produce extremely optimized and high-performing HFT applications. We will cover the following topics in this chapter:

- Understanding context switches
- Building lock-free data structures
- Pre-fetching and pre-allocating memory

Performance mental model

When we talk about HFT optimizations, we could use an endless number of techniques to reach the lowest possible latency. The most important question to ask is what we are trying to achieve – what level of performance is good enough for HFT trading strategies? In this book, we present a lot of optimizations and it would be overwhelming and time consuming to implement all of them. In order to guide the readers through all the optimizations, we will differentiate optimizations by considering them in terms of three groups that lowers the latency by a specific number of microseconds, represented by the following icons:

- ⏱: Lower than 20 microseconds
- ✈: Lower than 5 microseconds
- 🚀: Lower than 500 nanoseconds

Let's get started!

Understanding context switches ⏱

A context switch in computer science is the operation or set of tasks by which all the states associated with a running process or thread is saved and the state associated with a different process or thread to be run next is restored so that it can resume where the execution left off. The principle of context switching is the cornerstone on which modern **Operating Systems' (OSs')** support for *multitasking* is based, and which gives the illusion of running a lot more processes than the number of CPU cores available in the hardware.

Types of context switches

Context switches can be grouped into different types depending on which aspect of the context switching process we look at. We will briefly discuss them as follows.

Hardware or software context switches

Context switches can be performed in hardware or software. In hardware context switching, special hardware features such as **Task State Segments (TSSs)** can be used to save the register and processor state for the currently running process and then jump to a different process. In software context switches, the current stack pointer is saved and the new stack pointer is loaded to execute the new code. Registers, flags, data segments, and all other relevant registers are also pushed onto the old stack and popped off the new stack.

Hardware context switching requires special registers and/or processor instructions to implement and can be expected to be faster than software context switching due to the availability of special registers and instructions. However, in some cases, hardware context switches can be slower than software context switches since it needs to save all registers. Modern OSs, however, choose to implement context switching in software due to better fault tolerance and the ability to customize what registers are saved and restored.

Context switches between threads or processes

Another way to classify different types of context switching is whether it occurs between threads or processes. The latency associated with context switching between processes is referred to as *process switching latency* and between threads is referred to as *thread switching latency*. If threads or processes share the same address space, then the context switching is faster because the code to be executed is most likely already loaded in the cache/memory due to the shared address space. During context switching, not only does the OS need to remove and reload code from the cache and memory; it also has to clean/flush the data structure that holds the memory address mapping known as **virtual memory space**. So, context switching between threads is generally faster since they share the virtual memory space, and flushing and cleaning/invalidating the **Translation Lookaside Buffer (TLB)** is not necessary. The details of virtual memory space and the TLB are advanced OS concepts and out of the scope of this book, so we will not dive into too many details on those topics.

Why are context switches good

Context switching is worthwhile functionality for most applications that have a good mixture of user inputs, disk **Input/Output (I/O)**, and CPU-intensive processing, such as the Microsoft Office suite of applications, video games, or browsers. Within the HFT ecosystem, some (but not all) components such as logging processes, **Graphical User Interface (GUI)** applications, and so on benefit from context switching. As mentioned previously, supporting multitasking in modern OSs would not have been possible without context switching. The most important ones would be multitasking, interrupt handling in the OS, and switching between user and kernel modes (often invoked when handling interrupts). We will discuss them in the following sections.

Multitasking

All modern OSs have a task scheduler that switches out one process for another to be processed in the CPU. There can be several reasons for a running process to be switched out. For example, when the process is completed, or it is stuck on an I/O or synchronization operation – in both cases, waiting for input from another process, thread, or disk. It is possible for a thread or process to be switched out to prevent a single CPU-intensive thread or process from hogging all the CPU resources and preventing other waiting tasks from being finished, which is known as *CPU starvation*.

Interrupt handling

Interrupt-driven data flow is common in most modern architectures. When processes need to access resources, such as fetching something from or writing something to disk (disk I/O) or sockets/**Network Interface Cards (NICs)** – the process does not sit around consuming CPU resources waiting for the operations to finish. This is mainly because disk and network I/O operations are orders of magnitude slower than CPU operations, so this would waste a tremendous amount of CPU resources.

In the interrupt-driven architecture, such a process initiates the I/O operation and is blocked on that operation. Then the scheduler context switches out that process and resumes another waiting process. Behind the scenes, the OS also installs an interrupt handler with the hardware, which will interrupt the running process at the time the operation finishes and wake up the process that initiated the request and let it handle the request completion.

User and kernel mode switching

In the previous section, we saw an interrupt-driven example where the disk or packet read finishes and then the interrupt handler wakes up the process that initiated the request. In that sequence of events, part of the operation is carried out in kernel space, namely invoking the interrupt handler with the necessary signals, and the new process acquiring some CPU resources and starting to process the data. The actual data processing usually takes place in user space and depends on the application itself. This is not the only case where there are switches made between kernel and user space; some instructions invoked by a process running in user space also force a transition into kernel mode. For most systems, this switching does not invoke a context switch, but it might happen for some systems when switching between user and kernel mode. In the next section, we will look at the sequence of actions involved in a context switch operation. A good understanding of this is important because it then becomes clear how context switching can become expensive in the context of HFT applications.

Steps and operations involved in a context switch operation

Let's look at some of the operations involved in a context switch – specifically the tasks involved in saving the state of the currently running thread or process and restoring the state of the next thread or process to be run, as decided by the task scheduler. Please note that this section provides a high-level view of tasks involved and might be missing a few specific details for specific architectures; that is, each architecture and OS has caveats specific to them aside from this list, but this list still serves as a generic list of steps involved:

1. Saving the state of the current process involves saving the state in what is often known as a **Process Control Block (PCB)**. That contains the registers, **Stack Pointer register (SP)**, **Program Counter (PC)**, and memory maps. There are also various tables and lists for the current thread or process.

2. There are likely a few steps to flush and/or invalidate the cache and flush the TLB, which handles the virtual memory address to physical memory address translations.

3. Restoring the state for the next thread or process to be run is the opposite step of what it takes to save the state, that is, restoring the registers and data contained in the PCB for the thread or process to be restored.

This section presented a higher-level view of the all the steps involved in facilitating a context switch. In practice, there can be additional steps depending on the hardware architecture and OS and these can get quite complex and expensive. For an extremely low-latency application like HFT, these can lead to a large overhead. We will see the drawbacks of context switches in the next section.

Why are context switches bad for HFT?

Now that we have a good background on context switching, let's look at why context switches are not ideal for HFT applications.

Default CPU task scheduler behavior

Default CPU task-scheduling algorithms for a multi-core server are often not the best scheduling mechanisms for HFT. The different task-scheduling mechanisms try to consider several factors such as maintaining fairness in terms of CPU resources allocated across all threads and processes available to run, conserving energy/improving energy consumption efficiency, and maximizing CPU throughput/efficiency by either running the shortest jobs first or the longest jobs first, among others.

These tasks are often at odds with what is critical for HFT applications:

- We would rather not conserve energy and put measures in place so that the server does not overheat.

- We want to support overclocked servers, which again are not energy efficient.

- We want to control the scheduling/priority of processes so that it's preferred that very low priority tasks rarely get CPU time and/or get starved over the HFT application not getting as much CPU time as possible.

- We do not pre-empty the HFT thread or process even when it has already consumed a lot of CPU resources, that is, no need to be fair, and so on.

In general, most of these objectives are achieved for HFT servers by changing the kernel and OS parameters and having multi-core servers where the critical HFT processes are pinned to specific isolated and dedicated cores so that they never get pre-empted, often in combination with moving non-HFT processes to a specific tiny subset of available cores.

Expensive tasks in context switching

We have outlined the operations that need to take place when a context switch happens to save the PCB for the thread or process being removed from the CPU and to restore the PCB for the thread or process to be scheduled next on that CPU. Any work is more expensive than no work, but some of the steps in the case of context switching are very computationally intensive. We discussed task scheduling in the previous section, and it is one of the overheads of a context switch. Flushing the TLB and the cache if needed during a context switch are expensive tasks as well. Cache invalidation is another task when performing context switches. We saw TLB invalidation in a previous section; cache invalidation works very similar to that. During cache invalidation, data that has been edited in the cache but not written in memory is written to memory. Also, as new code replaces the space used by the old code, new code has to be fetched from memory and brought into the cache, which takes longer than accessing the cache (known as a **cache miss**). These cache invalidation steps cause the next thread or process to have quite a few initial cache misses, leading to a slow resumption for the process that got the CPU resource assigned after the context switch.

Techniques to avoid or minimize context switches

Finally, let's discuss how to design and configure a server/system for HFT with the aim of avoiding or minimizing context switches as much as possible.

Pinning threads to CPU cores

We discussed this in the *Default CPU task scheduler behavior* section, but to reiterate here, by explicitly implementing CPU isolation and pinning critical or CPU-intensive threads (a.k.a. hot or spinning threads) to specific cores, it is possible to make sure that little to no context switches occur on the hot threads/processes.

Avoiding system calls that lead to pre-emption

Another item we discussed before is that system calls that block disk or network I/O cause the calling thread to block and cause a context switch followed by a kernel interrupt when the data request is finished. To minimize these context switches, one obvious solution is to minimize the use of blocking system calls as much as possible. The other solution is to use a *kernel bypass*, to which we dedicate an entire section named *Using kernel bypass* in the following chapter. To introduce it quickly here, it avoids system calls altogether as far as network I/O operations are concerned (which are very prevalent in HFT applications) by trading in system call overhead for CPU utilization and thus avoiding context switches.

This section discussed context switching in great detail. We covered the following topics:

- Types of context switches
- Which applications benefit from context switches
- The tasks involved in performing a context switch
- Why context switches are not ideal for HFT applications
- Techniques to maximize HFT application performance by minimizing context switching

In the next section, we will discuss another fundamental computer science concept of locks. We will also design lock-free data structures and understand how avoiding locks maximizes HFT application performance.

Building lock-free data structures

In this section, we will discuss data structures that are shared between threads or between processes in an HFT ecosystem and the concurrency and synchronization considerations involved, especially given the extremely high-throughput and low-latency requirements of HFT systems. We will also design and discuss the performance implications of lock-free data structures. A lock-free data structure is a mechanism to share data between producers and consumers running in different threads and/or processes. The interesting point here is that it achieves this by avoiding locks altogether and thus performs significantly better for HFT purposes. We will investigate these items in more detail in the sections that follow.

When/why are locks needed (non-HFT applications)

Let's look at why locks are needed in a traditional multi-threaded/multi-process programming paradigm. The reason comes down fundamentally to the need to allow concurrent access to shared data structures and the use of synchronization primitives on shared resources. We will look at synchronization primitives including mutexes, semaphores, and critical sections in the following *Types of synchronization mechanisms* section. These help ensure that certain thread-unsafe sections of code do not execute concurrently if doing so could corrupt shared data structures. When using locks, if one thread attempts to acquire a lock that is already held by another thread, the second thread will block until the lock is freed by the first thread. We will see in the *Problems and inefficiencies with using locks* section the performance implications of using locks, as well as how we can get around them, especially when it comes to HFT systems.

Types of synchronization mechanisms

In this section, we will look at some of the common synchronization methods available to achieve concurrent access using some form of locking/blocking/waiting mechanism.

Memory barriers

A memory barrier a.k.a. memory fence or fence is used to instruct the compiler and processors to not reorder the loads and stores. This boosts performance, which is perfectly fine for single-threaded applications but can lead to strange, unpredictable, incorrect, and inconsistent behavior in multi-threaded applications. Using memory barriers disallows the compiler and preprocessor from reordering the sequence of loads and stores for a specific critical section, which can cause performance penalties in a multi-threaded HFT environment. Memory barriers are often lower-level instructions on top of which synchronization primitives and lock-free data structures are built.

test-and-set

`test-and-set` is a computer science primitive (basic code/instruction) that takes a pointer to a Boolean variable, sets it to `true`, and returns the old value as a single atomic/non-interruptible operation. The atomic nature of the operation makes it a perfect primitive to use to build synchronization mechanisms.

fetch-and-add

`fetch-and-add` is a primitive that takes a pointer to a variable, adds a number to it, and returns the old value as a single atomic/non-interruptible operation. It is used to build synchronization mechanisms where counting is required.

Compare-and-swap

`compare-and-swap` (**CAS**) is the most widely used primitive. It only stores a value to an address if the variable at the address has a given value. The steps of fetching the value, comparing it, and updating it are one atomic operation. CAS does not acquire a lock on the data structure but returns `true` if the update was successful and `false` otherwise.

Problems and inefficiencies with using locks

In this section, we will investigate some of the complications/problems and inefficiencies associated with using locks for synchronization for concurrent access of shared data structures by threads and processes.

Application programming and debugging skill requirements

Programming with locks is not trivial from a software development perspective. A simple task of atomically deleting something from one data structure and inserting it into a different data structure requires managing multiple concurrent locks and elaborate software support and rigorous validations to make sure all edge cases have been mapped out and handled since it is difficult to reproduce the edge cases in a multi-threaded application.

To reiterate, bugs associated with or caused by locks depend on the timing of the operations and the code path. Overall, they can be very subtle and extremely difficult to reproduce, such as deadlocks. Therefore, debugging applications that use synchronization mechanisms is quite a daunting task.

It is important to strike an optimal balance between *lock overhead* (extra memory/CPU resources to use locks) and *lock contention* (instances where a thread tries to acquire a lock that is already in an acquired state from another thread/process) and it depends on the problem domain, the design, the implementation of the solution, and the low-level architectural designs. During the life cycle of an application, as use cases change, there might be significant changes to these design considerations as well as how to achieve/maintain the optimal balance between lock overhead versus lock contention.

Lock overhead and performance

Using locks requires extra resources such as memory space for the locks, and the CPU resources to initialize, destroy, acquire, and release locks. As we discussed before, even trivial tasks can often require multiple locks and multiple lock acquisition and release operations to do correctly, hence as application complexity grows, so does the overhead associated with the locks. Although the chance for contention is rare, anywhere we use locks to protect access to a shared resource, there is additional overhead. However, modern processors are often able to avoid context switches during lock acquisition or release operations when contention does not exist at the time of the operation.

Lock contention

When a process or thread tries to acquire a lock that is already held by another thread or process, lock contention occurs. The more fine-grained locks (that is, individual locks that lock smaller code regions or data structure pieces) the lower the contention, but the higher the lock overhead (since a higher number of locks means more resources required).

There are many things to be considered with lock contention. Threads or processes that are waiting to acquire a lock (or locks) must wait till the locks are released, which introduces queuing delays. More importantly, if one of the threads or processes in that list dies, stalls, blocks, or enters an infinite loop, this will break the entire system since now the threads waiting on that lock will wait forever, leading to a *deadlock* condition.

Deadlock

We described the possibility of a deadlock scenario where if the thread holding the lock never finishes, all other threads waiting to acquire that lock will wait forever. The classic deadlock definition however is described as a scenario in which at least one of two tasks is stuck waiting to acquire a lock that the other process is holding on to. A simple example would be where process-1 holds lock-A and tries to acquire lock-B at the same time as process-2 holds lock-B and tries to acquire lock-A. In the absence of any external actions, the two tasks will be stuck forever.

Async signal safety, kill tolerance, and pre-emption tolerance

This section will revisit and expand on the concerns we raised in the *Application programming and debugging skill requirements* section about *lock contention* (instances where a thread tries to acquire a lock held by another) where if a thread or process that holds a lock dies or cannot finish for any reason, it brings the entire system down since no threads or processes that need to acquire that lock can ever make progress. The scenario where threads die or crash while holding locks and what would happen to the system in that case is referred to as its *kill tolerance*. Possible impacts can range from a lot of wasted time before the OS detects a deadlocked thread/process, to loss of progress due to the need to restart the whole system and possibly a complete halt to processing.

Signal handlers (an OS mechanism to handle unexpected scenarios/code paths) for instance cannot use lock-based primitives since it is impossible to guess what the state of the application might be in terms of which code was being executed/what locks were acquired at the time the asynchronous signal handler was invoked. A special example would be the C programming language functions `malloc()` and `free()`. For instance, if a thread is holding a lock during a memory allocation task and it happens to receive a signal, the context is switched right away to the signal handler, so the thread never gets an opportunity to release the lock. Then, if the signal handler executes and calls `malloc()`, requiring a lock, then we are in a deadlock situation again. In this scenario where the original thread is pre-empted (or in general when a thread is pre-empted while holding a lock for any other reason), the expected behavior of the component or system is referred to as *Pre-emption tolerance*.

Priority inversion

Priority inversion is a scenario where a low-priority thread or process holds a common lock that it shares with a higher priority thread or process. The low-priority thread holding the lock can slow down or prevent the progress of the higher priority thread or process. This is because in some cases the lower priority process holding the lock might not be picked up by the scheduler to be run due to its lower priority but each time the higher priority process gets picked up to be run, it blocks on the lock acquisition and does not make progress anyway.

Priority inheritance is one solution where if a high-priority process is waiting on a low-priority process due to a shared lock as described above, the scheduler assigns either the same priority or the highest priority to the low-priority process to handle the priority inversion issue. Priority ceiling protocol is a similar solution designed more for systems with a single processor. It aims to minimize the worst-case duration and possibly prevent deadlocks when priority inversion scenarios happen.

Convoying

Convoying refers to another case that causes degradation in software/application performance when using synchronization primitives. If multiple processes/code paths attempt to acquire the same locks in similar order and then somehow a slower process manages to get to the lock first, then all the other processes will be held back (in terms of making progress) to the speed of the first one, because even though the other processes finish their operations quickly, they still need to wait on the slow leading process for the lock acquisition operations. Also, if the thread holding the lock is context switched out for any reason (such as the thread holding the lock invokes an I/O operation, a higher priority process starts up, or an interrupt handler is invoked), then that will again add more latency to the completion of the other processes.

To summarize this section, building applications that use synchronization mechanisms is complicated, each lock instance and lock operation adds additional overhead, there are risks of deadlocks, and some peculiar scenarios where the system can slow down, requiring special solutions. Thus, locks are often inefficient and expensive and given their blocking, unblocking, and context switching nature are often not the preferred mechanisms for HFT applications.

Prototype for lock-free data structure

In this section, we will discuss lock-free data structure design to avoid all the problems and inefficiencies that come with using synchronization primitives in HFT applications. In general, designing generalized lock-free algorithms is hard, so the usual approach is to design lock-free data structures instead – some examples of which are lock-free lists, stacks, queues, maps, and deques. We can then use these lock-free data structures in spots where the HFT system requires interaction or data sharing between different threads and/or processes. In this section, we will design and understand the details of lock-free producer-consumer data structures. Producer-consumer data structures are basically queues where producers can write data to and consumers can read data from – a common task when passing data between HFT components. When there is a single producer and a single consumer, it is referred to as **Single Producer Single Consumer** (**SPSC**) and when there are multiple producers and consumers, it is referred to as **Multiple Producer Multiple Consumer** (**MPMC**).

There is a good amount of research on thread-safe `malloc()` and `free()` with no locks as well. *Michael (PLDI 2004), Scalable Lock-Free Dynamic Memory Allocation* is one such instance. The thread-safe `malloc()` and `free()` scale almost perfectly when adding additional processors. They also handle different contention levels well and offer very low latency when compared to other specialized `malloc()` implementations. As we will see in the *Pre-fetching and pre-allocating memory* section, this is not necessarily a huge win for HFT applications since they generally avoid dynamic memory allocations as far as possible, but this can still be quite valuable in cases where we need to use thread-safe and lock-free `malloc()` and `free()`.

Fundamentally, the main argument for lock-free data structures is to maximize concurrency. For containers that use locks, there always exists the possibility of a thread having to block on a lock acquisition step and wait and incur expensive context-switching latencies before it can make progress since mutual exclusion is the goal of mutex locks anyway. With lock-free data structures, a thread makes progress each time it runs, and this is effectively implemented as a *spin lock*. A spin lock does not block but instead repeatedly keeps checking if the lock is available. This behavior is known as *busy wait*.

SPSC and MPMC

To discuss what a lock-free data structure might look like, we will discuss a simple lock-free **SPSC** example – although the same ideas we discuss here can be extended all the way to **MPMC**. We can improve SPSC by turning it into MPMC by having different queues in memory per producer and having different location tracking variables per consumer. In the MPMC design, each producer writes new data to its own queue and each consumer has its own variables that track what the last element consumed was. With that design, the producers can produce and write data independent of each other without worrying about trampling on other producers' toes, and each consumer can consume data independent of each other from one or more of these queues.

Here is a diagram that describes how the **Producer** and **Consumer** track memory slots being written to and read from in a lock-free SPSC design:

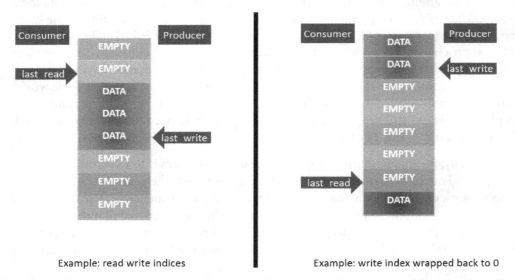

Figure 6.1 – Producer and consumer track memory slots being written to and read from in a lock-free SPSC design

In the most common implementation of lock-free SPSC or MPSC, new data is added to the back of the queue by the producer(s) and old data is consumed from the front of the queue by the consumer(s) – so it is a **First In, First Out (FIFO)** style queue. Quite often the underlying data structure/memory store for the queue is chosen to be a large, fixed-size, pre-allocated array, which has a lot of advantages such as no dynamic memory allocation and contiguous memory access. We will discuss this further in the *Memory pools* section.

There is a variable that the producer uses – `last_write` – to track which index in that array the last data was written to, or the next data will be written to – conceptually they both get the job done. The producer adds the nodes and increments the variable that tracks the last slot that data was written to. The consumer has a variable – `last_read` – which it uses to track the index that it last read data from. The consumer checks if there is new data available to read by comparing the `last_write` and `last_read` variables and consumes data till there is no more data left to consume.

Here, the producer will often use a CAS atomic operation to increment `last_write` (and similarly the consumer will use a CAS atomic operation to increment the `last_read` variable), but that is not necessary in an SPSC setup since the worst-case possibility is that the new node has been added to the queue but `last_write` has not been updated when the consumer checks for data, in which case it will just be read the next time the consumer checks for data and `last_write` has been updated.

When the producer and consumer read the end of the array, the indices wrap around and start from 0 again. The one invariant that is maintained is `last_read <= last_write`. This design works best when the array size chosen is large enough and the consumer is fast enough to process the data so that it is not struggling to keep up with the producer and/or slowing the producer down in its ability to write data to the queue.

Applications of lock-free data structures in HFT

We shall reiterate this point one last time, but lock-free data structures (and operations on them) have significantly higher throughput (no contention) as well as lower latencies (no overhead) compared to alternatives that use locks under periods of heavy load. If a process holding a lock to a critical section gets context-switched out, it will end up blocking other threads/processes that need to access that lock before proceeding. These threads wait until the original thread is scheduled to run again, finishes its tasks in the critical section, and releases the lock. The same sequence of events in a lock-free algorithm does not waste any time since they can change the shared variable without waiting. The original thread that wanted to modify the variable now must loop at least once more and try it again.

Lock-free Single Producer Single Consumer (SPSC), Single Producer Multiple Consumers (SPMC), Multiple Producers Single Consumer (MPSC) and **Multiple Producers Multiple Consumers (MPMC)** are used in various places in an HFT system. Without listing all applications, the following sections cover some of the important ones and it should not be hard for you to extrapolate from these examples where you want to use one of these lock-free data structures.

Market data dissemination on a critical path

Depending on how many market data feed handler processes a strategy is consuming market data from, we can have an MPSC-style setup per trading process that is consuming market data from multiple sources over a lock-free queue. If there are multiple trading processes running per trading server, then that setup can become an MPMC-style setup where the different market data feed handlers are the multiple producers and the different trading processes are the multiple consumers.

Order requests on critical path

The setup here is identical to the one described in the *Market data dissemination on critical path* section, except that here the flow of data is from the trading processes to the order gateways. Here, again depending on the number of trading processes and order gateways, it can be set up as a lock-free SPSC, MPSC, or MPMC.

Logging and online computation of statistics

Logging is another interesting application of these lock-free data structures we discussed in this section. A lot of the tasks in logging can be slow and not ideal on a critical performance path, such as the following:

- Formatting data into some human-readable format – this is not always necessary but when needed, it involves slow string operations.

- Writing logs to disk – this involves the use of super slow disk I/O operations.

- Computing running statistics – this can be slow depending on the amount of data and the nature of the statistics themselves.

Due to the slow and non-deterministic nature of these tasks, it is not uncommon for the different processes involved in the HFT ecosystem to ship off data in its simplest format to a separate logging thread or process that does the slower tasks off the hot path. Here again, lock-free data structures come in handy. We will discuss logging and statistical computations in Chapter 7, *HFT Optimization – Logging, Performance, and Networking*, in the *Diving into logging and statistics* section, since that is a particularly key component in HFT applications. The diagram that follows shows the different components that can use lock-free queues for efficient data transfer:

- From market data feed handlers to trading process(es)

- From the trading process to order gateway(s)

- Also from market data feed handlers, trading processes, order gateways, and other components to offload the logging to the logging processes

Let's look at the following diagram that shows the different types of lock-free queues:

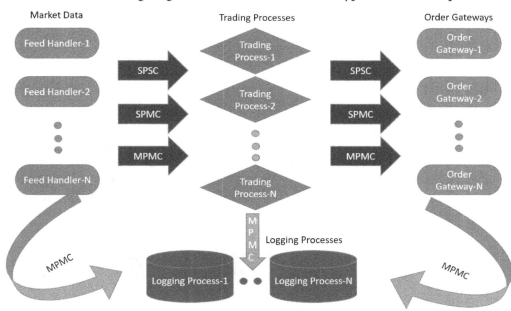

Figure 6.2 – The layout and use of different types of lock-free queues (SPSC, SPMC, and MPMC) in a complete HFT ecosystem

In this section, we discussed traditional computer science concurrency/synchronization mechanisms and why they are needed in multi-threaded applications. We then looked at why the use of locks is inefficient for HFT applications. Finally, we designed a lock-free data structure to be used in the presence of multiple producers of data and multiple consumers of that data and saw how that fits into an HFT ecosystem. In the next section, we will look at another important topic concerning all applications in general, but especially relevant to HFT applications – memory allocation during the course of an HFT application's life cycle.

Pre-fetching and pre-allocating memory

In this section, we will look at two things when it comes to accessing and allocating memory used by HFT applications mostly from the perspective of improving memory access and allocation latencies, especially on the critical path.

We will start off by discussing the hierarchy of memory – all the way from memory with super-fast access but that is expensive and limited in capacity, to those offering super-slow access but cheaply and of huge capacity. We will also discuss some strategies to design HFT applications to aim for optimal memory access latencies.

The other topic of discussion will be how dynamic memory allocation works, why dynamically allocating memory on the hot path is inefficient, and what techniques are employed to extract maximum performance without sacrificing too much of the flexibility that dynamic memory allocation allows.

Memory hierarchy

First, we will discuss the memory hierarchy in modern architecture. We will start from the storage closest to the processor, which has the lowest access latencies (but the highest cost and lowest storage capacity) and move further out from processor registers to various levels of caches to main memory (RAM) and then finally to the disk storage where applications reside before they are loaded into memory on startup. Note that these numbers vary from architecture to architecture and processor to processor and are in a constant state of evolution, so these are meant to be rough approximations of what to expect and are likely to change in the future.

First, let's look at a diagram that describes the pyramid of memory hierarchy from fastest, smallest, and most expensive at the top to slowest, largest, and least expensive at the bottom:

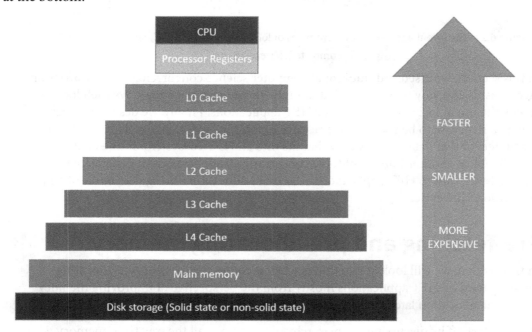

Figure 6.3 – Memory hierarchy in a modern architecture

As we move from the bottom to the top, the memory/storage options become faster, lower in capacity, and more expensive.

Processor registers

Processor registers have the fastest possible access (usually 1 CPU cycle). The processor register banks can hold up to a few bytes in size per register.

Caches

After the processor registers comes the cache bank, which comprises a few different cache levels. We will discuss those here in order from fastest (and smallest) to slowest (and largest).

L0 cache

Level 0 (L0) cache – this is accessed after the processor registers. The L0 cache is around 6 kilobytes in size.

L1 cache

Level 1 (L1) caches (the instruction and data caches) is 128 kilobytes in size. Access times are around 0.5 nanoseconds for the data cache and 5 nanoseconds for a *branch misprediction* for the instruction cache. *Branch prediction* is an advanced computer architecture feature where, based on previous access patterns, the processor/OS tries to guess which code path will be taken next. When it guesses the path correctly, it can pre-fetch the code before it is needed, thus speeding up access and execution when it is finally needed. Since it is a guess, sometimes it is incorrect, which is known as branch misprediction. We will not dive into too many details on branch prediction since that is outside the scope of this book.

L2 cache

Level 2 (L2) caches - instruction and data (shared) – sizes vary here but can range from 256 kilobytes to 8 megabytes. L2 cache access takes around 5-7 nanoseconds.

L3 Cache

Level 3 (L3) shared cache – L3 caches can vary in size from 32 to 64 megabytes. The L3 cache is the largest but also the slowest, with access times of around 12 nanoseconds. The L3 cache can exist on the CPU itself, however, there are L1 and L2 caches for each core, while the L3 cache is more of a shared cache for all cores on the chip.

L4 Cache

Level 4 (L4) shared cache – these can vary from 64 to 128 megabytes. Access times are around 40 nanoseconds.

Main memory

Main memory (primary storage) – this varies in size from 16 to 256 gigabytes. Access times are around 60 nanoseconds. **Non-Uniform Memory Access (NUMA)** machines experience non-uniform access times. NUMA is an advanced concept where in a multi-threaded environment the access times depend on the memory location relative to the processor, but diving into NUMA is outside the scope of this book.

Disk storage

Disk storage (secondary storage) – This goes up to terabytes in size. For solid-state storage, access speeds are around 100 microseconds, and for non-solid-state storage, around 300 microseconds.

Inefficiencies with memory access

In the previous section, we discussed the memory hierarchy and latencies incurred when fetching data from the different storages – basically, when an application requests a data for the first time, it might not be available in the registers or the caches and possibly (we will discuss why we use the word *possibly* in the *Pre-fetching based alternatives to boost performance* section) not even in the main memory, in which case it is loaded from disk to main memory (incurring the 100-300 microseconds latency), then from main memory to the L0 to L4 caches. Data is not loaded a few bytes at a time but one or few pages (a few kilobytes) at a time, so subsequent references to the same data (or data residing at a memory address close to that data) lead to cache hits and experience significantly lower access latencies.

So, the worst-case access time latencies are incurred when we experience a miss at the faster storage levels and must go to the slower storage, fetch it, cache it into the faster storage, and then access the requested data, yielding a few hundred microseconds in access latency.

The best-case scenario is when the data is already present in the L0/L1 cache and access times drop to less than a nanosecond. The average-case latency (referred to as **Average Access Time) (AAT)**), which is what we are really trying to optimize, is the average of access times over the course of an application's life cycle.

Let's say we have a hypothetical setup where the main memory has an access time 60 nanoseconds, the L1 cache has an access time of 0.5 nanoseconds but a miss rate of 10%, the L2 cache has an access time of 5 nanoseconds with a miss rate of 1%, and the L3 cache has an access time of 12 nanoseconds and a miss rate of 0.1%, then the AAT will be as follows for the different scenarios:

- **No cache**: AAT-no-cache = 60 nanoseconds

- **L1 cache**: AAT-L1 = L1-hit-time + (L1-miss-rate * AAT-no-cache) = 0.5 + (0.1 * 60) = 6.5 nanoseconds

- **L2 cache**: AAT-L2 = L1-hit-time + (L1-miss-rate * (L2-hit-time + L2-miss-rate * AAT-no-cache)) = 0.5 + (0.1 * (5 + 0.01 * 60)) = 1.06 nanoseconds

- **L3 cache**: AAT-L3 = 0.5 + (0.1 * (5 + 0.01 * (12 + 0.0001 * 60))) = 1.012 nanoseconds

The takeaway here is that applications that have memory access patterns that lead to a lot more cache hits (and thus fewer cache misses) will have significantly better performance in terms of accessing memory than an application that has access patterns that lead to a lot more cache misses (and thus fewer cache hits).

Pre-fetching based alternatives to boost performance

In the previous section, we discussed how cache hits affect memory access performance. So, to get the most out of cache performance, HFT application developers need to focus on writing cache-friendly code, the most important aspect of which is the *principle of locality*, which basically describes why related datasets placed near each other in memory allow for more efficient caching. You must be aware of how big each of the caches are, how much data fits in a cache line, and cache access times for the specific architecture where the HFT ecosystem lives.

Temporal locality

Temporal locality refers to the principle that given that a certain memory location was accessed, it is highly likely that the same location will be referenced/accessed again soon. So based on that principle, it makes sense to cache data that was recently accessed since there is a good chance that it will be accessed again and likely that it will still be cached at that point.

Spatial locality

Spatial locality refers to the principle of placing related pieces of data close to each other. Typically, memory loaded into RAM is fetched in large chunks (larger than what the application requested) and similarly for hard disk drives and CPU caches. The reasoning here is that application code is often executed serially (instead of jumping around randomly across memory addresses) and so the program will most likely require the data from the large chunk that was fetched in the previous instance. Thus, it is likely to produce cache hits or memory hits instead of having to fetch it from disk.

Appropriate containers

It is important to think carefully about the containers being used when writing cache-friendly low-latency HFT code. A quite simple example often presented is the choice between the C++ **Standard Template Library** (**STL**) vectors and lists. While both might appear to be serving similar purposes from the API perspective, the elements of a vector are saved in contiguous memory locations and they are much more cache friendly when it comes to accessing them compared to lists where the elements are not necessarily stored in contiguous memory and often all over the place in memory. Here, the principle of spatial locality kicks in and causes vector element access to perform significantly better than list element access.

Cache-friendly data structures and algorithms

This is a generalization of the previous point – when designing data structures and algorithms, it is important to be cognizant of cache and cache performance and try to tailor the design in a way that maximizes the use and performance of the cache, especially for HFT applications.

Exploit the implicit structure of data

Another simple example that is often presented when discussing spatial locality is the classic 2D array, which can be column-major (where elements of a column are next to each other in memory) or row-major (where elements of a row are next to each other in memory). We should consider this and access the element accordingly – for example, for column-major 2D arrays, accessing elements in the same column is much better than accessing elements in the same row, and the reverse is true for row-major 2D arrays. Data that is fetched from the main memory and cached in the cache bank is fetched in units of blocks. So, when a certain element of a matrix is accessed, elements near it in memory locations are also fetched and cached. Exploiting this ordering allows us to perform operations with fewer memory accesses because computations that need to access the subsequent elements already find them in the cache line.

Avoid unpredictable branches

Modern compilers, processor pipelines, and architecture are extremely good at prefetching data and reordering code to minimize memory access delays. But one place where they suffer in performance is if the critical code contains unpredictable branches since it is impossible to pre-fetch data and exploit temporal or spatial locality and pre-fetch data. This therefore leads to significantly more cache misses compared to code without a lot of unpredictable branches.

Avoid virtual functions

Virtual functions in the context of C++ are something that we try to avoid when writing low-latency HFT software in general, mostly because they make a lot of especially important compiler optimizations impossible simply because the compiler cannot determine which method implementation will get called at compile time, so it cannot inline the methods and processors cannot pre-fetch data. This results in a lot more cache misses during lookup if the specific method is not called often (otherwise at least the method body is likely to be cached and will not incur cache misses). The presence of virtual functions is not the biggest problem when it comes to cache friendliness, but still, this is something to be cognizant of.

In the next section, we will look at another topic related to memory allocation and access – dynamic memory allocation. Dynamic memory allocation is quite common in complex large-scale applications, so it is important to build a good understanding of that concept. You should build a good understanding of the fact that there are multiple steps involved each time a dynamic memory allocation operation is invoked and that can have performance penalties for HFT applications.

Dynamic memory allocation

Dynamic memory management is an excellent feature that has existed since the beginning of C – it allows applications to manage (allocate/move/deallocate) memory blocks of dynamic sizes determined at runtime. The actual internal implementation and performance impact, however, makes it less than ideal for extremely low latency HFT applications that need very tight (low variance on latencies on operations) performance. The memory allocated during dynamic memory allocation lives on the heap segment and when memory is freed, it is returned to the heap. However, in practice working with dynamic memory management is non-trivial and small mistakes in the application implementation can lead to subtle memory leak issues and performance issues on the critical path.

Steps in dynamic memory allocation

The OS maintains the free heap memory blocks using two linked lists – one is a freed list of heap memory blocks that are not currently allocated, and the other is an allocated list of heap memory blocks. When a request comes in for a new memory block, it traverses the freed list till it finds a memory block that is large enough to service the request, then moves part or all of the memory block from the freed list to the allocated list and returns the now allocated memory address back to the caller.

Over the course of a program's life cycle there can be any number of allocations and deallocations of random amounts in random orders. Due to these operations, the freed list can have holes when previously allocated memory is returned to the free list in between still allocated memory blocks. A new request for dynamically allocated memory can return something from one of the holes. This concept of the freed heap block list developing holes is known as memory fragmentation. In some rare cases it is possible for a lot of fragmentation and due to the presence of too many holes, memory is wasted and the holes cannot be used to satisfy dynamic memory allocation requests because each hole individually might be too small to satisfy the request. There are some techniques and strategies that the allocator invokes periodically to collect and consolidate such chunks to prevent heap fragmentation, but covering those is outside of the scope of this chapter.

Memory leaks are another problem for dynamic memory allocation, whereby a memory block is allocated but remains unused and is never freed by the application and hence not returned to the free pool. This is known as a memory leak and it causes memory usage to balloon, along with worsened performance due to the gigantic memory footprint, and might even cause the OS to terminate the process that is leaking memory and/or starve all processes that need dynamic memory to be allocated.

To summarize this section, dynamic memory management introduces application complexity, the potential for bugs, has an overhead and latency (due to the tracking/updating of the linked lists tracking the memory blocks), and can have performance issues due to memory fragmentation. The performance implications make dynamic memory management less than ideal for HFT applications.

Pre-allocation-based alternatives to dynamic memory allocation

In this section, we will investigate some alternatives when it comes to dynamic memory management. Here we want to preserve the flexibility of being able to allocate and deallocate an arbitrary number of elements at runtime, but we will try to see how we might be able to achieve this without encountering the performance issues of the dynamic memory management provided by the OS.

Some solutions to the dynamic memory management problem are listed here.

Limit memory to stack

One obvious solution is to limit dynamic memory allocation on the heap. What that means is that if something can be allocated on the stack, that should be the preference. Simple techniques such as having an upper bound on the number of elements and having a local variable on the stack to handle up to that number of elements can help eliminate the drawbacks of using dynamic memory allocation anytime an unknown number (at compile time) of elements could be needed.

Memory pools

If the type of object is known (as is quite frequently the case; for example, an `Order` object type that contains details about an order in market data, such as price, side, and quantity), it is often much more efficient to create a memory pool, allocate a huge block of memory, and manage the memory in software ourselves. Since the type and size of the object are known, the actual memory pool implementation can be made generic but super-efficient by using templates. Also, since the size of each element, we do not have to worry about holes/memory fragmentation. Additionally, we can use a LIFO stack-style deallocation/allocation scheme instead of a linked list, which is likely to give much better cache performance as well. Finally, using huge pages can help with the TLB translation efficiency in scenarios where we expect to create many specific kinds of objects.

In this section, we addressed details around accessing memory on modern architectures and OSs – the design of memory hierarchy, the inefficiencies of normal access patterns, and some techniques to maximize performance for HFT application requirements. We also discussed dynamic memory allocation, the drawbacks of using it on performance-critical paths, and techniques to use it without impacting performance for HFT applications.

Summary

We discussed the implementation details of various computer science constructs such as context switching, synchronization, and concurrency primitives. We also discussed the implications that these features have on HFT applications and found that often the default behavior that works best for most applications is not the optimal setup for HFT applications.

Finally, we discussed approaches/tools/techniques/optimizations for optimal HFT ecosystem performance. We hope this chapter provides you insight into advanced HFT optimization techniques and their impact on the HFT ecosystem's performance.

For developers and traders that want to build HFT systems and trading strategies, it is imperative that you understand the use of these HFT optimization techniques. The biggest edge in HFT comes from ultra-low latency algorithms/software and to be able to compete in that space, you will need to employ these techniques.

The next chapter will continue on the subject of HFT optimization technologies/techniques. We will discuss HFT optimizations that apply to kernel bypass technology, networking, logging, and performance measurement.

7

HFT Optimization – Logging, Performance, and Networking

In the previous chapter, we investigated a lot of lower-level HFT optimization tasks and optimization tips and techniques. In this chapter, we will continue the discussion and look at more topics in HFT optimization. The focus here will be on kernel and user space operations and optimizations related to them. We will also explore kernel bypass as well as optimization topics related to networking, logging, and measuring performance.

Some of the operations and constructs that we will discuss will be memory, disk, and network access operations at the **operating system** (**OS**) and server hardware levels and network architectures between data centers in different physical locations (microwave/fiber options). We will also discuss topics related to logging and statistical metrics around real-time performance measurement. Including the topics covered in the last chapter, by the end of this chapter, you will have a very good understanding of all the modern performance optimization tools, technologies, and techniques involved in HFT trading architectures.

In this chapter, we will cover the following topics:

- Comparing kernel space and user space
- Using kernel bypass
- Learning about memory-mapped files
- Using cable fiber, hollow fiber, and microwave technologies
- Diving into logging and statistics
- Measuring performance

Important Note

In order to guide you through all the optimizations, you can refer to the following list of icons that represent a group of optimizations lowering the latency by a specific number of microseconds:

: Lower than 20 microseconds

: Lower than 5 microseconds

: Lower than 500 nanoseconds

You will find these icons in the headings of this chapter.

It is important to understand these topics well since no modern HFT system is complete without incorporating these techniques to maximize performance. Understanding these topics is essential to building a competitive HFT business.

Comparing kernel space and user space

We touched upon the concepts of kernel and user space in the previous chapter. To refresh our memory, some privileged commands/system calls can only be made from kernel space, and this design is intentional so that errant user applications cannot harm the entire system by running whatever commands they want. The inefficiency from the perspective of an HFT application is that if it needs to make system calls, it requires a switch to kernel mode and possible context switches, which slows it down, especially if the system calls are made quite often on the critical code path. Let's formally wrap up the discussion in this section.

What is kernel and user space?

The kernel is the core component of all modern OSs. It has access to all the resources – memory, hardware devices, and interfaces, essentially everything on the machine. Kernel code has to be the most tested code that is allowed to run in kernel mode or kernel space to maintain machine stability and robustness. User space is where normal user processes run. The OS kernel still manages user space applications and polices the resources they are allowed to access. The virtual memory space is also divided into kernel space and user space. While the physical memory does not distinguish between the two spaces, the OS controls access. User space does not have access to kernel space, but the reverse is true, that is kernel space has access to user space. The diagram that follows will help you to understand the layout of these components:

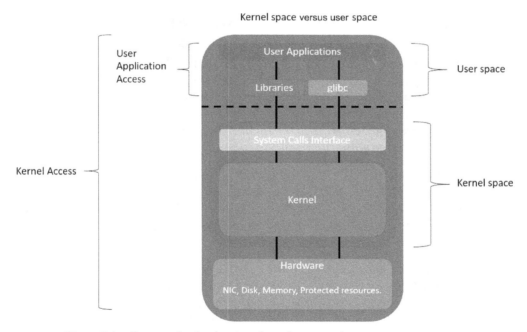

Figure 7.1 – Communication between kernel space and user space components

When processes running in user space need to execute system calls such as disk I/O, network I/O, and protected mode routine calls, they do so via system calls. In that design, system calls are the part of the kernel interface exposed by the kernel to user space processes. When a system call is invoked from a user space process, first an interrupt is sent to the kernel for the system call. The kernel finds the correct interrupt handler for the system call and launches the handler to handle the request. Once the interrupt handler is finished, processing continues onto the next set of tasks. This is not the only case where there are switches made between kernel and user space; some instructions invoked by a process running in user space also force a transition into kernel mode. For most systems, this switching does not invoke a context switch, but for some systems that might happen when switching between user and kernel mode.

Investigating performance – kernel versus user space

In general, code that runs in kernel space runs at the same speed as code in user space. The difference in performance comes into play when system calls are made – code executing in kernel space executes more quickly when system calls are involved and code executing in user space executes more slowly since when it encounters a system call, it needs to switch to kernel/supervisor mode and that switch is slow and can trigger even more expensive context switches. So, for user applications, it makes sense to minimize the use of system calls and try to eliminate them altogether if possible.

Another example is `gettimeofday()` and `clock_gettime()`, which, under the hood, invoke system calls. Since HFT applications update time very frequently, this can add up to a lot of system calls. Alternatives to that approach that would eliminate system calls are `rdtsc()` instructions, and on some architectures, even `chrono` time calls are able to avoid system calls.

Overall, there can be many opportunities during HFT application development where it is possible to eliminate or minimize (the latter being more realistic) system calls invoked from the user space application. You just need to give some thought to what methods are being called, if they invoke system calls, and if there is a better way to have the same functionality but without invoking system calls – at least as far as code in the critical hot path is concerned.

We will see an example of eliminating system calls in the section on *Learning about memory-mapped files*. By loading up the file into memory and allowing the processes to make changes directly to the memory and delay/throttle how often changes get committed to disk, the design minimizes system calls. Another example of eliminating systems calls altogether for network read/write operations is kernel bypass, which we will discuss shortly in the *Using kernel bypass* section.

We will discuss the latency improvements achieved by using that technique; however, you should know that a part of the improvement is achieved by eliminating unnecessary copies of data buffers. Before we look into the details, we will present some data here regarding the improvements. UDP read/write times without kernel bypass range between 1.5 to 10 microseconds, and with kernel bypass, range between 0.5 and 2 microseconds. TCP read/write times also have similar performance increases, except a tiny bit slower. Let's start by discussing the details of kernel bypass technology and its benefits next.

Using kernel bypass

In this section, we will discuss using the kernel bypass technique to improve the performance of **User Datagram Protocol** (**UDP**) sockets to process inbound market data updates from the exchanges and **Transmission Control Protocol** (**TCP**) sockets to send outbound order flow/requests to the exchange. Fundamentally, kernel bypass looks to eliminate the expensive context switches and mode switches between kernel mode and user mode as well as duplicate copying of data from the **Network Interface Card** (**NIC**) to user space, each of which ends up reducing the latency quite a bit.

Network processing driven by system calls/interrupts in the non-kernel bypass design, threads, or processes that want to read incoming data on UDP or TCP socket block on the read call, as described in the *Understanding context switches – interrupt handling* section in the previous chapter. That leads the blocked thread or process being context switched out, and then it is woken up by the interrupt handler when data is available on the socket. We discussed in the previous chapter, how the context switching of threads and switches between kernel mode to user space are inefficient since it adds latency on every single packet read.

For HFT applications that process market data and order responses, millions of such packet reads occur throughout the day and hence the delay adds up and causes significant performance degradation. Additionally, data is copied from the NIC buffers from kernel space to application buffers in user space, so the additional copy is another source of latency. A similar copy mechanism exists on outgoing UDP or TCP packets (TCP is the most common protocol for HFT applications, but outgoing UDP packets can exist depending on how the applications are designed).

Understanding why kernel bypass is the alternative

The alternative to eliminate the latencies incurred in traditional socket programming, which make it a bad fit for HFT, has two aspects: *spinning* on a CPU core in user space and *zero copy* of incoming and outgoing data. Both require special NICs and accompanying **Application Programming Interfaces** (**APIs**) that support these features – some examples are *Solarflare* NICs and the *OpenOnload/TCPDirect/ef_vi* API to support kernel bypass, *Mellanox* NICs and **Mellanox Messaging Accelerator** (**VMA**) APIs, and *Chelsio* adapters and **WireDirect/TCP Offload Engine** (**TOE**) APIs. Let's look at them in more detail in the following sections.

User space spinning

The alternative to the blocking and context switching design is for the calling thread or process to spin in user space while constantly polling the UDP and/or TCP sockets that are enabled for kernel bypass. This comes at the price of constantly polling and utilizing 100% of the CPU core. The good news is that polling is strictly in the user space, that is, no system calls or kernel time and CPU cores are plentiful in modern HFT trading servers, so this is a good trade-off. In this design, the NIC buffer mirrored into user space is polled constantly for new packets/data.

Zero copy

After user space spinning, the second part of the optimization eliminates the need to copy from the NIC kernel space buffers to the process's user space buffers. This is also part of the NIC, and the NIC buffers are just forwarded/duplicated straight into user space as soon as packets arrive (or packets are sent out); there is no extra copy step involved. This lack of copying is referred to as *zero copy* in the kernel bypass lingo.

Presenting kernel bypass latencies

UDP read/write times without kernel bypass latencies range between 1.5 to 10 microseconds, and with kernel bypass, latencies range between 0.5 to 2 microseconds. TCP read/write times have a similar performance increase, except a tiny bit slower. Peak latencies have an even better performance increase for UDP and TCP read/write. Over the course of millions of UDP reads and thousands of TCP reads/writes, the performance adds up and makes an enormous difference.

In this section, we introduced kernel bypass technologies to move NIC reads/writes to user space. We also discussed advanced kernel bypass techniques and presented empirical evidence of the achievable latency reductions. While single-digit microsecond latency reduction might seem small, for HFT applications it makes a big difference. We will dive into this in more depth in the *Reducing latencies with FPGA* section in *Chapter 11, High-Frequency FPGA and Crypto*, where we will look at nanosecond-level performance. In the next section, we will dive into more details about using memory-mapped files which allows us to eliminate/reduce system calls and boost performance for HFT applications.

Learning about memory-mapped files

In this section, we will discuss memory-mapped files, which are a neat abstraction that most modern OSs provide and have some benefits in terms of ease of use, ease of sharing between threads and/or processes, and performance compared to regular files. Due to their improved performance, they are used in HFT ecosystems, which we will discuss in the *Applications of memory-mapped files* section, after we investigate what they are and their benefits and drawbacks.

What are memory-mapped files?

A memory-mapped file is a mirror of a portion (or all) of a file on disk that is held in virtual memory. It has a byte-for-byte mapping in virtual memory corresponding to a file on disk, or a device, or shared memory, or anything that can be referenced through a file descriptor in UNIX/Linux-based OSs. Due to the mapping between the physical file and the memory space associated with it, it allows applications consisting of multiple threads/processes to read/modify the file by directly reading/modifying the memory that the file is mapped to. Behind the scenes, the OS takes care of committing changes to the memory to the file on disk. It updates the memory mapping when the file on disk changes, among other tasks. The application(s) themselves do not have to manage any of these tasks.

In C, memory-mapped files are created using the mmap() system call, which lets us read and write files on disk by reading and writing memory addresses. The two primary modes supported here are private to the process (the MAP_PRIVATE attribute) and shared between processes (the MAP_SHARED attribute). In the private mode, changes made to the memory map are not written to the disk, but in shared mode, changes made to the memory map are eventually committed to disk (not instantaneously, because that would be just as inefficient as reading/writing to the file on disk directly).

Types of memory-mapped files

There are two types of memory-mapped files:

- Persisted memory-mapped files
- Non-persisted memory-mapped files

Let's look at each of these in detail in the following sections.

Persisted memory-mapped files

Persisted memory-mapped files should be thought of as memory maps for which the files do/will exist on disk. When the application finishes working with the memory map of the file, then changes are committed to the actual file on disk – the functionality we have been discussing so far. This is a convenient and efficient way to work with large files or for applications where some end-of-process/end-of-day data needs to be saved to a file.

Non-persisted memory-mapped files

Non-persisted memory-mapped files are more like temporary files that only exist in memory and are not associated with an actual file on disk. So, these are not *files* at all – they are simply memory blocks that look like memory-mapped files, and they are used mostly for temporary data storage as well as sharing data using shared memory between processes – **Inter-Process Communication (IPC)**. This option is used in cases where memory-mapped files are just protocols that two or more processes communicate over but the data does not need to be saved/persisted.

Advantages of memory-mapped files

Let's look at some of the advantages of memory-mapped files – most of which are related to performance and access latency, which are quite important for HFT applications.

Improving I/O performance

The primary benefit, which should be obvious by now, is improving I/O performance. Accessing memory-mapped files is orders of magnitudes faster than a system call to read/modify something on disk, which takes an extremely long time compared to an operation in the main memory, as we saw in the previous chapter in the *Pre-fetching and pre-allocating memory*, *Memory hierarchy*, and *Inefficiencies with memory access* sections. Also, since the OS handles reloading/writing files to disks, it can do so efficiently and at optimal times (for example, when the system is not too busy with other tasks).

Understanding random access and lazy loading

Accessing a specific location in a large file on disk is slow because it involves seeking operations to find the correct location to read from/write to. However, with memory-mapped files, this is much faster since applications have direct read/write access to the data in the file in memory. Updates are also *in-place*, that is, they do not need additional temporary copies. Seeking a location in memory is fast since when page boundaries are crossed, the entire next page is brought into memory (which is slow) but then in-memory operations to that page following that are super-efficient.

Lazy loading is another benefit of memory-mapped files where tiny amounts of RAM can support large files. This is achieved by loading small page-sized sections into memory as data is being accessed/modified. This avoids loading a huge file into memory, which will cause other performance issues, such as cache misses and page faults.

Optimized OS-managed page file management

Modern OSs are extremely efficient at memory mapping and paging processes since that is the system that also deals with critical virtual memory management tasks – the virtual memory manager. For this reason, the OS can manage the memory mapping process very efficiently and select optimal *page sizes* (sizes of memory blocks/chunks), and so on.

Parallel access

Memory-mapped regions allow concurrent read/write access to different sections of the file from multiple threads and/or processes. Thus, parallel access is possible in this case.

Disadvantages of memory-mapped files

We saw the concept of cache misses in the previous chapter in the *Understanding context switches – Expensive tasks in a context switch* section. Cache misses are basically when code/data that a running process needs is not available in the cache bank and needs to be fetched from main memory. *Page faults* are a similar concept, except here the OS has to fetch data from the disk when it is not available in main memory. Page faults are the biggest concern with memory-mapped files. This is often the case where memory-mapped files are not being accessed sequentially. A page fault makes the thread wait until the I/O operation finishes, which slows things down. If address space availability is an issue (for instance, in a 32-bit OS), then too many or large memory-mapped files can cause the OS to run out of address space and make the page fault situation worse. Due to the extra operations and address space overhead described previously, sometimes standard file I/O can beat memory-mapped file I/O performance.

Applications of memory-mapped files

The most well-known application for memory-mapped files is the process loader that uses a memory-mapped file to bring the executable code, modules, data, and other things into memory.

Another well-known application for memory-mapped files is sharing memory between processes: IPC, as we discussed in the *Types of memory-mapped files* section under *Non-persisted memory-mapped files*. Memory-mapped files are one of the most popular IPC mechanisms to share memory/data between processes. This is used quite heavily in HFT applications, often in combination with lock-free queues, which we discussed in the previous chapter in the *Building a lock-free data structure* section. That design is used to set up a communication channel between different processes sharing high-throughput and latency-sensitive data. This is usually the non-persisted memory-mapped file option. Memory-mapped files in HFT applications are also used to persist information between runs using the persisted memory-mapped file option. This section covered the concepts, benefits, and applications of memory-mapped files that are used in a bunch of places in an efficient and performant HFT ecosystem. In the next section, we will transition from discussing low-latency communication options between processes on the same server/data center to network communication between different servers possibly in different locations.

Using cable fiber, hollow fiber, and microwave technologies ✐

Another key (but extremely expensive) area of competition in HFT is that of setting up connectivity between data centers sitting in different geographical locations – for example, Chicago, New York, London, Frankfurt, and so on. Let's take a look at the options that enable this connectivity:

- Cable fibers are a standard option – they have high bandwidth and extremely low packet losses, and they are slower and more expensive than some of the other options.

- Hollow fiber is a modern technology that is an improvement on solid cable fibers and provides lower latency for signal/data propagation between data centers.

- Microwave is another option, but it is often used for very specific purposes. It has extremely low bandwidth and suffers from packet losses in certain weather conditions and because of interference from other microwave transmissions. However, microwaves are the fastest way to transfer information and are cheaper to set up and move than the other two options.

Now that we have introduced the different network technologies that we shall be discussing, in the next section, let's look at the evolution of those technologies.

Evolution from cable fiber to hollow fiber to microwave

Let's quickly discuss the evolution of cable fiber to hollow fiber and microwave. It is important to see how the arms race to achieve ultra-low latencies in HFT drove the evolution from cable fiber to hollow fiber to microwave technologies because HFT will continue to evolve with technological improvements. Hollow fiber is the next step in the evolution of fiber optic cables. Hollow fibers are made of glass and carry beams of light that encode the data being transmitted. However, they are not solid like regular cable fibers: they are hollow (hence the name) and have parallel air-filled channels (we will see why shortly).

Microwave is an old technology, but it suffers from not having a lot of bandwidth and losing data during rain/bad weather. Microwave technology was abandoned in favor of solid cable fibers due to the reliability and huge bandwidth availability for most applications.

However, with the rise of HFT, a lot of participants realized that latency arbitrage strategies can rake in billions of dollars by employing microwave networks to transmit data a few milliseconds or microseconds faster than solid cable, even though they suffer from low bandwidth and experience much more frequent packet losses.

Finally, another advance in the landscape of HFT competition is hollow fiber, which still supports the high bandwidth and low packet loss behavior but is slightly faster than solid fiber cables. A while back, a company called Spread Networks laid a fiber-optic cable line from Chicago to New York, and the transmission latency for the route was 13 milliseconds. A few years after that, microwave networks were set up on the same route and reduced the transmission latency to less than 9 milliseconds.

How hollow fiber works

Hollow fiber technology simply tries to make better use of the fact that light travels 50% faster in air than in solid glass. There are some design limitations, however, so in practice, sending data through hollow fiber takes about 65% of the time of sending it through a standard fiber. As mentioned before, hollow fiber cables are hollow instead of solid, like standard fiber cables, and have parallel air-filled channels to allow light to travel through air and not glass.

In HFT, hollow fiber cables are used for brief stretches – several hundred yards at most – and are commonly used to connect data centers with nearby communication towers from where the rest of the path is connected via microwaves. Using hollow fiber cables results in speed-ups of a few hundred to a thousand nanoseconds – not a massive improvement, but still big enough to make a significant impact on the profitability of purely latency arbitrage trading strategies.

How microwave works

As mentioned before, microwave transmission technology is quite old (dating back to the 90s) and was abandoned for solid fiber cable transmission (since for most applications, that was the correct choice). However, HFT traders have found novel ways to utilize microwave transmissions between geographically distributed data centers to save microseconds and milliseconds and profit from being able to beat the competition by a tiny amount of time.

The reason for the lower latencies is two-fold – first, light travels 50% faster in air than it does in solid glass, and second, with microwaves it is possible to beam the signal from one location to another in a straight line, whereas with solid fiber cables, that is not possible in practice. With solid fiber cables, each time the path turns and deviates from a straight/optimal path, it introduces delays. In practice, microwave networks use *line-of-sight* transmissions and the sending and receiving microwave dishes must be able to see each other. For that reason, over long distances the earth's curvature means additional towers are required a few miles apart to relay the signal, and the towers need to be as tall as possible to use as few relay hops as possible.

Advantages and disadvantages of microwaves

So far, based on the discussion, it should be becoming obvious where microwave transmission has the upper hand on solid/hollow fiber cables and where it might suffer from some drawbacks. Let's formalize the advantages and disadvantages of microwave and fiber transmission in this section.

Advantages

The most important advantage of microwave transmission that makes it so useful in HFT is obviously the *speed of transmission*. This allows HFT traders to execute a few microseconds or milliseconds ahead of their competition and profit from that. Basically, being second in this game means losing the competition altogether.

Disadvantages

One of the disadvantages of microwave transmission is its *extremely limited bandwidth*. The extremely low bandwidth availability means HFT networking architecture and strategies need to be designed in such a way as to send only the most important/critical data over microwaves as well as engineering techniques to reduce the size of packet payloads as much as possible (we will look at this shortly).

The other big issue with microwave transmission is *the reliability of the transmission link*, especially in scenarios where anything that hampers the quality of the signal being sent makes it unusable. Anything from mountains, skyscrapers, rain, clouds, planes, and even other microwave networks operating around the same frequency can cause the signal to be dropped or garbled/corrupted. This leads to extra engineering requirements, such as larger dishes, hydrophobic coatings on the dishes, fail-over protocols (often in conjunction with a much more reliable transmission method, such as cable fiber), drop/corruption detection mechanisms in the network (packet) and HFT application layer, and so on.

Impact of microwave

Based on the speed of light, the theoretical limit for sending information between Carteret, New Jersey and Aurora, Illinois is 3.9 milliseconds. The theoretical limit is computed from the shortest straight line distance between Carteret and Aurora and the speed of light in a vacuum. Right now, the state-of-the-art among microwave service providers is about 3.982 milliseconds. The high-speed fiber-optic network between London and Frankfurt takes around 8.3 milliseconds and the microwave transmission network is less, 4.6 milliseconds, which means competitors with the microwave network will always beat cross-colocation latency arbitrage HFT participants who do not have access to the microwave network or do not have the best microwave network.

We are yet to figure out what the future of this space will look like, but there are efforts being made to use laser beam military technology to cut this latency down even further. This might show up between Britain and Germany or between New York and exchange locations around New York. In either case, the competition continues to tighten and HFT participants in the cross-colocation HFT latency arbitrage space continue to fight in the realm of nanoseconds.

In the next section, we will move on to mechanisms and techniques used for logging and statistics computation in HFT systems. Since HFT applications trade in the nanosecond and microsecond performance space, it is important to have an extremely robust and efficient logging system. Also important is a statistics computation system to gain insights into the strategy/system behavior and performance.

Diving into logging and statistics

Logging (outputting information from the various HFT components in some format and using some protocol/transport) and statistics generation (offline or online) on various performance data are less glamorous aspects of the HFT business but they are quite important, nonetheless. Implemented poorly, they can also bog down the system or reduce visibility into the system, so it is important to build a proper infrastructure for that. In this section, we will discuss logging and statistics generation from the perspective of the HFT ecosystem.

The need for logging in HFT

Logging in most software applications serves to provide the users and/or developers insights into the behavior and performance, alerting them to unexpected situations that might be a concern/need attention as far as the operation of the applications is concerned. For HFT applications, especially where thousands of complex decisions are being made each second, complex software components interact with each other, and a lot of money is at stake, proper logging and a proper logging infrastructure are extremely important. Logs generated by HFT applications vary in severity levels – critical errors, warnings, periodic logs, usual performance statistics – and they vary in verbosity as well. The less frequent the log types, the more verbose they might be – but this is not necessarily required to be true.

The need for online/live statistics computation in HFT

HFT applications execute thousands of instructions each second and make thousands of complex decisions related to processing market data, generating trading signals, generating trading decisions, and generating order flow, handling all of that every second. Also, HFT trading strategies in general do not seek to have a small number of trades on a few trading instruments that make a lot of money per trade but instead have an enormous number of trades across many trading instruments that make an average of tiny amounts of money per trade.

Given the nature of the HFT trading strategies' behavior/performance, summary statistics for various components in the system is an important way to evaluate system functionality. These summary statistics can apply to software latency performance statistics and statistics on trading signal outputs (per individual trading signal and aggregated across different signals and/or trading strategies). Additionally, there are statistics pertaining to order flow and/or executions on orders, statistics for trading strategy performance (**Profit and Loss (PnL)**) statistics, trading fee statistics, position size statistics, position duration statistics, passive versus aggressive trading, and so on – anything that provides insights into the strategies' behavior/performance. Many other statistics can be generated continuously in an online computed fashion or in an offline fashion (at the end of a trading session).

Problems with logging and live statistics

The fundamental issue with logging and statistics computation with regard to HFT applications is that they are extremely slow operations. Logging involves disk I/O at some level, which, as we saw in the section on memory hierarchy, is the slowest operation by far.

Offline/online computation of statistics can be expensive due to the nature of the computations themselves, which can be complex/expensive. Another reason for the slow computation of statistics is that they often involve a rolling window of past observations. These properties make both tasks too inefficient to be performed on the hot/critical thread.

HFT logging and statistics infrastructure design

Let's discuss the architecture/design of an efficient logging and statistics infrastructure that would be suitable for the processes that make up an efficient HFT system.

First, it is best to move the logging and the statistics computation threads or processes out of the critical trading thread or process. Then we can control how often the logging and stats computing threads are active by varying the sleep times, checking for system usage, deciding how real-time we want the logging and stats computation to be, and so on – factors that depend on the specific nature and expected utilization of the HFT system in question.

We will ideally avoid locks by using lock free-data structures and non-persistent memory-mapped files to transfer data from the critical threads to the logging threads, avoid context switches on the hot path by pinning the logging and statistics computation threads or processes to their own set of isolated CPU cores, and reduce the amount of time spent on disk I/O using persistent memory-mapped files and controlling when the write to disk occurs.

This is the overall architecture for the optimized logging and statistics computation framework for HFT applications. We saw parts of it in the previous chapter in the *Applications of lock-free data structures* section. However, there are some alternative design choices that we have seen in our experience. Instead of flat files, we can use different interfaces, such as SQL databases, especially when it comes to recording structured datasets for statistical computations. We have also seen the use of UDP- and TCP-based reliable multicast publishing-based logging setups to send log records over the network, the motivation here being to have them in a single centralized location, publish to trading/ monitoring GUIs, and so on. We do not use kernel bypass for this network traffic since it is not that latency sensitive and, overall, this is not the most popular design we have seen.

Measuring performance

No text on HFT optimization would be complete without discussing performance measurement. Due to the ultra-low latency nature of HFT applications, performance measurement infrastructure is often something that is built early on and maintained throughout the evolution of the HFT system. In this section, we will discuss in more detail why performance measurement is such a critical aspect, tools and techniques to measure performance for HFT systems, and what insights we can glean from the output of the measurements.

Motivation for measuring performance

Since HFT applications are incredibly reliant on super low average latency performance and low variance on the latency of their components, measuring the performance of each of their components on a regular basis is a particularly important task. As changes and improvements are made to the various components of an HFT system, there is always the possibility of introducing unexpected latency, so not having a robust and detailed performance management system can cause such detrimental changes to slip under the radar.

The other nuance of measuring performance, especially for HFT applications, is that the components of HFT applications themselves operate in the nanosecond and microsecond space. The implication is that the performance measurement system itself will have to make sure to introduce extremely few additional latencies. This is very important to make sure that invoking the performance measurement system does not change the performance itself.

Due to these reasons, performance measuring tools and infrastructure for HFT have the following characteristics:

- They are very precise in their measurements.

- They have extremely low overhead themselves.

- They often invoke special CPU instructions for target architectures to be very efficient.

- They sometimes resort to some non-trivial methods to measure performance such as mirroring network traffic and capturing it, inserting fields in outbound traffic to link with inbound traffic, and using hardware timestamping at NICs and switches.

One important principle when it comes to approaching HFT application (or any application) performance optimization is the 90/10 rule, which states that the program spends 90% of its run time in 10% of its code. This heuristic implies that certain code blocks/paths are executed very rarely, hence should not really be the target for optimizations (unless they are insanely inefficient/slow) and that certain code blocks/paths are executed very frequently, and these hot paths should be the targets for the majority of the optimization efforts. The key to finding these hot paths/critical code sections is measuring performance accurately, efficiently, and regularly. In the next section, we will cover the available tools to measure and profile Linux-based application performance. We will limit the tools to ones available on Linux since it is the most common platform for deploying/running HFT applications.

Linux tools for measuring performance

In this section, we will look at some tools/commands available in Linux that can be used to measure the performance of an HFT application. They vary widely in various ways:

- Ease of use

- Accuracy and precision

- Granularity of measurement (that is, measuring overall application performance, methods in applications, lines of code, instructions, and so on)

- Application overhead introduced by the measurement process by which resource utilization is tracked – cache, CPU, cache, stack memory, heap memory, and so on

It is important for you to get familiar with these tools and commands because application performance measurement is a key part of HFT system maintenance and improvement. The tools and commands are presented next.

Linux – time

This is a Linux command that requires code changes or compilation/linking changes. It can be used to determine the run time of a program, separately counting user time and system time, and CPU time and clock time. You can find more information here: `https://man7.org/linux/man-pages/man1/time.1.html`.

GNU Debugger – gdb

This is the **GNU Debugger (gdb)**. While this is not a traditional profiling tool, letting an application run and then break periodically and randomly can be used to see where the application spends most of its time. The probability of breaking at a specific code section is a fraction of the total time spent in that code region. So, performing these steps (randomly breaking in gdb) a few times is a good starting point. You can check out this link for reference: `https://www.sourceware.org/gdb/`.

GNU Profiler – gprof

The **GNU Profiler (gprof)** uses instrumentation inserted into the application by the compiler and runtime sampling. *Instrumentation* (adding additional code around function calls with the purpose of measurement) is used to gather function call information and *sampling* the measurements is used to gather profiling information at runtime. The **Program Counter (PC)** is checked at regular intervals by interrupting the program with interrupts to check the time since the last time the PC was probed. This tool outputs where the application spends its time and which functions are calling which other functions while it is executing. It is similar to `callgrind` (which we will discuss shortly), but it is different in that unlike `callgrind`, `gprof` does not do a simulation of the run. There are tools to visualize the output of `gprof` such as VCG tools and KProf. You can access `gprof` here: `https://ftp.gnu.org/old-gnu/Manuals/gprof-2.9.1/html_mono/gprof.html`.

Performance analysis tool for Linux – perf

`perf` is another Linux tool that is used to collect and analyze performance and trace data. This can operate on an even lower level than `gprof` by reading from hardware registers and getting an accurate idea of CPU cycles, cache performance, branch prediction, memory access, and so on. It uses a similar sampling-based approach to `gprof` in that it polls the program to see what functions are being called. You can refer to this link for further reading: `https://man7.org/linux/man-pages/man1/perf.1.html`.

Linux Trace Toolkit: next generation – LTTng

Linux Trace Toolkit: next generation (LTTng) is used for tracing Linux kernels and applications to get information regarding which kernel calls and application methods are called when an application runs to understand the system, libraries, and application performance. You can access it here: `https://lttng.org/`.

valgrind, cachegrind, and callgrind

`valgrind` and its suite of tools is a well-rounded set of tools that support the following:

- Debugging
- Profiling
- Detecting memory management and threading bugs
- Profiling cache and branch prediction performance (`cachegrind`)
- Collecting call-graphs and data on a number of instructions, correlating them with source code, functions callers and callees, frequency of calls, and so on (`callgrind`)
- Profile heap usage to try to reduce an application's memory usage/footprint (`massif`)

So, it is an instrumentation framework for everything you might need to debug and profile your applications. It acts as a virtual machine. It does not run the compiled machine code directly but instead simulates the execution of the application. It also has a bunch of visualization tools to analyze the output of the `valgrind` suite of tools (`KCachegrind` would be one particularly good example of a visualization tool). You can access `valgrind` here: `https://valgrind.org/`.

Google perftools – Gperftools

This is another set of tools from Google that helps analyze and improve performance, and it can work on multi-threaded applications as well. Offerings include a CPU profiler, memory leak detector, and heap profiler. You can access it here: `https://github.com/gperftools/gperftools`.

In this section, we looked at existing out-of-the-box solutions to measure HFT application performance. Next, we will explore custom techniques to instrument HFT code and measure performance. These involve adding/enabling additional architecture/OS/kernel parameters and adding additional code to the applications.

Custom techniques for measuring performance

We have seen some Linux tools that can help us profile most applications. It is common to add custom instrumentation code into the HFT applications in critical sections of the code. We have already discussed logging and statistics computation, and we mentioned that the latency performance of the different components/code paths of HFT applications is another application for that. Additionally, the data inside the HFT application that gets fed to the logging/stats infrastructure is often from custom timestamping/performance-measurement code.

In this section, let's discuss a few additional techniques to measure HFT application performance – how to make the performance measurement setup as consistent as possible between runs, C++ specific instrumentation libraries/functions, and finally, **Tick-To-Trade** (**TTT**), which is a standard and important way to measure an HFT system's end-to-end performance with as much granularity as required.

Getting consistent results on benchmarks

As with any process driven by repeated experiments and accurate readings from the experiments, performance measurement of HFT applications needs to be precise and consistently repeatable, that is, the experimentation process itself should not introduce too much noise/variance. Modern CPU, architecture, and OS features are intended to increase performance on higher demand, but they introduce *non-determinism* and higher variance in performance latencies. Non-deterministic performance is when similar input data and code paths trigger slightly different performance due to factors outside of the application developers' control, such as data in cache, memory, and instruction sets. For the purposes of benchmarking HFT application performance, we need to take steps to reduce the variance introduced by these features as much as possible (often by turning these features off). In summary, when doing benchmarking experiments, we disable potential sources of non-deterministic performance. A couple of the major features that can cause non-determinism are discussed next.

Intel Turbo Boost

Turbo Boost is a feature specific to Intel processors and architecture that raises CPU frequency when under heavy CPU load. While this is a good feature for most applications, when profiling/benchmarking extremely low-latency HFT applications, it introduces variance in the performance data by turning on and off at various times outside of the applications' controls, so it is best to disable it. This is achieved through the **Basic Input/Output System** (**BIOS**), which basically is used to control hardware parameters when booting up.

Hyper threading

Hyper threading allows modern CPU cores to have two threads of simultaneous execution inside a single physical core. Another feature that makes total sense for most applications except when benchmarking HFT applications' performance. Here some of the architecture resources – ALUs, caches, and so on are not replicated exactly as they should be. What this means is that one may observe non-deterministic behavior if, say, threads randomly get scheduled that steal resources from the process being measured. This is another modern feature that needs to be disabled when benchmarking HFT applications, which is another configuration option in the BIOS.

CPU power-saving options

When power-saving options are enabled, the kernel/OS can decide if it is better to save power and throttle. Disabling this feature is recommended to avoid sub-nominal CPU clocking kicking in unpredictably and causing degradation in performance (and performance measurements).

CPU isolation and affinity

We have touched upon this in the previous chapter under *Techniques to avoid or minimize context switches* in the *Pinning threads to CPU cores* section, but this is to make sure critical threads are pinned/bound to a specific CPU core and non-critical threads have no chance of interrupting those threads and causing context switches. This results in significantly greater determinism and lower variance in performance data.

Linux process priority

In Linux, we can change process priority using the `nice` command (more about the tool can be found at `https://man7.org/linux/man-pages/man1/nice.1.html`). By increasing process priority using the `nice` command, the process can get more CPU time. Additionally, the Linux scheduler prioritizes it above processes with normal/lower priority.

Address Space Layout Randomization

Address Space Layout Randomization (ASLR) is a security technique to prevent exploits based on memory locations of different sections (code, static data, constant data, stack, and so on) staying the same across multiple runs. A simple example of such an exploit/attack would be a malicious virus that steals or corrupts data written to a memory location if the memory location stays the same across application executions. The simple solution that ASLR adopts to prevent this is to randomly arrange the address space positions of key data areas of the process. But this introduces non-determinism and variance in performance data, so for the purposes of benchmarking HFT applications, this security feature needs to be disabled.

Measurement data statistics

Choosing the correct statistic for the performance data is also a key component. This can depend on a lot of factors, but the primary one is the objective of the optimization process: are we looking to reduce latency on an average, reduce maximum or minimum latency ever incurred, or somewhere in between (averages or percentiles such as 50% (median), top 90% latencies, and so on)? Depending on these factors, we might want to compute and compare any of the various statistical measures available – mean, median, variance, inter-quartile region, min, max, skew of distribution, and so on.

In the next section, we will discuss some additional performance measurement techniques specifically for the Linux environment when developing C++ applications, which is the optimal language and platform choice for HFT.

C++/Linux specific measurement routines/libraries

In this section, we will discuss some of the libraries/routines that can be used to insert instrumentation directly into source code when building HFT applications. Here, we will only cover Linux and C/C++ since that is the most common HFT setup, but analogous methods exist for most platforms and programming languages. For instance, a comprehensive guide to profiling applications running on Windows can be found at https://docs.microsoft.com/en-us/visualstudio/profiling/profiling-feature-tour?view=vs-2022.

gettimeofday

This has been used for a long time in C. It returns the time elapsed since 00:00:00 UTC on January 1st, 1970 (often called **Epoch** time). It returns both seconds and microseconds, but not nanoseconds. This is not the timestamping mechanism of choice in modern HFT applications C/C++ anymore, since this method invokes system calls and has larger overhead than more modern timestamping mechanisms.

Time Stamp Counter (TSC) using rdtsc

This is another method that was a high-resolution and low-overhead way to get CPU timing information but is no longer really accurate/used with multi-core, multi-CPU, and hyper-threaded processor architectures. The `chrono` library, which we will see next, overcomes the limitations mentioned here. `rdtsc()` is a CPU instruction that reads the **Time Stamp Counter** (TSC) register and returns the number of CPU cycles elapsed since reset. This cannot be directly used to extract the current time but can be used to calculate how many CPU cycles have elapsed between subsequent calls to `rdtsc()` and then that can be used (using CPU frequency) to compute how many microseconds have elapsed between the two calls to `rdtsc()` between the two locations in the code being measured.

chrono

This is the standard library in C++ used nowadays and it is easy to use and portable, has access to a multitude of clocks and resolutions, and needs C++ 11 or later versions. `Std::chrono::high_resolution_clock` from the `<chrono>` header file (available within the `chrono` library) contains a method called `now()` for extracting the current time using different clock resolutions, the most common of which is the `high_resolution_clock`, which provides the highest resolution clock so is the best fit for measuring HFT application performance.

End-to-end measurement – Tick-To-Trade (TTT)

We have seen a lot of performance measurement methods where the HFT application is profiled in a benchmark lab and/or simulation setting. But the thing that matters with performance measurement at the end of the day is how the application will run in a real production setting. We use the techniques mentioned in the previous section on C++/Linux-specific measurement routines/libraries with a combination of lock-free data structures, memory-mapped files, and the discussion in the *Diving into logging and statistics* section to build an end-to-end latency measurement system.

We measure the latencies of the various components (hops) in the system on the critical path, starting from when the market data update leaves the exchange infrastructure, hits the participants' trading server NIC, gets processed by the market data feed handler, gets transported to the trading strategy, gets processed in the sub-components inside the trading strategy (book building, trading signal updates, execution logic, order management, risk checks, and so on), then gets sent over to the order gateway, and finally sent out on the NIC to the exchange. This is referred to as **Tick-To-Trade** (TTT), where the tick is the incoming market data update and the trade is the outgoing order request to the exchange.

Here is a diagram that shows an example TTT measurement system. This assumes all trading decisions are made based on market data updates, which is not necessarily true but was assumed here for the sake of simplicity. The differences between the timestamps (t_1 to t_{10}) taken on various hops on the critical path can be used to derive the latencies of the various components of the system.

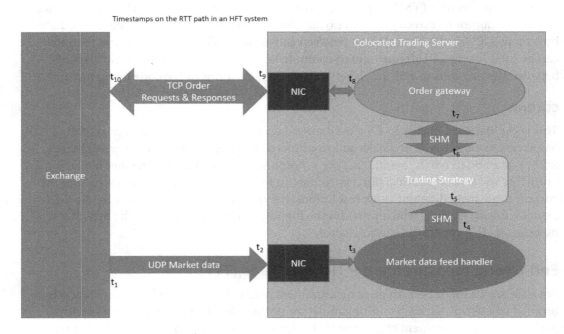

Figure 7.2 – Hops on the round trip path from the exchange to a participant and back to the exchange

The following table describes the different timestamps on the round trip path in greater detail. This outlines the different hopes when a single market data update generated from the exchange reaches a market participant and gets processed. On the path from the participant to the exchange, it describes the different hops for the order sent in reaction to the market update.

Timestamp	Description
t_1	Sending time when the exchange sends the market update out from its infrastructure – basically, when it puts it on the wire. Often, this timestamp is available as a field on the market data stream.
t_2	Receiving time when the market data packet hits the NIC on the participant'ts trading server.
t_3	This is when the market data packet is read and delivered to the market data feed handler.
t_4	This timestamp is taken after the market data feed handler has processed the market data update and generated an update for the trading strategy to consume. This time is when the update is written to the **shared memory** (**SHM**)/memory-mapped file from the feed handler to the trading strategy process.
t_5	This is when the trading strategy receives the market data update over SHM from the feed handler.
t_6	This timestamp is taken after the trading strategy processes the market update, produces trading signals, checks market conditions, and decides to send an order request out. This is the timestamp of the strategy writing the order request to the SHM from trading strategy to order gateway.
t_7	This is when the order gateway receives the order request from the trading strategy over SHM.
t_8	This is when the order gateway has finished processing the order request and wants to send out a message to the exchange. This timestamp is when the order gateway invokes a network write on the NIC.
t_9	This timestamp corresponds to when the TCP packet for the order request is put on the wire.
t_{10}	This timestamp corresponds to the exchange receiving the order request in its infrastructure. This timestamp is often also available on the TCP order response sent back by the exchange and sometimes also as a field on the market update generated corresponding to this order request.

Figure 7.3 – Details of timestamps captured at different hops on the round trip path between the exchange and a market participant

This section described a typical end-to-end measurement system for an HFT ecosystem. We also investigated the different timestamps captured on the hops between market participants and the exchange in detail.

Summary

We discussed the implementation details of various computer science constructs, such as memory access mechanisms, network traffic access from the application layer, disk I/O, network transmission methods, and performance measurement tools and techniques.

We also discussed the implications that these features have on HFT applications and found that, often, the default behavior that works best for most applications is not the optimal setup for HFT applications.

Finally, we discussed approaches, tools, techniques, and optimizations for optimal HFT ecosystem performance. We hope this chapter provided insights into advanced HFT optimization techniques and their impact on the HFT ecosystem's performance.

You should have a good idea of all the important optimization considerations in an HFT ecosystem. We also discussed in great detail the different performance measurement and optimization tools and techniques you can use to profile the performance of your HFT system and maintain and improve on it.

In the next chapter, we will dive into modern C++ programming language details, specifically with the goal of building super-low-latency HFT systems that use all the power that modern C++ has to offer.

Part 3: Implementation of a High-Frequency Trading System

This part will give you a hands-on experience by giving you the guidelines to implement a **high-frequency trading** (HFT) system in programming languages. We will start our journey with the most used language in HFT: C++. Then, we will continue with Java and its virtual machine. We will explain how Python can use HFT libraries. We will conclude this book by describing how **field programmable gate arrays** (FPGAs) reduce the tick-to-trade latency and by talking about HFT in cryptocurrencies.

This part comprises the following chapters:

- *Chapter 8, C++ – The Quest for Microsecond Latency*
- *Chapter 9, Java and JVM for Low-Latency Systems*
- *Chapter 10, Python – Interpreted but Open to High Performance*
- *Chapter 11, High-Frequency FPGA and Crypto*

8

C++ – The Quest for Microsecond Latency

In this chapter, we discuss some features and constructs available in C++. One disclaimer before we start is that covering a lot/most of what modern C++ (C++ 11/14/17) offers is beyond the scope of a single chapter (and often a single book), so we will focus on a few aspects that are important to developing, maintaining, and improving multi-threaded and ultra-low runtime latency HFT applications. Before starting to dig into this chapter, we recommend you to be fluent in C++. We recommend a couple of books to serve this purpose such as *Programming: Principles and Practice Using C++* written by Bjarne Stroustrup.

We will start out by looking into modern **C++ memory models**, which specify how shared memory interactions work in a multi-threaded environment, then look at static analysis, which is an important aspect of application development, testing, and maintenance. Then we will dive into how to optimize applications for runtime performance, before finally dedicating an entire section to templates, which are super important for top-tier HFT ecosystems.

In this chapter, we will cover the following topics:

- C++ memory model
- Removing runtime decisions
- Dynamic memory allocation
- Template for reducing runtime
- Static analysis

By the end of this chapter, you will be capable of optimizing your C++ code for HFT systems. Finally, we will review an industry use case. We will talk about the technology that we used to build a **Foreign Exchange (FX)** high-frequency hedge fund.

Important Note

In order to guide you through all the optimizations, you can refer to the following list of icons that represent a group of optimizations lowering the latency by a specific number of microseconds:

: Lower than 20 microseconds

: Lower than 5 microseconds

: Lower than 500 nanoseconds

You will find these icons in the headings of this chapter.

Let's first start by talking about the C++ memory model.

C++ 14/17 memory model

In this section, we will explore the definition and specification of the memory model for modern C++ (11, 14, and 17). We will investigate what it is, why it is needed for multi-threaded applications, and the important principles of the C++ memory model.

What is a memory model?

A **memory model,** a.k.a. a *memory consistency model,* specifies the allowed and expected behavior of multi-threaded applications that interact with shared memory. The memory model is the foundation of the concurrency semantics of shared memory systems. If there are two concurrent programs, one writing to and another reading from a shared memory space, the memory model defines the set of values that a read operation is allowed to return for any combination of reads and writes.

Implementation of the memory models (C++ or otherwise) must be constrained by the rules specified by the memory models, because if the outcome cannot be inferred from the order of reads and writes, then it is not an unambiguous memory model. Another way to think about the restrictions enforced by a memory model is that they define which instruction reordering is allowed by the compiler, the processor, and the architecture (the memory). Most research on memory models tries to maximize freedom for compiler, processor, and architecture optimizations.

Even if the optimizations become more and more complicated and complex, they must keep the semantics of what the developer wants to do. They should never break the constraints of the memory model.

At this point, let's formally define a few terms.

- **Source code order**

  This is the order of instructions and memory operations that the programmer has specified in the programming language of their choice. This is the code or set of instructions as it exists before the compiler has compiled the code.

- **Program order**

  This is the order of instructions and memory operations in the machine code that will be executed on the CPU after the compilation of the source code. The order of instructions and/or memory operations can be different here since, as mentioned previously, compilers will try to optimize and reorder instructions as part of the optimization process.

- **Execution order**

  This is the order of actual execution of instructions and memory references as executed on the CPU. This is different from the compiled program order because at this stage, the CPU and the architecture in general are allowed to reorder the instructions in the machine code generated by the compiler. The optimizations here depend on the memory model of the specific CPU and its architecture.

We will now discuss the need for a memory model.

The need for a memory model

Let's discuss why we need a well-defined memory model at all. The fundamental reason comes down to the fact that the code we wrote is not exactly the code that is output after the compilation process and also not the code that is run on the hardware. Modern compilers and CPUs are allowed to execute instructions out of order to maximize performance and resource utilization.

In a single-threaded environment, this does not matter but in a multi-threaded environment running over a multi-core (multi-processor) architecture, different threads trying to read and write to a shared memory location causes race conditions and can lead to undefined and unexpected behavior in the presence of instruction reordering. As we saw in *Chapter 4, HFT System Foundations – From Hardware to OS*, scheduling and context switching are non-deterministic. They can be controlled but when context switching occurs at extremely specific places, it is possible that the optimizations cause the instructions to be executed and the memory accesses to occur in an order that causes results to be different depending on the sequence of events.

Having a memory model gives optimizing compilers a high degree of freedom when applying optimizations. The memory model dictates the synchronization barriers that use synchronization primitives (mutexes, locks, synchronized blocks, barriers, and so on), which we saw in the previous *Chapter 7, HFT Optimization – Logging, Performance, and Networking*. When shared variables change, the change needs to be made visible to other threads when a synchronization barrier is reached; that is, the reordering cannot break this invariant. We will now describe in detail how the C++ memory model works.

The C++ 11 memory model and its rules

Before we investigate the details of the C++ 11 memory model, let's recap the previous two sections. A memory model is meant to do the following:

- Specify the possible outcomes of the interactions of threads through shared memory.
- Check whether a program has well-defined behavior.
- Specify constraints for compiler code generation.

The C++ memory model has minimal guarantees about memory access semantics. As expected, there is a limit on the acceptable effects of compiler processing and optimizations (optimizations that reorder instructions and memory accesses) and CPU/architecture that executes instructions and memory accesses out of order. The guarantees about memory access semantics in the C++ memory model itself are quite weak – weaker than you would expect and weaker than what is typically implemented in practice. The memory model in practice mirrors the rules the system imposes, such as **total store ordering** (**TSO**) for x86_64 or a relaxed ordering with ARM.

For the C++ memory model, there are three rules with regard to transferring data between main memory (shared) and memory per-thread. We will discuss those three rules as follows. We will address memory ordering along with **Sequential Consistency** in the next section.

Atomicity

We have seen this before in *Chapter 6, HFT Optimization – Architecture and Operating System,* in the *Lock-free data structures* section. It needs to be clear which operations are indivisible when working with global/static/shared variables/data structures.

Let's introduce some constructs available from C++ 11 onward to support atomicity that can be generalized to different types of objects (templates) and support atomic loads and stores. We will quickly introduce the memory ordering support that C++ 11 provides and will take a closer look at it later in the *Memory ordering* section under *C++ memory ordering principles.*

std::lock_guard

`std::lock_guard` is a simple mutex wrapper that uses the principle of **resource acquisition is initialization** (**RAII**) for owning a mutex within the scoped block. It tries to take ownership of the mutex as soon as it is created and the scope in which it was created is finished, the `lock_guard` destructor is called, which releases the mutex. For convenience C++ 11 provides the `std::atomic<T>` template class to support atomic loads and stores for objects of type `T`.

std::atomic

The generic class `std::atomic<T>` we mentioned before to support atomic operations on generic objects supports the following atomic operations (there are more but we list the most important ones):

- `load(std::memory_order order)`, which loads and returns the current value but does so atomically
- `store(T value, std::memory_order order)`, which saves the current value atomically
- `exchange(T value, std::memory_order order)`, which does a similar job as `store` but performs a read-modify-write operation

For integral and pointer types it also provides the following operations:

- `fetch_add(T arg, std::memory_order order)`, which takes an additional argument `arg` and atomically sets the value to the arithmetic addition of the value and `arg`
- `fetch_sub(T arg, std::memory_order order)`, which is like `fetch_add` except it subtracts instead of adding

And exclusively for integral types, it provides the following additional logical operations:

- `fetch_and(T arg, std::memory_order order)`, which is like `fetch_add` except it performs the bitwise `AND` operation.

- `fetch_or(T arg, std::memory_order order)`, which is like `fetch_and` except it performs the bitwise `OR` operation.

- `fetch_xor(T arg, std::memory_order order)`, which is like `fetch_and` except it performs the bitwise `XOR` operation.

The default value for the `std::memory_order` order parameter is `std::memory_order_seq_cst` (**Sequential Consistency**). There are other values that can be specified here instead of Sequential Consistency to define a weaker memory model. The different options and their effects will be discussed in the *Memory ordering* section of *C++ memory model principles*.

Properties of atomic operations

The properties of atomic operations are as follows:

- Operations can be performed concurrently from multiple threads without risking undefined behavior.

- Atomic load sees either the initial value of a variable or the value written to it via an atomic store.

- Atomic stores for the same object are ordered identically in all threads.

Let's look at the next rule.

Visibility

We briefly touched upon visibility in the prior section, where we mentioned that when there are read and write operations happening on shared data, the effects of one thread writing to the variable needs to be made visible to threads reading from it at the boundary of the synchronization barrier.

Let's discuss the rules with regard to visibility of changes made by one thread to another thread. Changes made by one thread are visible to other threads under the following conditions:

- The writing thread releases the synchronization lock, and the reading thread acquires it after that. Releasing the lock flushes all writes and acquiring the lock loads or reloads the values.

- For atomic variables, values written to it are flushed immediately before the next memory operation on the writer's side, but readers must call a load instruction before each access.

- When a writing thread terminates, all written variables are flushed, so threads that have synchronized with this thread's termination (join) will see the correct values written by this thread.

The following are some additional items to be cautious of with regard to visibility:

- When there are long stretches of code that use no synchronization with other dependent threads, the threads can be quite out of sync with the values of shared data members.

- Loops that wait or check against values written by other threads are wrong unless they use atomic or synchronization.

- Visibility failures and safety violations in the absence of correct synchronization are not guaranteed or required, merely a possibility. It might not happen in practice, only extremely rarely, or only on certain architectures or due to some specific external factors. Overall, it is almost impossible to be a 100% confident that there are no visibility-based errors.

We will now discuss instruction ordering.

Ordering

Since memory accesses are reordered by the compiler or CPU, the memory model needs to define when the effects of the assignment operations can appear out of order to a given thread:

- *Sequential Consistency* is a C++ machine memory model that requires that all instructions from all threads appear like they are being executed in an order consistent with the program or source code order on each thread.

- *Memory ordering* is another concept we will explore shortly in some detail. It describes the sequence of memory access instructions. The term can be used to refer to memory access ordering during compile time or runtime. Memory ordering allows the compiler and CPU to reorder memory operations, so they are out of order and that leads to optimal utilization of the different layers of the memory hierarchy (registers, caches, main memory, and so on) as well maximizing the use of the data transfer architecture and its bandwidth.

Let's learn about the principles of the C++ memory model and memory order concepts in the following section.

C++ memory model principles

In this section, we will look at the different options available to us in the modern C++ memory model paradigm with regard to accessing and writing to shared data structures in a multi-threaded and multi-processing environment.

Memory order concepts

The memory model is important to understand when using threads in HFTs since we may modify the semantics of a piece of software if we are not using the model accurately. We start by introducing some notations and concepts in the following list, and then dive into the different control options:

- **Relaxed memory order**: In the default system, memory operations are ordered quite loosely, and the CPU has a lot of leeway to reorder them. Compilers can likewise arrange the instructions they output in whatever sequence they choose, as long as it doesn't impair the program's apparent execution. Memory operations executed on the same memory region by the same thread are not reordered according to the modification order.

- **Acquire/Release**: All load-acquire operations reading the stored value synchronize with a store-release action. Any activities in the releasing thread that occur before the store-release occur before all operations in the acquiring thread that occur after the load-acquire.

- **Consume**: Consume is Acquire/Release's lighter variant. If X depends on the value loaded, all operations in the releasing thread before the store-release happen before an operation X in the consuming thread.

We looked at some features of memory ordering in this section. We will now focus on defining memory ordering in C++.

Memory ordering

Table 1 provides a quick introduction to the different memory ordering tags, which we will explore in greater detail in the subsequent sections.

`std::memory_order`	Description
`std::memory_order_relaxed`	No additional memory ordering restrictions.
`std::memory_order_release` `std::memory_order_acquire`	If load-acquire sees the value stored by store-release, then stores before the store-release happen before loads after the load acquire.
`std::memory_order_consume`	Like `memory_order_acquire` but only for dependent loads.
`std::memory_order_acq_rel`	Combines load-acquire and store-release.
`std::memory_order_seq_cst`	Sequential Consistency; provides read and write ordering globally.

Figure 8.1 – C++ memory model

These memory order tags allow four different memory ordering modes: *Sequential Consistency, Relaxed* and *Release-Acquire,* and the similar *Release-Consume.* Let's explore those next.

Sequential Consistency

Sequential Consistency (**SC**) is the principle that states that all threads involved in a multi-threaded application agree on the order in which memory operations have occurred or will occur. Another requirement is that the order is consistent with the order of operations in the source program. The technique to achieve this in modern C++ is to declare the shared variables as C++ 11 atomic types with memory ordering constraints. The result of any execution should be the same as if the operations of all processors were executed in sequential order.

Additionally, operations executed on each processor also follow program order. SC in a multi-threaded and multi-processor environment means that all threads are on the same page with regard to the order in which memory operations occurred and that this is consistent each time the program is run.

One way to achieve this in, say, Java is to declare shared variables as volatile and the C++ 11 equivalent would be to declare shared variables as atomic types with memory ordering constraints. When this is done, the compiler takes care of enforcing these ordering constraints by introducing additional instructions behind the scenes like *memory fences* (please check the *Fences* section in this chapter). The default memory order for atomic operations is sequential consistency, which is the `std::memory_order_seq_cst` operation.

> **Note**
>
> Although this mode is easy to understand, it will lead to the maximum performance penalty because it prevents compiler optimizations that might try to reorder operations past the atomic operations.

Relaxed Ordering

Relaxed Ordering is the opposite of SC, activated using the `std::memory_order_relaxed` tag. This mode of atomic operation will impose no restrictions on memory operations. However, the operation itself is still atomic.

Release-Acquire Ordering

In the *Release-Acquire Ordering* design, atomic store or write operations, a.k.a. store-release, use `std::memory_order_release`, and atomic load or read operations, a.k.a. load-acquire, use `std::memory_order_acquire`. The compiler is not allowed to move store operations after a store-release operation, and it is not allowed to move load operations before load-acquire operations. When the load-acquire operation sees values written by a store-release operation, the compiler makes sure that all the operations before the store-release happen before the load operations after the load-acquire.

Release-Consume Ordering

Release-Consume Ordering is like Release-Acquire Ordering but here the atomic load uses `std::memory_order_consume` and becomes an atomic load-consume operation. The behavior of this mode is the same as Release-Acquire except that the load operations that come after the load-consume operation and depend on the value loaded by the load-consume operation are ordered/sorted correctly.

We have seen that atomic objects have store and load methods for atomically writing to and reading from shared data and the default mode is Sequential Consistency. Under the hood, the compiler adds additional instructions to create memory fences after each store. We also discussed that adding a lot of memory fences creates inefficient code by preventing compiler optimizations. These fences are also not necessary for publication safety, in which case the question becomes how do we write code that generates minimal fencing operations (and hence much more efficient code)?

Here is what the compiler knows when it comes to memory access and operations on shared data:

- All memory operations in each thread and what they do, as well as any data dependencies

- Which memory locations are shared and which variables are mutable variables, that is, could change asynchronously due to memory operations in another thread.

So, then the solution to minimizing memory fences is to simply tell the compiler which operations on mutable and shared locations can be reordered and which cannot. Independent memory operations can be performed in random order with no implications as before.

Fences

Fences in programming are a sort of barrier instructions. They force the processor to enforce a specific ordering on memory operations. These operations will be modified based on the fences. Memory operations can be ordered between threads using fences. A fence can be either Release or Acquire. If the Acquire fence comes before the Release fence, then the stores take place before the loads following the acquire fence. We employ other synchronization primitives that allow atomic operations to ensure that the release fence comes before the acquire fence.

Like operations on atomic objects, the `atomic_thread_fence` operation has a `memory_order` parameter, which can take on the following values:

- If `memory_order` is `memory_order_relaxed`, this has no effects.

- If `memory_order` is `memory_order_acquire` or `memory_order_consume`, then it is an acquire fence.

- If `memory_order` is `memory_order_release`, then it is a release fence.

- If `memory_order` is `memory_order_acq_rel`, then it is both an acquire fence and a release fence.

- If `memory_order` is `memory_order_seq_cst`, then it is a sequentially consistent acquire and release fence.

We reviewed the order of the operation for fences. We will now finish off this section by talking about the changes in C++20.

C++ 20 memory model changes

There are some minor changes in C++ 20 as far as memory models are concerned. Some issues were discovered after the formalization of the C++ 11 memory model. The old model was defined with the objective that different regimes of memory access could be implemented on common architectures using costly hardware instructions. Specifically, memory_order_acquire and memory_order_release were supposed to be implementable on ARM and Power CPU architectures using lightweight fence instructions. Unfortunately, it turns out that they cannot, and this is also true for NVIDIA GPUs, although those were not really targeted a decade ago.

So that fundamentally leaves us with two options:

- Implement the standard as is. This is possible but will suffer from performance degradation, which goes against the purpose of why we have these memory models in the first place, and would degrade the efficiency of C++.

- Fix the standard to better handle the new architecture without messing up the concepts and ideas of memory models.

Option 2 being the more sensible choice was finally chosen by the C++ standards committee as the solution

In this section about memory models, we reviewed the different models. Since HFT processes run concurrently, it is important to know how the memory model works in the context of multi-threaded software. As part of our journey toward achieving peak performance for HFTs, we now need to learn how to reduce the execution time by removing the decision which could happen during runtime. That's going to be the topic for our next section.

Removing runtime decisions ⏱

As C++ is a compiled language, it can optimize the source code during the compilation process and generate machine code with as much code and data resolved at compile time. In this section, we will look at the motivation for removing runtime decisions, consider some C++ constructs that are resolved at runtime, and see how an ultra-low latency HFT application tries to minimize or substitute runtime decisions.

Motivation for removing runtime decisions

The more code that lies on the critical path and can be resolved at compile time (instead of being resolved at runtime), the better the application performance – a key element in optimizing HFT applications. Here we discuss the advantages obtained by the compiler, CPUs, and memory architecture in terms of performance when the application has minimal runtime decisions and most of the code can be resolved at compile time.

Compiler optimizations

If the compiler can resolve the source and constant/static data at compile time, it opens up the possibility of a lot of compile-time optimization. Resolving at compile time means it knows at compile time what each object type is, which method/functions/subroutines are called at each invocation, how much memory is required and where when executing each method, and so on. Compile-time resolution allows the compiler to apply a lot of optimizations, including the following:

- *Inlining*: This is where the compiler replaces the function call with the body of the called function.

- *Dead code removal*: The compiler removes code that doesn't affect the program result.

- *Instruction reordering*: This allows us to break dependencies and run a code faster.

- *Replacing compile time macros*: These are very similar to inlining except technically, uses of macros are replaced by the actual code for the macros in the pre-processing step that precedes the compiler optimization steps.

This leads to the generation of machine code that is massively faster than if the compiler was unable to optimize due to a failure of compile-time resolution.

CPU and architecture optimizations

Not only is the machine code generated by the compiler significantly more optimized, but it works much better with the prefetching and branch prediction optimizations at the CPU, pipeline, and architecture hardware levels.

Due to the CPU pipeline, modern CPUs prefetch instructions and data that will be required to be accessed and executed shortly. This works significantly better when the data and instructions are known at compile time – think about inlined versus non-inlined methods. If the objects that will be accessed and/or the methods that will be needed are not known at compile time (because they're resolved at runtime), this process is hard to do correctly and often ends up prefetching the incorrect data and instructions from caches or main memory.

Another prefetching-related optimization is the *branch prediction optimization*, where the CPUs try to predict which branch will be taken (conditional switches, function calls, and so on). This is harder in the presence of dynamic resolution, as is the case when C++ applications use *virtual* functions, **Run Time Type Identification (RTTI)**, and so on. This is because it is either impossible to predict the branches that will be taken since the type of object might not be known, and/or the method body might not be known or is just super difficult to get right most of the time. When the branch prediction is incorrect, it incurs a penalty since the data and code that was prefetched now needs to be evicted from the CPU pipeline, caches, memory, and so on. And then the correct data and code needs to be fetched at the call. We recommend reading the book *Computer Architecture: A Quantitative Approach* if you would like to know more about the theory of branch prediction.

Virtual functions

Virtual functions are key to one of C++'s particularly important features – *dynamic polymorphism*. This is an excellent feature that reduces code duplication, lends semantics to control and data flow program design, and lets us have generic interfaces that can be overridden and customized for specific object types. It is an important principle in **Object-Oriented Programming (OOP)** design, but unfortunately it comes with a runtime performance penalty. Due to the runtime resolution of virtual functions and the associated runtime performance penalty, HFT applications are typically extremely careful with regard to when and where virtual functions are used and try to eliminate unnecessary virtual functions. This section explores C++ virtual function performance in more detail.

How they work

Let's discuss how virtual functions are implemented from the compiler and operating system's perspective. When the compiler is compiling the source code, it knows which functions are virtual and their addresses. For each object that is created that has at least one virtual function, a table (called the **virtual table**, or vtable for short) is created that holds pointers to the virtual functions the type has. Objects of types that have virtual functions have a pointer referred to as a vptr that points to the virtual table for that object. When virtual functions are overridden by a derived class, the vtable entries for those overridden virtual functions point to the derived class implementation. At runtime, calling virtual functions requires a few additional steps over non-virtual functions: the runtime accesses the vptr, finds the vtable for that corresponding object type, figures out the address of the function it needs to call, and performs the virtual function call.

Performance penalties

In the previous section, we described how virtual functions are set up and how they are called. Since the runtime needs to access the `vtable`, virtual function calls have a little bit more overhead than non-virtual functions, but in this section, we will explore the biggest performance penalties that are incurred in the presence of virtual functions.

Compiler optimizations

One big source of performance penalty when using virtual functions is that it prevents compiler optimizations. To recap, the address of the virtual function depends on the type of the object, which is often not known till runtime. What that means is that the address and body of the virtual function that needs to be called are also not known till runtime. So, the compiler has no chance of inlining the function. That would save a few instructions for the call to the function and the return from it. Additionally, inlining would eliminate unused parameters and variables, often then eliminating operations before the call to the function. This becomes significantly worse when there are multiple objects with different virtual functions being called in a loop. In that case not only is inlining the calls not possible, but unrolling the loop is also impossible, as is exploiting the hardware for performance. We will discuss this in another section shortly, but this also kills the CPU pipeline and cache performance.

Prefetching and branch prediction

We mentioned before how the hardware tries to prefetch data and code that might be accessed and executed shortly. It also tries to predict which branches might be taken (a.k.a. *speculative execution*) and tries to prefetch the data and code from the branch that might be taken. In the case of objects with virtual functions and virtual function calls, it does not know the jump destination till the actual object type and virtual function address are resolved at runtime.

By this time, it has already prefetched instructions based on the branch it predicted and started executing those instructions already. If it happened to have predicted the branch correctly then it is all good, but if not then all the work done from the prefetch has to be stopped and reversed, and the correct instructions must now be fetched and executed after the fetch finishes.

This makes the program slower on branch mispredictions due to not only having to fetch the instructions once the correct addresses are resolved, but also since it must undo the effect of incorrect instructions being prefetched and executed. Also, the shorter the virtual function, the greater the slowdown observed since the overhead of branch misprediction becomes a larger fraction of total function call time.

Cache evictions and performance

We discussed the design and performance benefits derived from having different cache layers in the *Memory hierarchy* section in *Chapter 6, HFT Optimization – Architecture and Operating System*. We have also mentioned that L1 and L2 caches have instruction caches that cache frequently and recently used instructions. There is another cache that holds the comparison results for branch instructions – it is used to predict the destination branch from the previous executions of the same instructions and speed up computations by prefetching instructions and speculatively executing them.

Cache performance is best when the required instructions and branch results are in the appropriate caches, but virtual functions (especially large virtual functions with different implementations for each object type) are problematic here. This is especially bad if, say, there is a container of base class pointers and each one of them is pointing to potentially different object types or is randomly arranged (that is, the container is not sorted by type). This is bad because most calls to the virtual functions will result in calls to a different function in a potentially random memory location.

So, if the functions are large enough, each call to a virtual function will cause the cache to evict the data and instructions from the previous function call and load data and instructions for the new one. This is on top of the branch prediction penalties being paid (quite frequently). Virtual functions may cause a lot of cache evictions and cache misses and significantly hurt performance. But this is not always the case since if we have a function invocation through a `vtable`, and we perform this in a tight loop, the CPU will cover up the latency from accessing the `vtable` through the power of branch prediction and cache locality. It is always important to analyze where the performance issues of code occur.

Figure 8.2 describes this situation better. Let's assume the following class structure where a single base class with a virtual function gets derived by different implementations that override the virtual function.

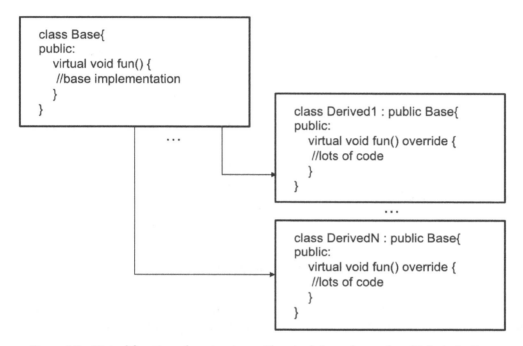

Figure 8.2 – Virtual function: class structure with a single base class and multiple derivations

Let's say there is a container of base class pointers that point to different derived class implementations that are potentially in different memory locations. If the code tries to loop through this container and call the virtual function, it will lead to a lot of cache evictions, cache misses, and overall terrible runtime performance. This is on top of the compiler not being able to unroll the loop and the branch misprediction penalties.

Figure 8.3 shows how the `vtable` can impact the performance by having different memory locations for the different virtual functions.

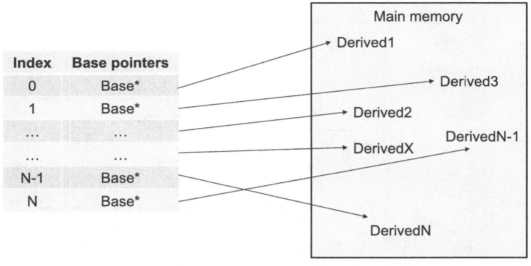

Figure 8.3 – Container of base pointers pointing to different derived objects at random memory locations

Since we saw that using virtual functions can be detrimental to performance, we will now talk about a method to remove them: the **curiously recurring template pattern** (**CRTP**).

Curiously recurring template pattern (CRTP)

We often oppose the **CRTP** method with virtual functions. We should first say that the virtual functions discover interface implementation at runtime, which is not the case for the CRTP. The CRTP is an example of **static polymorphism** as opposed to virtual functions, which are examples of **dynamic polymorphism**. The CRTP is a compile-time construct, which means it has no runtime overhead. It is used with a base class exposing an interface and the derived classes implementing that interface. As we saw in this section, invoking a virtual function via a base class reference frequently necessitates a call via a pointer to function, incurring indirection costs and preventing inlining.

In summary, we learned how to remove the latency that might be introduced by virtual functions. The use of virtual functions needs to be done very carefully. The CRTP is a way to avoid using virtual functions by opting for static polymorphism.

We will now introduce another type of latency that could cause slowdowns at runtime.

Run Time Type Identification (RTTI)

The previous section on virtual functions outlined the impact of having objects and function calls that are resolved at runtime on performance. Most of the performance penalties outlined in that section apply to all object types resolved at runtime. In C++, **Run Time Type Identification** (**RTTI**) is the term used to describe the feature by which the types of objects are checked at runtime for objects where the types are not known at compile time.

What is RTTI?

C++'s RTTI is the mechanism that tracks and extracts information about an object's type when required at runtime. This only makes sense for classes that have at least one virtual function, meaning there is a possibility of base class pointers pointing to different types of derived class objects at runtime. So RTTI allows you to find the type of an object dynamically at runtime from the available pointer or reference of the base class type. This was introduced into C++ when exceptions and exception handling were added to C++ because knowing the runtime type of an object was critical to exception handling. Thus, RTTI allows applications to explicitly check for runtime types instead of relying on dynamic polymorphism, which implicitly deals with runtime type resolution.

C++ provides the `dynamic_cast` built-in operator for safely downcasting base class objects in an inheritance hierarchy. When downcasting pointers, it returns a valid pointer of the converted type on success and a `nullptr` on failure. `dynamic_cast<Derived*>(base_ptr)` attempts to convert the value of `base_ptr` to type `Derived*`. When downcasting references, it returns a valid reference of the converted type on success and raises an *exception* on failure. We will cover this in the *Exceptions impeding performance* section later in this chapter.

Another C++ built-in operator `typeid` is used fetch the runtime information of an object and returns it as a `std::type_info` object. The `std::type_info` object contains information about the type, type name, check equality between two object types, and so on. For polymorphic types, the `typeid` operator provides additional information about the derived types. `typeid(*base_ptr) == typeid(Derived)` returns `true` if `base_ptr` points to an object of type `Derived`.

Performance penalties

Let's discuss the performance penalties associated with the C++ RTTI mechanism.

- There is some additional space allocated per class and object, which is not a huge deal, but can become an issue if there are a lot of objects, and causes reduced cache performance.

- The typeid call can be quite slow as it usually involves fetching type information that is not often accessed.

- The dynamic_cast operation can be extremely slow. It involves fetching type information and checking for casting rules, which can lead to exceptions that are extremely expensive themselves (we will discuss that shortly).

In the following section, let's understand dynamic memory allocation.

Dynamic memory allocation ⏱

Allocation in the heap (or dynamic allocation) is common in programming. We need dynamic allocation for the flexibility to allocate at runtime. The operating system implements the dynamic memory management structures, algorithms, and routines. All dynamically allocated memory goes to the heap section of main memory. The OS maintains a few linked lists of memory blocks, primarily the free list to track contiguous blocks of free/unallocated memory and the allocated list to track blocks that have been allocated to the applications. On new memory allocation requests (malloc()/new), it traverses the free list to find a block free enough, then updates the free list (by removing that block) and adds it to the allocated list and then returns the memory block to the program. On memory deallocation requests (free()/delete), it removes the freed block from the allocated list and moves it back to the free list.

Runtime performance penalty

Let's recap the performance penalties associated with dynamic memory management that makes it unfit for use on the critical/hot path, especially for super latency-sensitive HFT applications.

Heap tracking overhead

Serving dynamic memory allocation/deallocation requests requires traversing lists of free memory blocks, which is not as efficient as using already available CPU registers or pushing additional variables onto a stack. So, the heap tracking mechanism adds some overhead and often the latencies are non-deterministic depending on the contents of the free list, how fragmented the memory is, the memory block size requested, and so on. In summary, metadata created by heap memory management can get quite involved to manage, and a lot of operations are performed just to free that block of memory.

Heap fragmentation

Over the course of many allocations and deallocations of varying sizes, the heap memory can get fragmented, meaning there are many small memory blocks with holes in between, which makes the free list long and can make it difficult and time-consuming, and in the worst case, impossible to service a memory allocation request that is larger than any of the free blocks, even though there is plenty of free memory available across the different free blocks. The OS employs some heap de-fragmentation techniques to manage these potential issues, but again that comes at a performance cost.

Cache performance

Dynamically allocated memory blocks can often be randomly distributed in heap memory. This can lead to significant cache performance degradation, higher cache evictions, and cache misses, among others. Application developers should be conscious of this and try to request dynamic memory in a cache-friendly way – often by requesting a large block of contiguous memory and then managing the objects in that memory to improve cache performance.

Alternatives/solutions for dynamic memory allocation

Not all parts of an HFT system are time critical. So, we need to be concerned about the speed of dynamic allocation and deallocation only on the time-critical hot paths.

Most high-performance dynamic memory allocation techniques come down to moving dynamic memory allocations off the critical path either by pre-allocating huge blocks of memory or managing them in the application themselves (*Memory pools*). Memory pools are basically data structures where an application allocates a huge chunk of memory at startup and then manages the use of this memory in critical code paths. The advantage here is that this allows the application to use very specialized allocation and deallocation techniques that maximize performance for the specific use case the applications are built for.

Another technique is to thoroughly inspect dynamic memory management uses and minimize them as much as possible, often at the cost of some assumptions that might make the application less flexible or generic.

We can also redefine the C++ new and delete operators, although this is not the recommended approach – it is better to have custom new and delete methods (my_new() and my_delete() methods would be examples) and call them explicitly. We can also talk about placement new, which gives us most of the semantic benefits of invoking new / delete, but with control over where the operator places the object. The downside is that you have to manage the memory life cycle separately.

Using constexpr efficiently

constexpr in C++ is used to make functions run at compile time – not as a guarantee, but it provides the possibility. There are a few restrictions to constexpr functions – they must not use static or thread_local variables, exception handling, or goto statements, and all variables must be of literal types and must be initialized – in short, everything the compiler needs to resolve the entire function body at compile time.

As we mentioned, declaring a constexpr function does not mean that it must run at compile time. It means that the function has the potential to be run at compile time. A constexpr function must be executed at compile time if used in a constant expression – for instance, if the result of the function call is assigned to a constexpr variable, then it must be evaluated at compile time.

The benefits of constexpr functions are along the same lines as has been discussed so far. Allowing the compiler to resolve and evaluate the function at compile time means no runtime costs for evaluating that function.

Exceptions impeding performance

Exceptions are the modern C++ mechanism for error handling and seek to improve upon the traditional error-code and if/else statement-based error handling from C. In this section, we will investigate what advantages they bring, what drawbacks and performance penalties they impose, and why that is suboptimal for HFT applications.

Why use exceptions?

Let's discuss the reasons for and benefits of using C++ exceptions for error handling:

- Using exceptions for error handling makes the source code simpler, cleaner, and better at handling errors. It is a more elegant solution to a long-nested list of if-else statements that grow over time and lead to spaghetti code, require tests for each scenario, and so on. Overall, requiring handling for each error code (and associated tests) leads to slower development.

- There is some code that cannot be done elegantly or cleanly without exceptions. The classic example is an error in a constructor – since it returns no value, how do we report the error? The elegant solution is to throw an exception and that serves as the basis for the **Resource Acquisition Is Initialization** (**RAII**) principle in modern C++ design. The alternative would be to set an error flag that needs to be checked each time an object is created after the constructor returns, which is ugly and requires a lot more code to check each time any object is created. Similar ideas apply even to regular functions, where you would have to return an error code or set a global variable. Returning error codes works but every time we add a new failure case, it requires updating code in a bunch of locations and leads to the if-else spaghetti code mentioned before. Setting global variables comes with its own set of issues – the variable must be checked after the function returns, would take on different values for different failures, is hard to maintain, and fails in a multi-threaded application.

- Exceptions are difficult to ignore, unlike return error codes, which often get ignored if application developers are not careful. Failure to catch an exception leads to program termination.

- Exceptions propagate automatically over method boundaries – that is, they can be caught and re-thrown up the caller stack.

We now know why exceptions should be used from the software engineering point of view. Next, we will explain what the performance impact is.

Drawbacks and performance penalties

Let's discuss some complexities, drawbacks, and performance penalties related to the use of C++ exceptions for error handling:

- Exception handling takes discipline and practice, especially for developers used to a more traditional error-code, if-else statement-driven type of error handling. So, as with any other programming construct, it needs good developers and careful consideration during application design.

- As far as performance is concerned, the good thing with C++ exceptions is that on the path where exceptions are not raised, there is no additional cost. However, when exceptions are thrown, it has an extremely prohibitive cost compared to, say, a function call and requires thousands of CPU cycles.

  For HFT, if the applications are designed carefully so that exceptions are raised only for the rarest and most critical errors where it is unsafe to continue normally anyway, then the additional performance penalty is not an issue. However, if exceptions are treated lightly and raised as part of the normal functioning of the algorithm, then that can lead to major performance issues and what was initially thought to be rare might end up being performed quite frequently, leading to major performance degradation.

To continue with the runtime decision impacting performance, we will now talk about templates whose goal is to actually replace any runtime decision by generating multiple specialized versions of code.

Templates reducing the runtime

In this section, we will continue our discussion on removing or minimizing runtime decisions on the critical or hot path by introducing another important C++ feature. We will discuss what templates are, the motivation for using them, their advantages and disadvantages, and their performance relative to the alternatives.

What are templates?

Templates are the C++ mechanism to implement generic functions and classes. *Generic programming* is when generic types are used as arguments in algorithms and classes for compatibility with different data types. This eliminates code duplication and the need to repeatedly write similar or shared code that is independent of data type. Templates not only work with different data types, but based on what different types are needed at compile time, the source code for the classes and methods for those data types is generated automatically at compile time, just as with C macros. Unlike macros, however, the compiler can check for types instead of blindly substituting as with macros.

There are a few different types of templates:

- *Function templates*: Function templates are like normal C++ functions, except with a key difference. Normal functions work only with the defined data types inside the function, whereas function templates are designed to make them independent of data types, so they can work with any data type.

- *Class templates*: Class templates are also like regular classes, except they have members of one or more generic types passed as template parameters. These class templates can be used to store and manage any type of data. Instead of creating a new class each time for a different type, we define a generic class template that can work with most data types. This helps with code reusability, runs faster, and is more efficient.

- *Variadic templates*: This is another important template type and applies to both functions and classes. It supports a variable number of arguments, as opposed to non-variadic templates, which support only a fixed number of arguments. Variadic templates are usually used to create functional, list-processing constructs with template metaprogramming.

We will now talk about another advanced template-related technique, template specialization.

Template specialization

So far, we have been discussing the idea that a single template class or function can handle all data types. But it is also possible to have customized behavior based on some specific data types, which is known as *template specialization*. Template specializations are mechanisms by which we can customize function, class, and variadic templates for specific types. When the compiler encounters a template instantiation with specific data types, it creates a template instance for that type or set of types. If a template specialization exists, then the compiler uses that specialized version by matching the passed-in parameters with the data types specified. If it cannot match it to a template specialization, then it uses the non-specialized template to create an instance.

Why use templates?

Let's discuss the motivation behind using C++ templates to reduce latency at runtime.

Generic programming

The main advantage of using templates is obviously **generic programming** and producing code that is efficient, reusable, and extensible. One particularly good implementation of the generic programming paradigm using templates is the **Standard Template Library (STL)**. This supports a wide range of data *containers*, *algorithms*, *iterators*, *functors*, and so on that are generic and operate on all data types.

Compile-time substitution

The substitution takes place during compile time and only the class or function bodies needed in the program are generated – that is, only the data types for which the template has been used in the application produce an instance of this template class at compile time. Knowing the parameters at compile time also makes template classes significantly more type-safe compared to runtime-resolved objects or functions.

Development cost, time, and lines of code (LOC)

Since we can implement a class or a function a single time that works with all data types, it cuts down on development effort, time, and source code complexity. It also makes debugging easy because there is less code, and it is contained in a single class or function.

Better than C macros and void pointers

C used preprocessor macros and void pointers to support some form of generic programming. But templates are a much better solution in each case as they are significantly more readable, type-safe, and less error prone. Macros are also always expanded inline, but with templates, the compiler has the choice to expand inline only when appropriate, which is useful for preventing code bloat. Macros are also clunky and hard to write due to the need to fit onto a single logical line of code, but templates appear as regular functions in their implementation.

Compile-time polymorphism

This is one of the most important applications at least for HFT applications (on top of everything else that has been mentioned here). We discussed in detail how virtual functions and dynamic polymorphism have significant performance penalties. Templates and the generic *compile-time polymorphism* they offer are often used to eliminate virtual inheritance and dynamic polymorphism as much as possible. By moving the code resolution and construction to compile time instead of runtime, and more importantly allowing compiler, CPU, and architecture optimizations to kick in, the performance is improved significantly.

Template metaprogramming

This is a more advanced use of C++ templates and is often either not understood well or is abused (by converting existing code constructs to use template metaprogramming unnecessarily and prematurely). Template *metaprogramming* gives us the ability to write code that is expanded at compile time to yield the actual machine code that will be used at runtime, essentially using templates to pre-compute a results table that can be referenced later. *Expression templates* are another similar advanced use of templates that are used to evaluate mathematical expressions at compile time to produce more efficient code executed at runtime.

Disadvantages of templates

Now let's look at some of the disadvantages and drawbacks of using templates.

Compiler support

Historically, a lot of compilers have had poor support for templates and can lead to reduced code portability. Also, it is not clear what compilers should do when they detect template errors, which can increase development time when using templates. Some compilers still do not support nesting of templates.

Header only

Templates are header only, which means all the code sits in the header files and none in any compiled libraries. When changes are made, it requires a complete rebuild of all pieces of the project. Also, there is no way to hide code implementation information since it is all exposed in the header file.

Increased compilation times

As mentioned before, templates reside entirely in headers and cannot be compiled into a library; they are linked during the application compilation and linking process. The advantage we gain from compiled libraries is that when a change is made, only the components that are affected need to be rebuilt. However, with templates that is not true, so each time changes are made, all the templated code has to be rebuilt. This leads to increased compilation times and as application complexity grows and template usage increases, this can go up significantly and become a problem. However, this is manageable and a non-issue.

Difficult to understand

Templates confuse a lot of developers (advanced C++ programmers included) because the rules around their use are complex. Issues such as *name resolution* in templates, *template specialization matching*, and *template partial ordering* can be confusing to understand and implement correctly. In general, generic programming is a different programming paradigm and requires time, effort, and practice to get used to – it does not come naturally if you are used to *imperative programming* in C++ (which is what 90% of C++ programmers use regularly). Overall, templates have a lot of advantages including development and debugging speed, but it takes a while to get to that point as there is quite a learning curve to understand templates properly.

Tough to debug

Debugging code that has a lot of templates can be difficult. Since the compiler replaces the template instantiation and calls with the substituted implementation, it is difficult for the debugger to find the actual code at runtime. This is similar in nature to how it can be difficult to debug inlined methods at runtime since the source code does not match what the debugger sees exactly. Error messages are extremely verbose and very confusing and time-consuming to understand. Even most modern compilers produce large, unhelpful, and confusing error messages.

Code bloat

Templates are expanded at the source code level and compiled into the source code. The compiler generates additional code for each template type or instance. If we have a lot of templated classes and functions or a lot of different data types that generate instances, the code generated by the compiler can grow quite large. This is known as *code bloat*, which also contributes to increased compilation times. The more subtle issue that hurts runtime performance from over-templated code bases is that since the size of the application itself is so large, it can have poor cache performance since there is a greater chance of cache evictions, misses, and so on.

Performance of templates

Fundamentally, the runtime performance of templates is as efficient and low latency as possible since it moves away from runtime object resolution and function calls to compile-time resolution. As mentioned before, this opens up a world of compiler optimization opportunities, such as inlining (among many others), and when executed, works much better with CPU and architecture optimizations such as prefetching and branch prediction to yield particularly superior performance.

It's important to avoid using the template and virtual keywords in the same class declaration. When a class template is used for the first time, it creates a copy of all member functions (applied to that new type). Having virtual functions means that even the vtable and RTTI will be duplicated, leading to additional code bloat (on top of what templates already cause).

Standard Template Library (STL)

Let's explore the C++ STL, which has become quite common among recent C++ applications. There are also some variants and libraries that operate similarly to the STL but improve upon some issues and add some functionalities.

What is the STL?

The STL is a very widely used library that provides containers and algorithms using templates for all data types. The STL is a repository of template classes that implement commonly used algorithms and data structures and work well with user-defined types as well as built-in types, and its algorithms are container independent. They are implemented as compile-time polymorphism, not runtime polymorphism.

Commonly used containers

Let's explore the most popular and commonly used C++ STL containers and when they are used:

- vector: This is the default go-to for a lot of applications, has the simplest data structure (C-array-style contiguous memory layout), and provides random access.

- deque: deque implements a double linked list and has better performance than a vector when elements are inserted and removed from the beginning or the end. deque is also efficient with memory and usually uses only as much memory as needed based on the number of elements. Accessing random elements is slower since it involves traversing the list and walking over potentially random memory locations (poor cache performance).

- list: list is like deque in that it is also implemented as a linked list and has similar benefits and drawbacks as deque. The difference here is that list does not invalidate iterators that refer to elements when elements are added or removed, unlike vector and deque.

- `set`, `unordered_set`, and `multiset`: These are **associative** containers that are used to track whether an element exists in the container or not. Associative containers are basically ones that are designed specifically to support quick and easy storage and retrieval of values referred to by keys. `unordered_set` uses hashes on the elements to perform lookup in amortized constant time but have no ordering. Amortized constant time lookup means under normal conditions, it takes constant time to perform the operation regardless of the size of the container. `set` and `multiset` on the order hand have keys that are ordered/sorted. `multiset` and `set` are identical except the former allows multiple elements with the same value to be saved.

- `unordered_map` and `map`, and `unordered_multimap` and `multimap`: These are also associative containers as discussed in the previous point, except they track key-value pairs. `unordered_map` and `map` save single key-value pairs, with the difference being that the former has no ordering on keys and the latter is ordered by key values. `Unordered_multimap` and `multimap` are like `unordered_map` and `map` respectively, except they allow multiple values per key.

Performance at runtime

Let's look at the performance of the STL at runtime:

- The STL, being a templated library, has particularly good runtime performance compared to C-style solutions or dynamic polymorphism-based solutions. Another way to squeeze performance from the STL is to optimize the user-defined structures to work exactly as we need them in the context of the HFT application.

- Using the STL effectively to build low-latency HFT applications requires the developers to understand the working of the STL properly and design programs carefully. Often developers misuse the STL and without understanding the computational complexity involved, they blame the library.

- Another problem with the STL is that many calls to STL library functions allocate memory internally, and without being careful to build and pass allocators to the STL containers, non-deterministic performance can result, especially for HFT applications (if they use the default dynamic memory allocators).

In this section, we studied data structures that can help to reduce latency because they are already optimized for performance. In this next section, we will learn how to improve performance by doing static analysis.

Static analysis

In this section, we will look at the development and testing techniques of *static analysis*. This is a set of tools and techniques to aid in the software development/testing/maintenance life cycle. It applies to all software application development processes in general, but especially to HFT applications where it is important to make changes quickly (adapting to changing market conditions and inefficiencies is key to being profitable) but very carefully without breaking existing expected functionality (bugs/errors/mistakes can lead to significant monetary losses).

What is C++ static analysis?

Static code analysis means debugging software applications by examining the code and using tools to automatically detect errors without actually executing the application or providing inputs. This can also be thought of as a code review-style debugging process that examines the code and tries to check the code structure and coding standards. Having automated tools and processes in place that can do this means we can make significantly more thorough checks for vulnerabilities while validating the code than a team of developers could. The algorithms and techniques used to analyze the source code and automatically spit out errors and warnings are similar in spirit to compiler warnings, except taken a few steps forward to find issues that dynamic testing at runtime would have revealed. There has been a good amount of progress with static analysis tools, from basic syntax checkers to something that can find even subtle bugs.

Static analysis aims to find software development issues such as programming errors, coding guideline violations, syntax violations, buffer overflow type issues, and security vulnerabilities, among others.

Let's explain why we need static analysis.

The need for static analysis

The motivation behind static analysis is to find errors and issues explained previously that dynamic analysis (unit tests/test environments/simulations that seek to uncover errors when the program is executed) does not find. Thus static analysis can uncover an issue that might have caused a major problem down the road when the system encounters data and scenarios that were not encountered during dynamic testing, triggering a failure (potentially a huge failure). Note that static analysis is just the first step in a large list of tools and practices to enforce software quality control.

In addition to static analysis, dynamic analysis relies on setting up enough test scenarios and feeding enough input and data to hopefully cover all the use cases for the application. Some coding errors might not surface during dynamic analysis (since we did not think of them when writing or carrying out the unit tests). These are the defects that dynamic analysis would miss, and the hope is that static analysis would find them.

Types of static analysis

One way of classifying types of static analysis based on the errors they aim to find is as follows:

- **Control flow analysis**: Here, the focus is on the caller-callee relationships and the flow of the control in the calling structure, such as process, thread, method, function, subroutine, instructions, and so on.

- **Data flow analysis**: Here, the focus is on the input, intermediate, and output data – the structure, the validation of types, and correct and expected operation.

- **Failure analysis**: This tries to understand faults and failures in different components (that do not fall into the first two categories).

- **Interface analysis**: This aims to make sure the components fit in with the overall pipeline – that they implement interfaces comprehensively and correctly. In HFT, this means a trading strategy process is correctly implemented with all the interfaces it needs to operate correctly and optimally in simulations and live trading.

Another way to break down static analysis types is as follows:

- **Formal**: The goal here is to answer the question, is the code correct?

- **Cosmetic**: The question here is, does the code *look* consistent? Does it align with the coding standards to the required degree?

- **Design**: The question here is, based on established firm-wide standards, have the components (such as class structures, method sizes, and organization) been designed correctly?

- **Error checking**: This is self-explanatory and focuses on faults, failures, and code violations.

- **Predictive**: This is more advanced, but the goal is to predict how the application will behave when executed, preparing for dynamic analysis.

In the following section, we will give a walkthrough of static analysis.

Steps in static analysis

The goal of static analysis is to automate it so that it is easy, fast, and thorough when applied to large code bases. Hence the process itself needs to be simple and algorithmic enough to be automated. Once the source code is ready or semi-ready from the developer's perspective, a static code analyzer runs through the code and flags compilation issues, issues with coding standards, code or data flow errors, design warnings, and so on. False positives are common, so the output of the static code analyzer is analyzed manually (by the developers) and once all real (true positive) issues are fixed, it is run through the static code analyzer again and then progresses to the dynamic analysis phase.

Static analysis is nowhere near perfect – it produces false positives and misses issues as well – but it is a good orthogonal debugging and troubleshooting tool that can save developers and code reviewers time and thus yield a more efficient work environment.

Benefits and drawbacks of static analysis

Let's look at the benefits and drawbacks of static analysis. The benefits have been discussed before, so we simply formalize and list them in this section. You can also likely guess what some of the drawbacks might be, but we will formally discuss them here as well.

Benefits

We present the list of the benefits of static analysis:

- **Standardized and uniform code**: Static analyzer tools started out as linters, so they are extremely good at flagging when new code does not meet coding guidelines and design standards. This yields a uniform code base that complies with established (firm-wide or industry-wide) coding standards and design patterns.

- **Speed**: Manual code reviews are extremely time consuming for the entire team of developers. Automated static analysis can help eliminate a lot of the issues before the code goes into code review. Additionally, it finds these issues early on, when errors are always easier and faster to fix. Overall, this leads to higher development, review, and maintenance speed across the entire software development life cycle for the entire team.

- **Depth**: We have mentioned this before, but building unit tests or running dynamic analysis such that they cover all edge cases and all code execution paths is downright impossible. Static code analyzers do much better in these cases as they can check for bugs and errors that are non-trivial or *deep*.

- **Accuracy**: Another obvious advantage of having an automated static analysis approach is that it is extremely accurate where manual code reviews and dynamic analysis cannot be. Accuracy helps with both thoroughness and quality.

- **Offline**: In most real-world applications (especially HFT applications), there are many moving pieces, so dynamic analysis in a simulated, test, or lab environment requires a lot of setup and resources. For HFT, this means different processes and components (feed handlers, order gateways, simulated exchanges, and loggers), along with network, IPC, and disk resources. That can be painful, expensive, and time consuming. Static code analysis on the other hand is performed offline in the absence of all these moving pieces so it is easy, cheap, and quick.

We described in detail what the benefits of static analysis are, so we will now talk about its weaknesses.

Drawbacks

The drawbacks of static analysis are as follows:

- *Understanding semantics/developer intent is difficult*

  Consider the following code:

  ```
  int area(int l, int w) {
      return l + w;
  }
  ```

  A static analyzer here can detect that for some combination of l and w int values, their sum will yield an overflow, but it cannot determine that the function is incorrect to compute area.

- *Coding rules are complex*

  A lot of coding rules are too complex for a static analyzer to statically enforce or detect. They might depend on external documentation, be subjective, depend on the firm or the application, and so on.

- *False positives*

  We mentioned this before: false-positive detections can occur, and waste developers' time.

- *Static analysis is not free or instantaneous*

  Like the compilation process, it takes time to run a static analyzer on the entire application. The larger and more complex the code base is, the longer it takes to run.

- *Static analysis can never replace dynamic analysis*

  Despite their utility, static analyzers can never guarantee what will happen when the application is executed, so static analysis can supplement but never replace dynamic analysis, unit testing, simulations, or testbeds.

- *System and third-party libraries*

  These often throw off static analyzers since the source might not be easily available or accessible.

We have seen the benefits and weaknesses of static analysis, so we will now consider the tools used to perform this kind of analysis.

Tools for static analysis

Let's quickly introduce some of the best and well known static code analyzers available for C and C++:

- **Klocwork** by **Perforce**

  Klocwork is one of the best C++ static code analyzers out there. It works well with large code bases, has an enormous number of checkers, allows the customization of checkers, supports differential analysis (to help analysis times when only a small amount of code in a large code base has changed), and integrates with many IDEs and CI/CD tools.

- **Cppcheck**

  Cppcheck is a free, open source, cross-platform static code analyzer for C and C++.

- **CppDepend** by **CoderGears**

  CppDepend is a commercial C++ static code analyzer. Its strengths are in analyzing and visualizing the code base architecture (dependencies, control, and data flow layers). It has a dependency graph feature and monitoring capabilities to report differences between builds. It also supports rule checker customization.

- **Parasoft**

  Parasoft has a commercial set of testing tools for C and C++ featuring a static code analyzer and supporting dynamic code analysis, unit tests, code coverage, and runtime analysis. It has a large, rich set of techniques and rules for static code analysis. It also lets you manage the analysis results in an organized manner, thus offering a comprehensive set of tools for the software development process.

- **PVS Studio**

  This is another commercial tool that supports a lot of programming languages, C and C++ included. It detects non-trivial bugs, integrates with popular CI tools, and is well documented.

- **Clang Static Analyzer**

  The Clang C and C++ compiler comes with a static analyzer that can be used to find bugs using path-sensitive analysis.

Finding a single recipe that works for all aspects of an HFT system is impossible. Learning how to analyze performance and run static analysis helps you to avoid the biggest mistakes we can make when coding in C++. By removing the biggest issues our code can have, we can focus on things that are critical for performance.

By combining static analysis and the runtime optimizations we talked about, such as using a proper memory model and reducing the number of function calls, we will reach an acceptable level of performance for an HFT system.

Use case - Building an FX high-frequency trading system

A company needs an HFT system capable of sending an order within 20 microseconds. To do this, the company can follow this approach:

- Choose a multi-process architecture over a multi-core architecture.

- Ensure each process is pinned to a specific core to reduce context switches.

- Have processes communicating over a circular buffer (lock-free data structure) in shared memory.

- Design the network stack using *Solarflare OpenOnload* for network acceleration.

- Increase the page size to reduce the number of TLB cache misses.

- Disable hyperthreading to get more control over the concurrency execution of the processes.

- Use the CRTP to reduce the number of virtual functions.

- Remove runtime decisions by using templated data structures.

- Pre-allocate data structures to avoid any allocation on the critical path.

- Send fake orders to keep caches hot and allow an order to go out at the last moment.

In any trading system, the number of orders is way lower than the amount of market data received. The critical path from getting market data to sending an order is exercised very infrequently. The cache will be overtaken by non-critical path data and instructions. That's why it is very important to run a dummy path to send orders through the entire system to keep the data cache and instruction cache primed. This will also keep the branch predictors hot.

The main idea of all these optimizations is to reduce the number of costly operations. Removing function calls, using lock-free data structures, and reducing the number of context switches are a part of this strategy.

Additionally, any decision taken at runtime is costly. That's why templated functions and inlining will be part of the common code in any HFT system. The most costly operations are those involving networking communications. Using an end-to-end kernel bypass such as *Solarflare* optimizes the network latency within the trading system. By using these optimizations, this company could achieve 20 microseconds for the tick-to-trade. The latency distribution is very important to measure. We need to be sure that 20 microseconds is the latency upper bound. We should never consider the average values because it is difficult to assess high latency with this value.

In HFTs, some strategies are very profitable when a lot of trades occur. If most of the time a trading system works as expected, there is no guarantee that the system will always perform well. When a trading system receives a lot of data, if it is not built correctly, the maximum latency can be 10 times more than the average. We should keep in mind that any optimization is not guaranteed to be faster if we have not measured it ourselves in production.

Summary

In this chapter, we covered a lot of modern C++ 14, 17, and 20 features for multi-threaded and ultra-low latency applications that deal with shared memory interactions. We also covered static analysis for application development. Finally, we discussed runtime performance optimization techniques that move as much decision, code evaluation, and code branching away from runtime into compile time as possible. The contents of this chapter address the major design and development decisions and techniques critical to the development and performance of C++ HFT applications.

We also saw how to build an HFT system for a small hedge fund specialized in FX. In the next chapter, we will learn about the usage of Java in an ultra-low-latency system such as an HFT system.

9
Java and JVM for Low-Latency Systems

When people think about **high-frequency trading (HFT)**, **Java** does not often come to mind. The **Java virtual machine (JVM)** warm-up, the fact that it is running on a virtual machine, and the infamous garbage collector have been big deterrents for programmers. However, if you smartly understand those limitations and code, Java can be used in a low-latency environment. You will then be able to benefit from all the advantages that come with Java:

- A very active and deep offering of free third-party libraries.

- Write it once, and compile and run it everywhere.

- Greater stability, avoiding the infamous *segmentation fault* due to bad memory management.

In this chapter, you will learn how to tune Java for HFT. The performance at runtime is largely based on the performance of the JVM. We will explain in depth how to optimize this critical component.

We will cover the following topics:

- Garbage collection
- JVM warm-up
- Measuring performance in Java
- Java threading
- High-performance data structures
- Logging and **Database** (**DB**) access

> **Important Note**
>
> In order to guide you through all the optimizations, you can refer to the following list of icons that represent a group of optimizations lowering the latency by a specific number of microseconds:
>
> 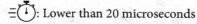: Lower than 20 microseconds
>
> : Lower than 5 microseconds
>
> : Lower than 500 nanoseconds
>
> You will find these icons in the headings of this chapter.

Before getting into the optimization, we would like to remind you how Java works. In the next section, we will describe the basics of Java.

Introducing the basics of Java

Java was created by Sun Microsystems in 1991. The first public version was released 5 years later. The main purpose of Java was to be portable and highly performant in internet applications. Unlike C++, Java is platform independent. The JVM ensures any architecture and operating system's portability.

Figure 9.1 shows the compilation chain for Java. We can observe that the Java compiler doesn't produce an executable but a bytecode. JVM will run this bytecode to run the software.

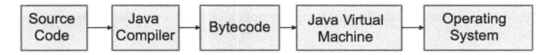

Figure 9.1 – Java compilation chain

We recommend reading the Packt book *Java Programming for Beginners*, written by Mark Lassof, to learn the characteristics of this language in detail. In this chapter, we will talk about the factors that will affect the performance of HFT. As we described for C++, one critical component is the memory management structure. Unlike C++, where the developer must handle memory manually, Java has a **garbage collector** (**GC**). The main purpose of the GC is to free objects (memory segments) from the heap when these objects are not used anymore.

Figure 9.2 describes how the memory is divided into different functional parts. The heap area is created when the JVM starts. To improve the data structures, objects at runtime are added to the heap area. In the section on the GC, we will see how to resize the heap to improve the performance at runtime. Like the heap, the method area is created at startup and stores class structures and methods.

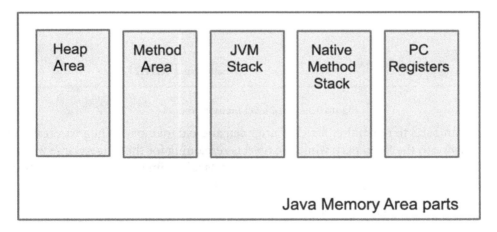

Figure 9.2 – JVM memory area parts

When we create a thread, the JVM stack is used. This part of memory is used to store data temporarily. Native stack and PC registers are also created when the JVM starts but will not be a critical component for performance in HFT.

The component that is critical for performance is the GC. JVM triggers the garbage collection to automatically deallocate the memory of objects that are not used anymore in the heap.

Figure 9.3 represents the organization of the Java heap memory. The garbage collection will manage the object allocation on this part of the memory.

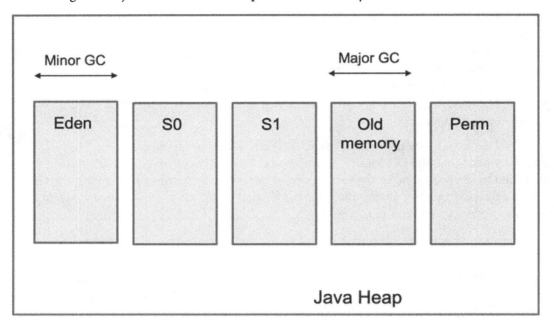

Figure 9.3 – JVM heap memory model

The two main parts to remember for HFT are Eden and old memory. When we create new objects, they go to the Eden part, while the objects remaining for the longest time will stay in the old memory. Allocating and deallocating objects takes time; that's why the garbage collection will be the main performance component in HFT.

We will now talk about garbage collection.

Reducing the impact of the GC ⏱

When Java was released in 1996, one of the big promises was the end of the dreadful `segFault` error, so familiar to all C/C++ developers. Java decided to remove all the objects and pointer life cycle out of the hands of the developer and entrust the logic to the JVM. This gave birth to the GC.

There is not a single type of garbage collection. There have been multiple versions developed; all have different specifications to offer either low-latency pauses, predictability, or high throughput.

One of the biggest parts of tuning Java is to find the most appropriate GC for your application as well as the best parameters for it. The main GC algorithms are as follows:

- **Serial GC**: Recommended for the small dataset or single-threaded with no pause time requirements.

- **Parallel/throughput collector**: Recommended for peak performance and not pause time requirements.

- **Concurrent Mark Sweep collector**: Recommended for minimum GC pause time.

- **G1 GC**: Recommended for minimum GC pause time.

- **Shenandoah collector**: Improved version of G1 GC, where pause time is no more proportional to the heap size. You can find more information here: `https://wiki.openjdk.java.net/display/shenandoah`.

- **Z GC** (*Experimental*): Recommended for high response time, very large heap, and small pause time. You can find more information here: `https://wiki.openjdk.java.net/display/zgc/Main`.

- **Epsilon GC** (*Experimental*): For the bold and brave, this is known as Java's no-op GC. It has the lowest number of GC interventions possible with no memory reclamation. It is recommended for people that understand the complete life cycle of objects created in their application.

It is beyond the scope of this book to exactly recommend a specific GC. If you would like to have more information, we recommend Packt's *Garbage Collection Algorithms* by Dmitry Soshnikov (`https://www.packtpub.com/product/garbage-collection-algorithms/9781801074629`). In a high-frequency environment, the less often and the less time we spend in the GC state, the better. That is why we will prefer using concurrent algorithms such as Concurrent Mark Sweep, G1, Shenandoah, and Z.

The only way to choose the best GC for your needs is to try all of them. It is important to measure performance to establish which algorithms will work the best. When testing performance, we want to enable the different GCs and run in an environment as close as the one running in production. Each GC algorithm also comes with a multitude of options that will allow you to control and tweak its behavior. There are no options that are better than the others; you will need to experiment to find the ones that have the best results for your application. We will find the right balance between the frequency and the duration of the GC. Do you prefer GC for 2 ms every 30 minutes or 4 ms every 60 minutes? These are questions you will need to answer. For a more in-depth look at the different GC algorithms and options, you can refer to the latest documentation on the Oracle website: `https://docs.oracle.com/en/java/javase/18/gctuning/index.html`.

We will now look at how we can limit the GC events as much as we can.

What to do to keep GC events low and fast

In HFT, we want to limit the effect of the GC. When a GC is triggered, it is difficult to keep control of the execution. The performance can be impacted whenever the GC is triggered. Therefore, it is important to keep the number of GC interventions low, and when the intervention is inevitable, we need to make it fast. The best way to reduce the number and the duration of the GC depends on the coding style. The more objects you create, the more pressure you are going to put on the GC. It is important to keep in mind that the creation of an object on the critical path may end up in the removal of this object at some point. The key is to pre-allocate objects that will live during the entire execution of the software to avoid allocation/deallocation triggering the work of the GC. Your primary goal is to avoid the frequent creation of short-lived objects.

You first need to identify the **hot paths** (functions or pieces of code that are constantly called at a very high frequency) in your program; once identified, you need to look for all the object creations in that path. If you know you will be creating thousands of objects for a very short time span, you will need to consider adding these objects to a cache pool. They will be first allocated and will be used afterward. Ideally, the hot path is single-threaded and spinning on a specific core (as we explained in the *Reducing the number of contexts switched* section in *Chapter 6, HFT Optimization – Architecture and Operating System*. This design will remove the need for any locks on the pool, and a simple counter to get and return the object will be enough. In some situations, even if it is multithreaded, it might still be good to use a pool even though you will need a lock. We can offset the cost of using a lock with a smaller GC time. By caching, we will increase the heap size. It is important to consider the tradeoff between the number of objects created with the heap size.

We will continue this section by talking about other Java features increasing the number of objects allocated that can potentially trigger the use of the JVM.

Limiting the autoboxing effect

Another critical coding style to pay attention to is *autoboxing*. Moving back and forth between a primary type and its object wrapper will create a lot of unnecessary objects. When the compiler automatically converts the primitive types into their corresponding Java object wrapper, it is called autoboxing. For example, converting `int` to an Integer, `double` to a Double, and so on. *Inboxing* is when the conversion goes the other way. Even though some wrappers contain a cache, it is relatively small. For example, for Integer, it only caches values between `-127` and `127`. If you need to use a wrapper, it is recommended to use Integer, because it is the only wrapper that allows you to extend the cache (`-XX:AutoBoxCacheMax`).

By default, Java offers a multitude of **Collection**, **List**, and **Set** implementations that will solve most of your needs. Unfortunately, all those structures only support objects as parameters, and most of them are also creating new objects on each insert in order to implement the desired behavior. When coding, you need to keep this in mind. You can also use some third-party libraries (`https://fastutil.di.unimi.it/` or `https://github.com/real-logic/agrona`) that will implement the Java collection using the Java primary type. Depending on your needs this could greatly reduce the object creation in your program.

You also need to be mindful of the different objects that are created by either the code 's Java classes or any third-party libraries. You need to be aware of the object creations of which the *Iterator* is a perfect example. It will create a new object each time you call it. This is why you might give preference to a structure that supports a simple loop for each iteration. Another example is the libraries used to connect to databases. They are very dynamic but they could create a ton of objects on each insert.

The GC may be tweaked to reduce latency while increasing memory usage. After Oracle Java 11, the Epsilon option appeared. This option sets a GC that manages memory allocation but doesn't implement a memory reclamation mechanism. The JVM will shut down whenever the available Java heap is depleted. At the price of memory footprint and speed, this Epsilon provides a passive GC approach with a defined allocation limit and the lowest possible latency overhead. However, introducing manual memory management features in the Java language was not a goal.

Stop-the-world pause

In general, GC does not necessitate a **stop-the-world** (STW) pause. It means all the active threads pause and only the memory cleaner thread is running. It is called a stop-the-world pause because during that time, your program is not actively running. There are JVM implementations that do not have any pauses. Azul Zing JVM is one of them. The algorithm it employs determines whether or not JVM needs STW to collect trash.

Mark Sweep Compact (MSC) is a standard algorithm that is used by default in hot spots (a critical part of a code). It contains three steps and is implemented in an STW fashion:

- `Mark`: Traverses the live object graph to mark things that are accessible
- `Sweep`: Searches memory for unmarked memories
- `Compact`: Defragments memory by moving designated things

The JVM should fix all references to this object when shifting items in a heap. The object graph is inconsistent throughout the relocation process, so a STW pause is essential. An object graph is a list reporting the relationship between the different objects created. It allows them to know which objects are still needed and which ones are not referred to by any other and are free to be collected.

Concurrent Mark Sweep (CMS) is a HotSpot JVM technique that does not need the STW pause to gather old space (not the same thing as a full collection).

CMS does not use `Compact` and instead uses a write barrier (the trigger that acts each time you write a reference in the Java heap) to construct a concurrent version of `Mark`. Lack of compaction can cause fragmentation, and if background trash collection is not quick enough, the program may be halted. CMS will resort to STW MSC collection in certain circumstances.

We will now talk about how the Java primitive types can improve the garbage collection.

Primitive types and memory allocation

In addition to the previous methods to reduce the GC intervention, we can consider optimizing memory allocations. When primitive types are available, one technique to minimize latency is to employ them. Primitive types (often called **primitives**) use less memory than their object equivalents, which has the following benefits:

- It allows fitting more data into a single cache line. If the data the processor needs is not in the current cache line, a new 64-byte cache line will be loaded. If the CPU cannot anticipate the memory access, the retrieval operation might take 10 to 30 nanoseconds.

- If we can utilize less memory, we can keep the maximum heap size short, which means the collector has fewer live roots to search while doing a full GC with a lesser number of objects. A complete GC can easily take 1 second/gigabyte.

- Primitives decrease the amount of waste generated by a program. Most of the items you make will need to be gathered at some point. A minor GC is very quick at disposing of dead items; in fact, disposing of dead objects takes essentially no time at all because only living things are moved between (and into) the surviving areas; nonetheless, copying the live objects uses resources that may be utilized to conduct business logic.

- Assigning to a primitive is faster than generating a new object on the heap. Object creation in Java is extraordinarily fast, even faster than `malloc` in C, identifying a suitable portion of the main memory. The object is constructed in Java in the next accessible spot in a pre-existing buffer, referred to as the **Eden space**.

- Many functions return double values rather than a single number when building a pricing system. In a perfect world, objects would be preferred; however, this is not feasible because our computations occasionally fail, and we must produce an error or status code. If we need to return an object, in some cases, it could be re-used, so we could just pass it in the function as an argument.

We saw how primitives can help optimize the garbage collection; we will now talk about the profiling of memory.

Memory profiling

We talked about how to keep object creation to a minimum, but how do you keep track of the number of objects created by your program? The best way to do this is to use a **Java profiler**. There are many solutions (licensed or free) available:

- Profiler (`https://www.ej-technologies.com/products/jprofiler/overview.html`)

- Java Profiler: `https://www.yourkit.com/java/profiler`

- Visual VM: `https://visualvm.github.io`

- Apache NetBeans – Java profiler: `https://netbeans.apache.org/kb/docs/java/profiler-intro.html`

These software will give reports and graphs; they will be the primary visual evidence of a performance problem. Some will report the hotspots where most of the objects are created. They also incorporate performance measurement tools that could be helpful to find inefficiencies in your code. It is not recommended to use profiling software in a production environment. These tools are intrusive in terms of performance. They should run in a simulation environment, where we can recreate a mock of the production environment to make sure we explore all the paths in our code. We do not have to pound it with tons of data; profiling is not made to find what your system can handle, but how efficient it is with the resources.

Figure 9.4 represents the output of a Java profiler. We can actually see with the bars which part of the code is most time-consuming.

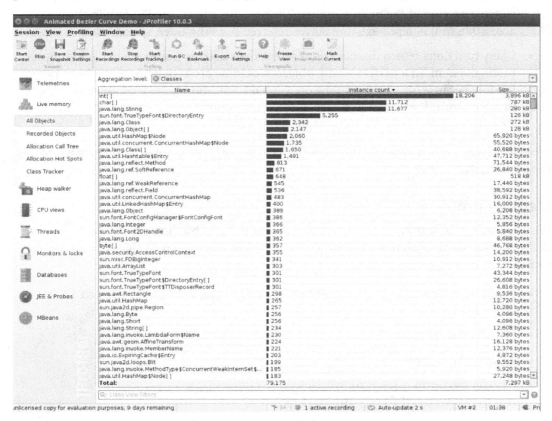

Figure 9.4 – Example of a Java profiler result

In this section, we talked in depth about the GC and its impact on performance. We saw how to limit its intervention by using coding techniques. We will now talk about the JVM warm-up, which is required to have performant code.

Warming up the JVM ≡⏱

Compileable languages, such as C++, are so named because the provided code is entirely binary and can be executed directly on the CPU. Because the interpreter (loaded on the destination machine) compiles each line of code as it runs, Python and Perl are referred to as interpreted languages. In *Figure 9.1*, we showed that Java is in the middle; it compiles the code into Java bytecode, which can then be turned into binary when necessary.

It's for long-term performance optimization that Java doesn't compile the code upon startup. Java builds frequently called code by watching the program run and analyzing real-time method invocations and class initializations. It might even make some educated guesses based on past experience. As a result, the compiled code is extremely quick. The main caveat for having an optimal execution time is to call the function many times.

Before a method can be optimized and compiled, it must be called a particular number of times to exceed the compilation threshold (the limit is configurable but typically around 10,000 calls). Unoptimized code will not run at *full speed* until then. There is a trade-off between getting a faster compilation and getting a better compilation (if the assumptions that the compiler takes in terms of execution were wrong, there would be a cost of recompilation).

We're back to square one when the Java application restarts, and we'll have to wait till we reach that threshold again. The HFT software has infrequent but crucial methods that are only called a few times but must be incredibly quick when they are.

Azul Zing solves these problems by allowing the JVM to store the state of compiled methods and classes in a profile. This one-of-a-kind feature, known as **ReadyNow!**®, ensures that Java programs always execute at maximum performance, even after a restart. You can find more information on *ReadyNow* on this website: https://www.azul. com/products/components/readynow.

When we resume a software (such as a trading system) with an existing profile, the Azul JVM remembers its prior decisions and compiles the described methods directly, which eliminates the Java warm-up problem.

We can also create a profile in a development environment to simulate production behavior. After that, the optimized profile can be deployed in production with the assurance that all key pathways have been compiled and optimized.

GraalVM recently also developed an **ahead-of-time** (**AOT**) project. We will not dive into the details, but it would allow you to pre-compile your binary code into native code. This would allow you to speed up the process at startup as the AOT native code would be used right away and until the tiered compilation kicked in. It was introduced in Java 9 as an experimental function. We will now explain how JVM optimizes the runtime using tiered compilation.

Tiered compilation in JVM

At runtime, the JVM understands and executes bytecode. In addition, **just-in-time** (**JIT**) **compilation** is used to improve performance. We had to manually pick between the two types of JIT compilers accessible in the HotSpot JVM in older versions of Java. One (**C1**) was designed to speed up application startup, while the other (**C2**) improved overall performance.

In order to attain the best of both worlds, Java 7 introduced *layered compilation*. For the most used parts, a JIT compiler converts bytecode to native code. HotSpot JVM gets its name from these parts, which are referred to as hotspots. As a result, Java may achieve performance comparable to a fully compiled language. There are two types of JIT compiler:

- C1 (client compiler), which optimizes the start-up time
- C2 (server compiler) is tuned for overall performance

In comparison to C1, C2 watches and analyzes the code for a longer length of time. This enables C2 to improve the compiled code's optimizations.

Compiling the same functions using the C2 compiler takes longer and uses more memory. However, it creates native code that is more optimized than C1. Java 7 was the first to introduce the idea of tiered compilation. Its objective was to achieve both rapid startup and strong long-term performance by combining C1 and C2 compilers.

Figure 9.5 shows the tiered compilation in JVM. When an application is first started, the JVM interprets all bytecode and accumulates profiling data. The acquired profiling information is then used by the JIT compiler to locate hotspots. To achieve native code speed, the JIT compiler first compiles the frequently performed parts of code using C1. When more profile data becomes available, C2 takes over. C2 recompiles the code using a more aggressive optimization algorithm.

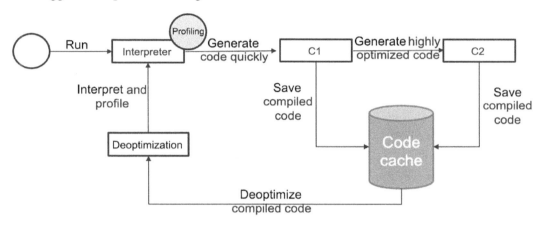

Figure 9.5 – Tiered compilation in JVM

Despite the fact that the JVM only has one interpreter and two JIT compilers, there are five layers of compilation, as shown in *Figure 9.6*. The reason is that the C1 compiler has three levels of operation. The quantity of profiling done is the difference between those three tiers.

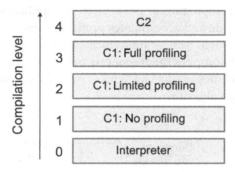

Figure 9.6 – Compilation levels

We are going to describe the JVM compilation levels more in depth.

Level 0 – Interpreted code

The JVM understands all Java code the first time the code is run. When compared to compiled languages, performance is typically worse at this phase. However, following the warm-up phase, the JIT compiler kicks in and compiles the hot code at runtime. The profiling information gathered at this stage is used by the JIT compiler to conduct optimizations.

Level 1 – Simple C1 compiled code

The JVM compiles the code using the C1 compiler at this level, but without gathering any profiling data. For functions that are considered trivial (such as arithmetic operations), the JVM employs the compilation level 1. The C2 compilation would not make it quicker due to the minimal method complexity. As a result, the JVM believes that gathering profiling data for code that cannot be further optimized is pointless.

Level 2 – Limited C1 compiled code

At level 2, the JVM uses the C1 compiler with mild profiling to compile the code. When the C2 queue is full, the JVM switches to this level. To boost performance, the objective is to compile the code as fast as feasible. The JVM then recompiles the code on level 3 with full profiling afterward. Finally, the JVM recompiles the C2 queue on level 4 once it is less crowded.

Level 3 – Full C1 compiled code

At level 3, the JVM compiles the code with complete profiling using the C1 compiler. Level 3 is included in the standard compilation process. As a result, except for basic operations or when compiler queues are full, the JVM utilizes this level of compilation in all circumstances. In JIT compilation, the most typical case is that the interpreted code goes straight from level 0 to level 3.

Level 4 – C2 compiled code

On this level, the JVM uses the C2 compiler to build the code for the best long-term performance. Level 4 is likewise included in the standard compilation process. Except for simple methods, the JVM compiles all methods at this level. The JVM stops gathering profiling information because level 4 code is considered completely optimized. It may, however, decide to deoptimize the code and return it to level 0.

To summarize, the JVM interprets the code until a method reaches `Tier3CompileThreshold`. The method is then compiled using the C1 compiler, while profiling data is still being gathered. When the method's invocations reach `Tier4CompileThreshold`, the JVM compiles it using the C2 compiler. The JVM may eventually decide to deoptimize C2 compiled code. That implies the entire procedure will be repeated.

Each compilation threshold is associated with number of iterations. To find out the default value we can ask the JVM to print them using `-XX:+PrintFlagsFinal`:

```
intx CompileThreshold = 10000
intx Tier2CompileThreshold = 0
intx Tier3CompileThreshold = 2000
intx Tier4CompileThreshold = 15000
```

You can change those values using the JVM options if you want to lower or increase them. There is no magic number, each program is unique, so it is best to monitor the performance using different parameter combinations and choose the one that best satisfies your performance requirements.

We will now show how to optimize the JVM as soon as we start the software.

Optimizing the JVM for better startup performance

In HFT, we don't want to be able to get the best performance as soon as we run the software. We will explain the different methods we can use to avoid intermediate compilation.

Tiered compilation

We can run the JVM with the `-XX:-Tiered Compilation` option. It disables intermediate compilation tiers (1, 2, and 3) so that a method is either interpreted or compiled at the maximum optimization level (C2):

- **ReservedCodeCacheSize**:

    The `-XX:ReservedCodeCacheSize=N` option specifies the maximum size of the code cache. The code cache is controlled in the same way as the rest of the JVM's memory: it has an initial size (given by `-XX:InitialCodeCacheSize=N`). The initial size of the code cache is allocated, and when the cache fills up, the size is increased. The code cache's initial size is determined by the architecture. This setting is useful because it has a small impact on speed.

- **CompileThreshold**:

    The value of the `-XX:CompileThreshold=N` option triggers standard compilation. Java can run in *client* or *server* mode, and the default value will depend on that mode; it is 1,500 for client applications and 10,000 for server applications. Lowering this number could speed up the compilation to native code. It needs to be tuned based on the needs of each application; pick a number too small and the JVM will generate native code with limited profiling information and maybe not create the most optimized code for the long term. The threshold is determined by adding the total of the back-edge loop counter and the method entrance counter, despite the fact that there is only one flag here.

- **Warm up your code**:

  You could write your own code *warmer*. As you are aware of the hot path in your program, you could write a wrapper that would execute that hot path in order to reach the minimum number of iterations for bytecode optimization. In an HFT system, the market data process is usually not an issue as you will very quickly reach the iteration threshold with the sheer amount of data you will receive. You should focus on the less frequent events such as new orders or execution of code that are called periodically, but you do not want to have them slow down your hot path. You need to be extremely careful about JVM warm-up in a live environment. To warm up the JVM, we can utilize a variety of techniques. The **Java Microbenchmark Harness (JMH)** is a toolkit that assists us in appropriately implementing Java microbenchmarks. For HFT, it could be a function on the critical path, such as the function in charge of sending orders. Once loaded, it continually executes a code snippet while keeping track of the warm-up iteration cycle. JMH was created by the same team that created the JVM. You can read about it here for your reference: `https://www.baeldung.com/java-jvm-warmup`.

The quickest approach to get started with JMH is to use the JMH Maven prototype to create a new JMH project. We will dive more into the details of JMH in the following section.

Measuring the performance of a Java software

JMH is a toolkit that assists you in appropriately implementing Java microbenchmarks. Let's now discuss them in detail.

Why are Java microbenchmarks difficult to create?

It's difficult to create benchmarks that accurately assess the performance of a tiny area of a bigger program. When the benchmark runs your component in isolation, the JVM or underlying hardware may apply a variety of optimizations to it. When the component is operating as part of a bigger application, certain optimizations may not be available. As a result, poorly designed microbenchmarks may lead you to assume that your component's performance is better than it actually is.

Writing a good Java microbenchmark often requires avoiding JVM and hardware optimizations that would not have been done in a genuine production system during microbenchmark execution. That's exactly what it is about. Benchmarks that correctly measure the performance of a tiny part of a larger application are challenging to come up with.

We are not going to dive into the details of how to implement JMH. There are multitudes of very good sources already available over the web. A must-read is the *JMH GitHub* (`https://github.com/openjdk/jmh`), which will provide you with instructions on how to install JMH but also has a multitude of examples. The JMH framework helps to reduce the warm-up period of an application. It could also be used to measure *offline* performances; it will help you in your design decisions. If you are hesitating between multiple design options or thinking about some optimizations, JMH can help you evaluate the performance and help confirm your choices. As we said a few times in this book, the key to optimization is to be sure that we measure the performance accurately to ensure that the optimization works. We will now talk about how to measure real-time performance.

Real-time performance measures

Harness testing will only allow you to make a decision on what is the best design to achieve the best throughput or speed. Once your code is released in a production environment, you need to keep track of the performance of the critical parts of your application.

A good measure that will not give you a pure performance report, but will let you spot quite easily changes in performance behavior, is to keep a **revolutions per minute** (**RPM**) on your hot threads. In an HFT application, you always have one or multiple threads that will be spinning on a core. You could keep a simple counter that will increment on each spin. If for any reason you have some code in that loop that starts misbehaving and it starts to add some drag, you will be able to detect it by observing a change in the RPM behavior.

The next measure to keep is **latency**. You want to keep simple latency measures in the critical part of your code, and if you have a distributed system, you also want to measure the communication latency between the different processes.

We need to be smart about collecting the latency and the RPM statistics. The last thing we want is to create more overhead and latency than in your standalone code when capturing statistics.

For this reason, the *statistics collector* should have very light and basic logic. There must be no lock or object creation at any time in the logic. You should have cumulative, incremental, and descriptive (`min`, `max`, `avg`, and `pctXX`) statistic collectors, as they will cover most of your needs.

Here are the different types of counters that we can use:

- **Cumulative** is an easy counter that could be incremented by any values.

- **Incremental** is a simple counter that can only be incremented by one.

- **Descriptive** keeps track of the minimum, maximum, average, and percentile X over the collection period.

You now need to collect the statistics for the period and store them to be able to analyze them. The best course of action is to have a periodic thread that awakens every X minutes (1 minute is a good number) that will grab and reset the statistics from all the collectors. It will then store the statistics to be able to visualize or analyze them. The storing must also be made in a smart way. Speed is not critical but object creation is; logs or database storage will generate a lot of object creations. A good solution is to send those statistics to a different process through either **Inter-Processing Communication** (**IPC**) or the **User Datagram Protocol** (**UDP**) and let the remote process take care of the storing. It is easy to send data to a remote process without creating any lock or object.

On the remote server, you are now free to use any software to store statistics and access the data easily, including databases and time-series data (for example, Graphite: `https://grafana.com/oss/graphite/`).

To visualize the stored data, a good option is the Grafana dashboard (`https://grafana.com/grafana/`). It is a frontend that can be linked to multiple data sources using different plugins. It will let you access those statistics through a nice website with lots of graph options and alert triggers. The raw data will be available on the box where Grafana is running or through a web API. The next section will talk about the performance that we can achieve with threading.

Java threading

Threads are the basic unit of concurrency in Java. Threads provide the advantage of reducing program execution time by allowing your program to either execute multiple tasks in parallel or execute on one portion of the job while another waits for something to happen (typically **input/output** (**I/O**)).

HFT architecture heavily uses threads to increase the throughput, as we mentioned in *Chapter 7, HFT Optimization – Logging, Performance, and Networking*. Multiple threads are created to do tasks in parallel. Adding threads to a program that is completely CPU bound can only slow it down. Adding threads may assist if it's totally or partially I/O bound, but there's a trade-off to consider between the overhead of adding threads and the increased work that will be done. We know that the underlying hardware (CPU and memory resource) will limit this throughput. If we increase the number of threads beyond a certain limit (such as the number of cores or the number of threading units), we deteriorate the performance by increasing the memory footprint (potentially decreasing the cache usage) or by increasing the number of context switches. If we notice that the latency of our trading system has been impacted and the memory usage has sharply increased, monitoring the number of threads will be required.

As we explained in *Chapter 8, C++ – The Quest for Microsecond Latency*, the rule of thumb to optimize HFT software is to be aware of bottlenecks. For instance, if an algorithm is susceptible to cache contention between multiple CPUs, it has the ability to wreak havoc on the thread's performance. When employing many CPUs to run a highly parallelized algorithm, cache contention is a critical consideration. There is no magic number for thread count; the goal is to minimize them while achieving the best throughput.

The use of a Java profiler will show the number of threads and list the GC threads that will be used within the trading system. This graphical tool has many features that could be useful to find objects or data structure being the contention of the tasks accomplished by the threads (finding bottlenecks). When using this tool, it is important to keep in mind that any profiler can be intrusive. There are simpler alternatives to query the number of threads in an application; for a Linux-based **operating system** (**OS**), the best one is **htop** (`https://htop.dev/`). It will give you an immediate view of how many threads are running within your Java process. For a Linux-based OS and other useful command-line tools, sending a `kill -3 pid` command will force the JVM to dump a list of all the threads in your program as well as what they are executing at the time of the call. This is a useful tool to use to diagnose blocked threads or unexpected behaviors.

Using a thread pool/queue with threads

Threads in Java are mapped to system-level threads, which are the resources of the OS. Creating too many threads can impact the performance, reduce the cache efficiency, and we can run out of these resources quickly. Because the OS will handle the scheduling of these threads, it is easy to conclude that these threads will have less time to do actual work.

The goal of the thread pool is to help resources and contain the parallelism in a certain capacity. When using thread pools, we write concurrent code that will be called in parallel when submitting tasks. The thread pool will perform these tasks by re-using threads. We will not pay the thread creation cost and we will be able to limit the number of threads. *Figure 9.7* represents code (a **submitter**) submitting tasks to a thread pool. The thread pool will handle these tasks. We can see that the number of threads is important since it will increase the concurrent executions of these tasks:

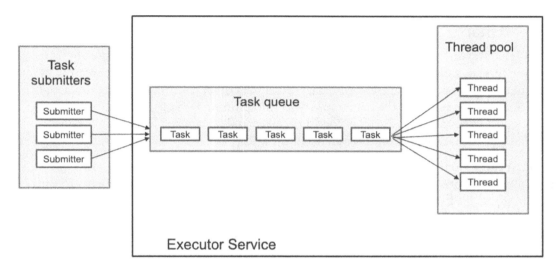

Figure 9.7 – Tasks with a thread pool

It is a good practice to keep two distinct pools of threads: a smaller one in charge of running the short-lived task, and a bigger one for the long tasks (I/O access, DB, and logging, for example), the one that could take multiple seconds or even used in a forever-spinning loop.

There is also the concept of the *scheduler* in Java, where you can *schedule* a task to run at a specific time or at a constant interval. The scheduler usually runs on its own thread, and when triggered, delivers the task to the thread pool. It is helpful when you add your task to the scheduler to designate the pool it should be assigned to. You could also designate the tasks that will take a couple of microseconds to run directly in the scheduler thread. A typical example would be a triggered task that adds an event in a lock-free event queue. There is no need to handle the *add* logic in an external intermediary thread.

We will now talk about the different types of executors that can help to create thread pools.

Executors, Executor, and ExecutorService

We will simplify the explanation of the `Executors` by saying that they contain methods to create preconfigured thread pool instances. We use them to work with different thread pool implementations in Java. The `ExecutorService` interface includes a significant number of ways for controlling task progress and managing service termination. We may submit tasks for execution and manage their execution using the returned `Future` instance using this interface.

Thread map

In an HFT system, there is always a hot path that logic should be *bound* to a specific looping thread, and that thread should be pinned to a core on the OS. If one thread is not enough to process the amount of data, we can start other spinning threads and assign to each of them a subset of the data to process. The spinning thread should never access blocking I/O or avoid any OS call or lock. OS calls could be blocked by other OS calls coming from other threads on the systems or the OS itself.

When it comes to thread affinity, we need to also be conscious of the CPU architecture: the number of cores, **Non-Uniform Memory Access** (**NUMA**) domain, and network card core binding. If threads need to communicate with each other or some other application over shared memory or network traffic, they should all be running on the same NUMA domain. When processes are running on the same NUMA domain, they are sharing the same memory cache and avoiding crossing NUMA boundaries, which will cost us more in terms of performance. We also want to isolate the core at the OS level, which will prevent the OS from scheduling any other process on the reserved core. On a Linux-based OS, this is done using the `isolcpu` functionality. It will exclude the designated cores to be accessed by the OS.

Utility threads (logging, timer, DB, and others) do not need to be bound to specific cores; they just need to make sure they will not be running on a core shared with the OS.

A very nice library to allow us to bind our Java thread to a specific core is found here: `https://github.com/OpenHFT/Java-Thread-Affinity`.

This library will allow you to pin threads to specific cores directly from Java. It is a pretty excellent tool with a simple API that will let you acquire a core when starting a thread. We have multiple options where you can ask for the next available core on the socket or lock a specific core number, or even pre-allocate a set of cores and have them assigned in the order of acquisition.

Let's see an example:

```
IRunnable command = new IRunnable() {
                @Override
                public void run() {
                                Affinity.acquireLock(true); //
Acquire the next free lock from the preallocated list
            s_log.info("Cpu Lock:" + Affinity.getCpu());
        s_log.info("On Next Core The assignment of CPUs is\n: "
+        AffinityLock.dumpLocks());
                        while (true) {
                                processInternalEvent();
                    }
                }
            };
```

A Linux-based OS offers another alternative: we could use *htop* (please see the previous reference) to manually assign a core for each thread. This is not ideal as it is a manual process and we need to redo the mapping each time the process is restarted. The advantage of this solution is that the assignment of the core is not final, so you could move your thread around to a different core. It is also a quick way to test the performance improvement or changes that your application could achieve when you are binding a thread to a core.

Taskset (https://man7.org/linux/man-pages/man1/taskset.1.html) on a Linux-based OS can also be used to limit which cores the Java application-free threads will be allowed to run on. This will apply to the main thread and all Java threads that are not bound to a core.

In *Figure 9.8*, the diagram is the best-case scenario:

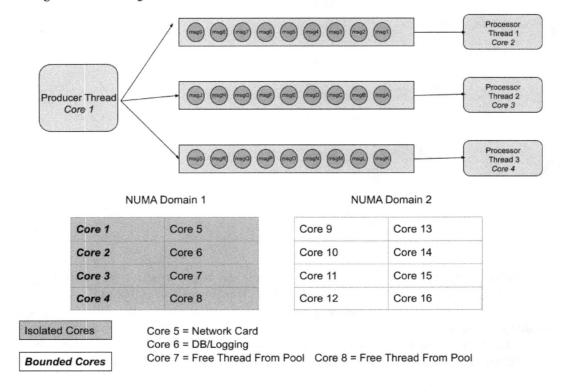

Figure 9.8 – Ideal scenario to execute a parallel program

We can run the entire program on one NUMA domain. If we start our Java application using `tasket --cpu-list 6-8`, the main starting thread and all non-bounded threads will be limited to run on CPU cores 6, 7, and 8, keeping them on the same NUMA domain.

In HFT, the principal component for performance is the data structure. We will now study which data structure we should use in Java to build an HFT system.

High-performance task queue ⏱

To achieve performance, any trading system must have processes and threads working in parallel. Processing many operations at the same time is a way to save time. The communication between processes is very challenging in terms of speed and complexity. As we saw in *Chapter 6, HFT Optimization - Architecture and Operating System*, it is easy to create a segment of shared memory and share data between them. As we know, there is a problem with the synchronization of the access to the data because shared memory doesn't have any synchronization mechanism. The temptation of using a lock is high but performance will be affected by this kind of object.

In this section, we are going to review the different Java data structures that we use in HFT. The first one is the simplest: the queue.

Queues

Queues generally have a write contention on the head and tail and have variable sizes. They are either full or empty but never operate on the middle ground where the number of writes is equivalent to the number of reads. They use locks to deal with the write contention. The lock can cause context switches in the kernel. Since any context switches save and load the local memory of a given process, the cache will lose the data. In order to use caching in the best way, we need to have one core writing. However, if two separate threads are writing, each core will invalidate the cache line of the other.

In *Chapter 6, HFT Optimization - Architecture and Operating System*, in the *Using lock-free data structures* section, we showed how lock-free data structures are the way to go for HFT. The circular buffer or ring buffer enables processes or threads to transfer data without any locks. We are going to talk first about the circular buffer.

Circular buffer

There are several names for a ring buffer. Circular buffers, circular queues, and cyclic buffers are all terms you've probably heard of. They all imply the same thing. It's essentially a linear data structure with the end pointing back to the beginning. It's simple to think of it as a circular array with no end.

A ring buffer, as you might expect, is mostly used as a queue. It has read and write positions, which the consumer and producer utilize separately. The read or write index is reset to 0 when it reaches the end of the underlying array. The problem comes when a reader is slower than a writer. We have two options: the first is to overwrite the data if we do not need the data anymore or to block the writer from writing (potentially having a write buffer).

The option to increase the size of a circular buffer is feasible. However, it must be done only if the read/write is blocked. In this situation, resizing will require moving all the elements to a newly allocated bigger array. This operation is very expensive and slow. It cannot be done on the critical path.

One of the implementations of the circular buffer is made by LMAX, and is called the LMAX disruptor.

LMAX disruptor

Disruptor uses a circular buffer. All events are broadcast (multicast) to all consumers for consumption concurrently via distinct downstream queues. Disruptors are similar to a multicast graph of queues in which producers send items to all consumers for concurrent consumption via distinct downstream queues. The consumer could be a chain of event handlers, allowing you to run multiple handlers for each consumed message. When we examine the network of queues more closely, we can see that it is actually a single data structure called a ring buffer. It is required to synchronize the dependencies between the consumers since they are all reading at the same time.

A sequence counter is used by producers and consumers to identify which slot in the buffer they are presently working on. Each producer/consumer can create their own sequence counters, but they may read the sequence counters of other producers/consumers. Producers and consumers check the counters to confirm that the slot they wish to write in is unlocked.

The disruptor is designed to address internal latency issues in Java processes. It is not a permanent store; messages remain in memory, and it is primarily intended to reduce latency between two or more worker threads serving as producers or consumers. It's faster than using `ArrayBlockingQueue`, which is Java's standard thread-safe class for this purpose. If we work with a high-throughput system that also has to ensure that each message is delivered as rapidly as feasible, this library becomes more appealing.

The disruptor is a lock-free data structure. The benefits are the same as the ones we described in *Chapter 6, HFT Optimization – Architecture and Operating System*, in the *Using lock-free data structures* section. In terms of Java, when compared to `LinkedList`, the disruptor ensures that elements are stored in a single contiguous block of memory and that elements are pre-fetched/loaded into the local CPU cache. Each logical item in memory is physically assigned to the next, and values are cached before they are needed. When compared to `LinkedList`, values are dispersed broadly across the heap memory when allocated, resulting in the loss of valuable CPU cache hits. A predetermined number of container objects are also pre-allocated in the ring buffer.

Because these containers are reference types or objects, they will reside on the heap, but they will be re-used once a buffer space is reclaimed. Because of this constant re-use, containers last indefinitely and are unaffected by the GC's STW pauses. To avoid indirectly allocating to the heap, we must remember that nested values on those objects are preserved as primitive values.

This section studied the LMAX disruptor; we will now review the conversant disruptor, another candidate for lock-free data structures.

Conversant disruptor

We will first talk about the design of a conversant disruptor. The underlying data structure of this disruptor is a ring buffer and a queue. The main advantage is to flush the entire queue as a batch using CAS comparison.

The conversant doesn't require any extract code; it is based on the Java `BlockingQueue` interface and is not domain-specific. It also works without the need for memory pre-allocation. The performance to push-pull an object in the multithreaded versions is 20 nanoseconds, whereas the push-pull variant takes 5 nanoseconds. This intrinsic quickness is primarily due to mechanical sympathy and simplicity. This implementation takes into account hardware specificities.

The conversant disruptor is different from the LMAX disruptor and is not a fork of the LMAX disruptor. They are essentially diverse in design and implementation, but they both have similar functionality. It makes sense to utilize the LMAX disruptor's implementation if we use the domain model. The conversant disruptor is the ideal choice for the typical use case of using a Java `BlockingQueue` interface as a fundamental data structure at the center of an application.

Agrona circular buffer

This is another available solution provided by the Agrona Project (`https://aeroncookbook.com/agrona/concurrent/`). Like the LMAX disruptor, it uses a specific interface, and we cannot simply swap classes that implement the Java queue interface with it. It offers one producer-one consumer (`OneToOneRingBuffer`), or many producers-one consumer (`ManyToOneRingBuffer`) solutions. It provides multiple options for the idle strategy, giving you more control over your reader and writer thread behavior. We reviewed the different lock-free data structures we can use in Java. We will now talk about the last part of this chapter, the logging and the DB access specific to Java programming.

Logging and DB access

As we explained in *Chapter 7, HFT Optimization – Logging, Performance, and Networking*, logging is critical for any trading system. It enables users to debug strategies, improve the return, compare theoretical and actual profit and loss, and store information in databases. It always requires a costly input/output. Therefore, logging cannot be done on the critical path. Like C++, a specific technique is needed to achieve performance in Java.

When creating a log, it can store trades in a database or build a string in a flat file. When generating a string to be pushed in the logging system, creating a string is a very time-consuming construction. It is essential to consider the speed of the system and the object's reaction. For instance, log4j zeroGC is a zero object creation logging framework, but it will generate the log message before putting it on the logger thread queue (in this case, the disruptor from LMAX). Your main application thread will need to generate the news, and this will have a cost on the performance. Nevertheless, this is still an acceptable solution for HFT systems.

You could develop your logging framework; we can still use the disruptor but store the unformatted log messages in the disruptor queue and then do the string creation in the consumer thread. You need to have objects added to the queue but writing the formatted logs into the appender can be done in a non-critical thread using a buffer without generating a string object.

We can find many frameworks, including java.util.logging, log4j, logback, and SLF4J. If we are building a microservice or another application with complete control over the execution environment, we oversee choosing a logging framework. Changing logging frameworks is usually as easy as searching and replacing, or in the worst-case scenario, a more complicated *structural* search and replace accessible in more powerful IDEs. If logging speed is crucial, which is the case in HFT, a logging API will always be better.

Choosing a framework will imply doing some benchmarking. When comparing the different frameworks, we need to keep in mind that the java.util.logging philosophy is that logging should be rare rather than the rule, while log4j 2.x and logback have a design for permanent logging.

Java util logging is less efficient than the logging API framework on the performance side because there is no buffer management, which affects logging speed significantly. The ability to buffer file I/O has the biggest influence on performance when configuring logging. The downside of activating buffer handling is the risk that the data is not pushed to disk if the process of writing this log fails. Another issue with buffering is that it might make it challenging to monitor the system in real time by tailing the log files. Buffering with a guaranteed maximum duration before flushing would be helpful if the various logging frameworks provided it. Having a flush every 100 ms would not have as large of an impact on system performance as flushing after each log statement, and it would allow humans to follow the log in real time.

Once we find the best logging infrastructure, we need to think about where to store the data. We can have a flat file or a database using the system logging framework.

We can review the advantages of these different media:

- `file`: Good for development and testing environments, but impacts the performance by the number of I/Os for the production environment. If the use of files is needed, we recommend a memory map file, which is blazing fast but not persisted.

- `Database`: Easy to retrieve and query but slow. The interaction with databases creates many objects. It might be better to send it on the wire (UDP or shared memory) and have an external process to do the logging. The downside is the need to ensure that the remote process keeps running.

- `Syslog`: Lets you send data on a UDP socket and is fast with low memory usage. We can configure `Syslog` in multiple ways. The logs can be kept locally or sent to a central server (`https://github.com/syslog-ng/syslog-ng`).

Let's see which process to choose for logging and database interactions.

External or internal thread?

When it comes to logging and database interactions, we have two choices: keep the logic in the main program using a dedicated thread or send the information to a reliable process using a straightforward and fast communication technique (UDP or shared memory).

If we choose to use logic in the main program, we add reliability, but we risk putting more pressure on the GC because of the object creations.

If we rely on a specialized external process, we risk sending information in an insecure way as we cannot guarantee that someone isn't listening on the other end. The benefit is that your main program does not need to worry about object creations coming from the logging or DB framework. We can send all the information from our main program as byte-encoded messages, which could be done with zero object creation. We are now free to code in the specialized node without worrying about having the GC kicking in too often. An excellent library to handle all the binary encoding can be found at `https://github.com/real-logic/simple-binary-encoding`.

For logging, fully encoding large messages could be too costly. A solution is to use a dictionary of the different messages assigned with numeric codes. When we want to send information to a specialized process, you encode the code and the values carrying the information. This can be done with zero objection creation and is amazingly fast. On the other hand, the specialized node is free to insert the data into the DB or recreate the string to log without having to worry about the pressure the object creation can have on the GC.

Summary

This chapter showed that JVM eases software developers' lives but impedes a trading system's performance. We demonstrated that by understanding how the JVM behaves under the hood, following good coding practice, and tuning the JVM, we could use Java as a serious programming language candidate for HFT. We studied in detail how to measure performance with Java. We know that measuring the execution time is the only evidence that code performs better after optimization. As we did with C++, we introduced high-performance data structures helping to get a performant code. We combined these data structures with the use of threads and thread pools. We concluded by discussing logging and database access, which are vital in HFT.

C++ and Java are the most used languages in HFT. The next chapter will talk about another programming language: **Python**. We will see how Python can be used in HFT and run fast using external libraries.

10

Python – Interpreted but Open to High Performance

In this chapter, we will introduce you to using **Python** in the **high-frequency trading** (**HFT**) system. Getting an HFT system using Python is problematic since Python was not built for speed and low latency. Because Python is the most used language and provides all the necessary libraries for data analysis, this language is the go-to in algorithmic trading. We will learn how to use HFT libraries in Python in this chapter.

We will cover the following topics:

- Introducing Python
- Python limitations in the context of HFT
- How to use a C++ library in Python

We will provide you with the tools capable of transforming any C++ code into code that can be used by Python.

We will start by explaining why we should use Python, even in HFT.

Introducing Python

Python is the most used programming language on the planet (one-third of all new code is written in Python). This language is used in software development. Python is a relatively simple language to learn and it is a high-level programming language that uses type inference, which is interpreted. Unlike C/C++, which requires you to concentrate on memory management and the hardware aspects of the computer you're programming, Python handles the internal implementation, such as memory management. As a consequence, this language will make it easier to concentrate on writing trading algorithms.

Python is a flexible language that can construct applications in any sector. Python has been extensively used for years. The Python community is vast enough to provide many important libraries for your trading strategy, spanning from data analytics, machine learning, data extraction, and runtime, to communication; the list of open source libraries is enormous.

Python also contains concepts seen in other languages, such as object-oriented, functional, and dynamic types on the software engineering side. Python has an abundance of online resources and a wealth of books that will guide you through every subject where Python may be used. For example, you can read *Learn Python Programming* published by Packt and written by Romano and Kruger. In trading, Python isn't the only language used. To undertake data analysis and construct trading models, we'll want to utilize Python. We'll utilize C, C++, or Java in production code. Source code will be compiled into an executable or bytecode using these languages and as a result, the program will be 100 times quicker than Python or R. Even though all three languages are slower than Python, we will utilize them to build libraries. These libraries will be wrapped so that they may be used with Python.

Python is an appropriate language for data analytics, which makes this language adaptable to create trading strategies. In the Packt book, *Learn Algorithmic Trading*, written by the authors of this book, we describe how to leverage this language and the pandas and NumPy libraries to create trading strategies.

Making use of Python for analytics

Python has all the features for quantitative researchers to be proficient in data analysis, and Python with `scrapy` or `beautifulsoup` can scrape websites (**data crawling**). It has many string libraries and the regular expression library, which can help clean data (**data cleaning**). The `sklearn` and `statsmodels` libraries help developers create models (**data modeling**). Matplotlib will help with **data visualization**.

Python is the go-to language for many developers in finance. It is essential to talk about this language in this chapter as Python is the most used programming language in the world. Raising the question of whether Python can do HFT is a fair question to ask. However, as we saw, it is difficult to use Python as it is because of its speed. We can, therefore, think about using other language libraries to exploit their speed.

Figure 10.1 represents the steps for building a trading strategy:

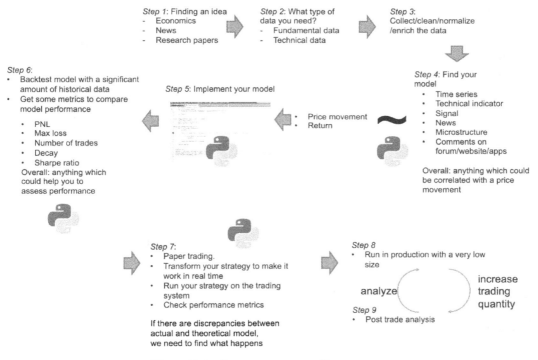

Figure 10.1 – Steps to create a trading strategy

HFT strategies are also made the same way by following these steps:

1. This part doesn't involve any programming since it just involves getting the trading idea which we will introduce in the market. In the case of an HFT strategy, we could use the example of a statistical arbitrage strategy. This strategy will assume that the derivative financial product and its underlying asset returns are correlated.

2. In this step, we can start getting market data to validate *Step 1*. From this moment, the use of Python will be beneficial for data analysis.

3. Any data transformations, such as normalizing and cleaning data to create the model, should be done with Python and the pandas and NumPy libraries.

4. We can use the `scikit-learn` package to build models. It is an open source Python-based machine learning package, and it supports classification, regression, clustering, and dimensionality reduction. In the case of our HFT strategy example, we will be able to correlate returns between the two assets by using regression models.

5. In *Steps 5* and *6*, we will implement a first model with the market data collected and backtest this model.

6. *Step 7* is essential to promote the need for speed in the trading strategy at this stage. Based on the prior data analytics done in the previous steps, we will be able to determine the time needed to enter and get out of a position to have a profitable trading strategy.

7. *Steps 8* and *9* are the final stage of the trading strategy, and will be an iteration between the actual profit and the predicted profit.

Looking at the last steps, we can observe that speed matters. We need to understand why Python has a slow execution; it will not be possible to use it for the last steps of the trading strategy.

Why is Python slow?

Python is a high-level language (higher than C or C++); therefore, it handles software such as memory allocation, memory deallocation, and pointers. Python memory management makes it easy for programmers to write Python programs. *Figure 10.2* depicts the Python chain. Python code is converted into Python bytecode initially and internally, the bytecode interpreter conversion occurs, and most of it is hidden from the developer. Bytecode is a lower-level programming language that is platform agnostic. The purpose of bytecode compilation is to speed up source code execution. The source code is converted to bytecode and then run one after another in Python's virtual machine to carry out the operations. Python's virtual machine is a built-in feature. Python code is interpreted rather than compiled to native code during execution; therefore, it is a little slower:

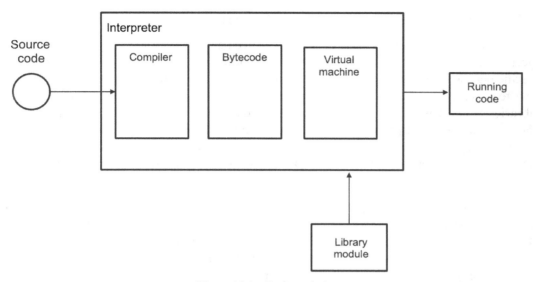

Figure 10.2 – Python chain

Python is first converted to bytecode. The **Python virtual machine** (**PVM**) then interprets and executes this bytecode.

Python is slow because of the following reasons:

- Python code is interpreted at runtime rather than converted to native code at compile time, unlike native languages such as C/C++. Python is an interpreted language, which means that the Python code we create must go through several abstraction steps before becoming machine code that can be executed.

- Compiler for **Just-in-Time** (**JIT**): Other interpreted languages, such as Java bytecode, run quicker than Python bytecode because they come with a JIT compiler that translates bytecode into native code at runtime, as explained in *Chapter 9, Java and JVM for Low-Latency Systems*. Python does not have a JIT compiler since it is challenging to create one due to the dynamic nature of the language. It's hard to predict what parameters will be supplied to a function, making optimization a difficult task.

- The **Global Interpreter Lock** (**GIL**) inhibits multi-threading by requiring the interpreter to run only one thread at a time inside a single process (that is, a Python interpreter instance).

Since we now understand why Python cannot achieve performance by itself, we will study how Python uses libraries in detail.

How do we use libraries in Python?

A library helps developers to reuse code that has been already created and tested for specific functionalities. We use libraries by downloading a pre-compiled version for a specific platform and by linking them to our software. By doing so, we don't have to rewrite code, and we increase the trust in our implementation by using tested code. Libraries can be statically linked to software, which increases the size of the executable. They can also be used dynamically, which means the executable will load the libraries when starting up. We can find these libraries with the **dynamic load library** (.dll) extension on Windows or with the **Shared Object** (.so) extension in the Linux world. Python uses dynamic libraries by using the import command.

Python standard modules are pretty numerous. The library includes built-in modules (written in C) that enable access to system capabilities such as file **input/output** (**I/O**) that would otherwise be unavailable to Python programmers, as well as Python modules that provide standardized solutions to many common programming issues. Some of these modules are specifically designed to promote and improve Python application portability by abstracting platform-specifics into platform-neutral **application programming interface** (**APIs**). Python has many other libraries that can help develop software. We introduce some of them here:

- **Google's TensorFlow library** was created in partnership with the Google Brain team. It's a high-level calculation library that's open source. It's also seen in deep learning and machine learning algorithms. There are a lot of Tensor operations in it.

- **Matplotlib** is a library that allows you to plot numerical data. This library is useful to display charts in data analytics. It is often used in designing trading strategies to visualize how they perform by having a visual presentation of important metrics such as profit and loss.

- **pandas**: For data scientists, pandas is an important library. It's an open source machine learning package with a range of analytic tools and configurable high-level data structures. It simplifies data analysis, processing, and cleansing. Sorting, re-indexing, iteration, concatenation, data conversion, visualizations, aggregations, and other operations are all supported by pandas.

- **NumPy**: **Numerical Python** is the name of the program. It is the most widely utilized library. It's a well-known machine learning package that can handle big matrices and multi-dimensional data. It has built-in mathematical functions for quick calculations. NumPy is used internally by libraries such as TensorFlow to conduct various Tensor operations. One of the most essential components of this library is the **array interface**.

- **SciPy**: **Scientific Python** is a high-level scientific computation package in Python that is open source. This library is based on a NumPy extension, and it uses NumPy to do complicated calculations. The numerical data code is kept in SciPy, whereas NumPy supports sorting and indexing array data. It is also commonly used by engineers and application developers.

- **Scrapy** is an open source toolkit for scraping information from web pages. It allows for highly rapid web crawling as well as high-level screen scraping. It's also suitable for data mining and automated data testing.

- **Scikit-learn** is a well-known Python toolkit for dealing with large amounts of data. Scikit-learn is a machine learning library that is open source. It supports a wide range of supervised and unsupervised methods, such as linear regression, classification, and clustering. NumPy and SciPy are often used in conjunction with this package.

We now know that Python can work efficiently with libraries. Let's now explain how C++ HFT libraries can work with Python.

Python and C++ for HFT

As we showed in the previous section, Python is too slow to be adequate for high-frequency trading. C++ is much faster and is the language of choice to get low latency. We are presenting in this section a means to integrate the two languages to unify both worlds. On one side, Python gives the developers ease and flexibility, and on the other side, C++ allows code to reach high performance and low latencies. In HFT, we need to have quantitative researchers and programmers build HFT strategies to run in the production environment. Having a Python ecosystem capable of using C++ libraries will allow **quants** (quantitative traders) to focus on their research and deploy code in production without the need for other resources. We will explain how to provide a standard interface to different C/C++ libraries. These C/C++ libraries will become Python modules. In other words, we will use them as dynamic libraries loaded in memory when we need them.

Let's first talk about motivation.

Using C++ in Python

We want to use C++ with Python for the following reasons:

- We already have a vast, well-tested, and reliable C++ library that we would like to use in Python. This might be a communication library or a library to help with a specific project goal, such as HFT.

- We want to transfer a vital portion of Python code to C++ to speed it up. C++ has a quicker execution speed, but it also lets us avoid the Python GIL restrictions.

- We wish to utilize Python test tools to test their systems on a wide scale.

We now know the motivation to use C++, and we will explain how we can achieve that next.

Using Python with C++

To use Python with C++, we have mainly two ways:

- **Extending** involves using C++ libraries with the `import` command. We will provide C++ libraries with a Python interface. The function prototypes are in Python and the implementation is in C++. It is equivalent to creating a shared C++ library that will be dynamically loaded when the software starts. This library will be used in a critical portion of a code.

- **Embedding** is a technique in which the end user runs a C++ application that calls the Python interpreter as a library procedure. It's the equivalent of adding scriptability to an existing program. Embedding is the process of adding calls into your C or C++ program after it has started up to set up the Python interpreter and invoke Python code later.

Extending modules is frequently the best approach to use highly performant code. The operation of creating a C++ library and using it will be the code solution to what we are proposing. Embedding requires more effort than simply extending. Unlike embedding, extending gives us more power and freedom. When we are embedding, many valuable Python tools and automation techniques become significantly more difficult, if not impossible, to employ.

A mapping of one object to another is referred to as **binding**. Binding is used to link one language with another one. For instance, if we create a library in C or C++, we can use this library with Python. The modification of these libraries requires their recompilation.

When an existing C or C++ library designed for a specific purpose has to be utilized from Python, Python bindings are employed.

To understand why Python bindings are necessary, consider how Python and C++ store data and the problems that this might generate. C or C++ saves data in memory in the most miniature feasible format. If you use `uint8_t`, the space required to store data is 8 bits if structure padding is not considered.

On the other hand, Python uses objects allocated in the heap. In Python, integers are large integers whose size varies depending on their data. This means that for each integer transmitted across the border, bindings convert a C integer to a Python integer.

When preparing data to be transported from Python to C or vice versa, Python bindings execute a method similar to marshaling by changing an object's memory representation to a data format acceptable for storage or transmission.

Boost.Python library

This library allows you to combine Python and C++. It enables you to use C++ objects and functions in Python and vice versa without using any further tools outside the C++ compiler. There is no need to modify the C++ code. The library is made to encapsulate C++ APIs without being intrusive:

1. To illustrate how this tool works, we will work on this example. This example illustrates how to compile the `add` function using a C++ compiler and how to use it in Python code. Let's assume we want to use the C++ `add` function defined as follows:

    ```
    int add(int x, int y)
    {
        return x+y;
    }
    ```

2. This function can be exposed to Python by writing a `Boost.Python` wrapper:

    ```
    #include <boost/python.hpp>

    BOOST_PYTHON_MODULE(math_ext)
    {
        using namespace boost::python;
        def("add", add);
    }
    ```

3. We will build a shared library with the preceding code, which will create a
    .dll or .so file. We will be able to use this library with Python by using the
    import command:

```
>>> import math_ext
>>> print math_ext.add(1,2)
3
```

As seen in the preceding example, the Boost.Python library is pretty easy to use and is
a comprehensive library. It allows us to perform practically anything the C-API provides
but in C++. With this package, we do not have to write C-API code, and when we bind
code, either it compiles perfectly or fails.

If we already have a C++ library to bind, it's undoubtedly one of the most acceptable
options currently available. However, when we simply need to rebuild a simple C/C++
code, Cython is recommended.

Cython

The **Cython** programming language is a Python superset that enables programmers to run
C/C++ functions and declare C/C++ types on variables and class properties. This allows
the compiler to build C code from a highly efficient Cython code. The C code is created
once and then compiled with all significant C/C++ compilers. Technically, we write code
in .pyx files, and those files are translated into C code, then compiled into CPython
modules. Cython code can resemble standard Python (and pure Python files are valid
.pyx Cython files), but it includes additional information such as variable types. Cython
can create speedier C code by using this optional type. Both pure Python functions and C
and C++ functions (and C++ methods) can be called from code in Cython files.

We are going to illustrate how to convert the add function into a more optimized
function. This function will be compiled by a C/C++ compiler, and then we will use the
function in regular Python code:

1. Let's reuse the same example we used earlier with the add function, and we will
    save this code to add.pyx:

```
def add(a,b):
    return a+b
add(3,4)
```

2. Then, we create the `setup.py` file, which works like a build automation tool such as Makefile:

```
from setuptools import setup
from Cython.Build import cythonize

setup(
    ext_modules = cythonize("add.pyx")
)
```

3. We will build the Cython file by using the command line:

```
$ python setup.py build_ext --inplace
```

It will create the `add.so` file in Unix or `add.pyd` in Windows.

4. We can now use this file by using the `import` command:

```
>>> import add
7
```

That's an example of how to compile C/C++ code based on Python code.

When designing Python bindings for C or C++, Cython is a highly complex tool that may provide you with a lot of power. It gives a Python-like technique for building code that manually manages the GIL, which may significantly speed up certain issues, but we didn't explore it fully here. However, because that Python-like language isn't precisely Python, there's a slight learning curve for figuring out which bits of C and Python go where.

Using ctypes/CFFI to accelerate Python code

ctypes is a tool in the standard library for creating Python bindings.

With this tool, we load the C library, and we call the function in the Python program. To create the Python bindings in ctypes, we can follow these steps:

1. Load your library.

2. Wrap the input parameters.

3. Indicate `ctypes` as the return type of the function.

The fact that ctypes is part of the standard library gives it a significant edge over the previous tools. It also doesn't necessitate any further steps because the Python application handles everything. Furthermore, the principles employed are simple. However, the absence of automation makes increasingly complicated jobs more complex, which was not the case with the previous tools we saw.

The **C Foreign Function Interface** for Python is known as **CFFI**. Python bindings are created using a more automated method. We design and utilize Python bindings in a variety of ways using CFFI. There are two modes to choose from:

- **API versus ABI**: API mode generates a complete Python module using a C compiler, but **Application Binary Interface** (**ABI**) mode imports the shared library and interacts with it directly. It's challenging to get the structures and arguments right without using the compiler, and the API model is strongly recommended in the manual.

- **Out-of-line versus inline**: The difference between these two modes is a speed versus convenience trade-off.

The Python bindings are compiled every time a script runs in inline mode. This is useful since it eliminates the need for a second construction phase; however, it will slow down the software.

Out-of-line mode necessitates an additional stage in which the Python bindings are generated once and then used each time the application is executed. This is far quicker, although that may not be a factor.

Ctypes appear to need less effort than CFFI. While this is true for simple use cases, due to the automation of most of the function wrapping, CFFI scales to more significant projects considerably better than ctypes. The user experience with CFFI is also pretty different. You can use ctypes to import a pre-existing C library into a Python application. CFFI, on the other hand, generates a new Python module that can be loaded in the same way as any other Python module.

SWIG

Simplified Wrapper and Interface Generator (**SWIG**) is not like any of the other tools listed previously. It's a comprehensive tool for creating C and C++ bindings for various languages, not just Python. In some applications, the ability to develop bindings for many languages might be pretty valuable. It does, of course, come at a cost in terms of complexity. The configuration file of SWIG is pretty cumbersome, and it takes some time to get it right.

We illustrate the use of SWIG with the following code. Suppose we have some C functions we want to be added to Python:

```c
/* File : math.c */

int add_1(int n) {
    return n+1;
}

int add(int n, int m) {
    return n+m;
}
```

The configuration file of SWIG is made by an interface file. We will now describe this interface.

Writing an interface file

With this method, we write an interface file that SWIG will use.

This is an example of the interface file:

```
/* example.i */
%module math
%{
/* Put header files here or function declarations like below
*/
extern int add_1(int n);
extern int add(int n, int m);
%}

extern int add_1(int n);
extern int add(int n, int m);
```

We will now build a Python module in the following section.

Building a Python module

The last step to turning C code into a Python module is as follows:

```
unix % swig -python math.i
unix % gcc -c math.c math_wrap.c \
       -I/usr/local/include/python3.7
unix % ld -shared example.o example_wrap.o -o _example.so
```

We will use this module by using the `import` command:

```
>>> import math
>>> math.add_1(5)
6
>>> math.add(5,2)
7
```

We can talk about many other ways of using C/C++ in Python. This part aims to build an exhaustive list of all the ways of accomplishing the migration of a C++ library for Python use but to tackle the problem of speed that Python has by using a high-speed library.

Improving the speed of Python code in HFT

The critical components we defined during the previous chapters must run at high speed. Using any of the tools we described previously will help you create C/C++-like code and create performant Python code using libraries. It is essential to begin constructing a new algorithm in Python utilizing NumPy and SciPy while avoiding looping code by leveraging the vectorized idioms of both libraries. In reality, this means attempting to replace any nested `for` loops with similar calls to NumPy array functions. The purpose is to prevent the CPU from wasting time on the Python interpreter instead of crunching numbers for trading strategies.

However, there are situations when an algorithm cannot be efficiently expressed in simple vectorized NumPy code. The following is the recommended method in this case:

1. Find the primary bottleneck in the Python implementation and isolate it in a dedicated module-level function.

2. If there is a small but well-maintained C/C++ version of the same algorithm, you may develop a Cython wrapper for it and include a copy of the library's source code. Or you can use any of the other techniques we talked about previously.

3. Place the Python version of the function in the tests and use it to ensure that the built extension's results match the gold standard, easy-to-debug Python version.

4. Check whether it is possible to create coarse-grained parallelism for multi-processing by utilizing the `joblib.Parallel` class once the code has been optimized (not a simple bottleneck spottable by profiling).

Figure 10.3 depicts the function calls to C++ when there is a need for low-latency functions for HFT:

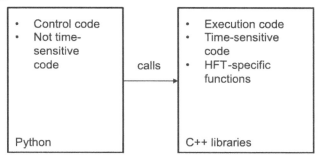

Figure 10.3 – Python and C++ interactions

The control code, which could be used to decide to liquidate a position, can be calculated in Python. C++ will be in charge of the execution of the liquidation by using the speed of these libraries.

The critical components include the following:

- Limit order book
- Order manager
- Gateways
- HFT execution algorithm

All these should be implemented in C/C++ or Cython.

Some companies that have compiler engineers invest in C++ code generation from Python. We will have a tool parsing Python code and generating C++ code in this situation. This C++ code will be compiled and run like any other code, and Python code, in general, can be used for coding trading strategies. Most people in charge of creating trading strategies have more Python skills than C++ knowledge. Therefore, it is easier for them to develop everything in Python than convert Python into C++ libraries used in the C++ trading system.

In this section, we learned how to improve Python code using C++. We will now wrap up this chapter.

Summary

In this chapter, we illustrated how to use Python in HFT. Python is not a language for performance and low latency, and we highlighted how to use other languages such as C++ to get to the same performance level. You are now capable of using any HFT-specific C/C++ code in your Python code.

We will now finish this book by opening up to some new topics in the next chapter, such as achieving less than 500 nanoseconds for tick-to-trade latency with **Field Programmable Gate Array** (**FPGA**), and opening HFT systems to cryptocurrencies.

11

High-Frequency FPGA and Crypto

Welcome to the final chapter of this book. In the previous chapters, we saw how to optimize traditional trading to obtain a **high-frequency trading (HFT)** system working with a tick-to-trade latency of 5 microseconds. In the next section, we will discuss how to improve this latency to 500 nanoseconds using advanced hardware optimization. Finally, we will conclude this book by exploring the difference between traditional and cryptocurrency trading.

Our goal in this chapter is to show that the software solution we used in the past chapters has limitations in achieving latency lower than 1 microsecond. Using a specific piece of hardware, we will show you that it is possible. The second goal is to apply the optimization we explained in this book to cryptocurrencies. We will elaborate by extending the design to the cloud.

In this chapter, we will cover the following topics:

- How **Field Programmable Gate Arrays** (**FPGAs**) hardware can perform for HFT to reduce latency

- How to trade cryptocurrencies with HFT techniques

- How to build a trading system in the cloud

Important Note

In order to guide you among all the optimizations, you can refer to the following list of icons that represent a group of optimizations lowering the latency by a specific number of microseconds:

: Lower than 20 microseconds

: Lower than 5 microseconds

: Lower than 500 nanoseconds

You will find these icons in the headings of this chapter.

Reducing latencies with FPGA

In this section, we will look at the **Field Programmable Gate Array** (**FPGA**), investigate the evolution of the fierce competition of speed in HFT, and then discuss the motivation for using FPGAs in modern HFT. We will also explore how an FPGA itself works, the design of an FPGA-based trading system, and the advantages and disadvantages of using FPGAs in HFT systems.

Evolution of the fierce competition of speed in HFT

As we have seen in this book, HFT has received a lot of attention, become extremely popular, and also grown to become a significant component of all financial market liquidity and trading. We have also seen that HFT (as the name implies) is all about speed/latency – the speed at which HFT systems and algorithms can analyze market data information, send order requests, and execute trades.

To summarize, **latency** refers to the total time to travel from one point to another for a data packet. However, specifically in trading, latency means the time, in *nanoseconds/ microseconds/milliseconds*, that it takes from when a market participant receives a market update to when they can get their order to the exchange. Improving technology is the key to winning on trades at the best prices before the price moves, or some other market participant trades against the orders at a cost, or before the orders at that price are canceled. This is true for all market participants – manual traders, market makers, statistical arbitrage traders, or high-frequency traders.

For HFT, since speed is the critical component, the faster a participant's system becomes at processing and trade execution, the higher the profit they receive. So, there is endless fierce competition in this space, with competitors constantly investing massive amounts of money allocated to more powerful and faster trading solutions approaching the ability to trade securities/derivatives/stocks/financial instruments in a few nanoseconds. In addition to increasing profits by increasing the speed of HFT systems, the firms that fall behind by failing to keep up with continuous technological innovations will be unable to compete and, therefore, might go out of business.

To keep up, investment banks, hedge funds, and HFT firms spend massive amounts of money on faster software, co-location setups closest to the exchanges, and networks with the lowest latencies – we saw these in *Chapter 7, HFT Optimization – Logging, Performance, and Networking*. Participants purchase the fastest servers, processors, memory, and network cards when optimizing the hardware itself. Still, even that is not enough anymore – now, they need to invest in hardware acceleration-based solutions. The approach to hardware acceleration is to offload compute/CPU-intensive portions of trading systems to custom processors, **graphics processing units** (**GPUs**), or FPGAs. There are numerous solutions to scaling hardware computing performance. But, finally, right now, FPGAs are responsible for the technological revolution as far as HFT systems and algorithms are concerned. FPGAs have exciting and specific characteristics that enable them to execute relatively simple trading strategies/algorithms magnitudes (1000x) faster than even the most highly-optimized software solutions.

Introduction to FPGA

In this section, we will introduce the FPGA and then investigate the details of the components of an FPGA and its characteristics. An FPGA is hardware (in this case, a chip) that can be programmed (although not easily) for whatever purpose is required. It can also be reprogrammed as needed and as mentioned already, has the advantages of ultra-low latency, high performance, and energy efficiency.

To understand where an FPGA fits in; you can think of a performance spectrum for processors/chips. We have **central processing units (CPUs)** on one end, which offer a generic and flexible instruction set. The instructions available can be combined in many different ways to perform almost any task, making them general purpose. But this flexibility leads to slow/poor performance when performing these tasks since it is not specialized; that is, a couple of instructions have to be executed to achieve any task.

On the other end, we have **application-specific integrated circuits (ASICs)**, which are extremely fast because they are custom built with a specific/single task in mind, but they cannot be changed once built. They also cost a lot of time and money to develop. For example, a chip is used to mine Bitcoin.

FPGAs are in between CPUs and ASICs on this performance spectrum.

What is an FPGA?

An FPGA is nothing more than a chip that contains thousands, sometimes millions, of **core logic blocks (CLBs)** – CLB is Xilinx terminology. A comparison can be drawn to the microprocessors in laptops and smartphones, among others, which are composed of millions of logic blocks called **Lookup Tables (LUTs)**. These contain Boolean logical operations such as AND, OR, NAND, and XOR, which are also referred to as **gates**. Additionally, LUTs work by acting as an n-input function that reduces to a single output. This means Xilinx's UltraScale CLB has a six-input LUT architecture (though this can be reconfigured to two five-input LUTs with unique outputs each). So, you can implement a sequence of Boolean operations in the LUT (that is, a six-input function can be reduced to a single LUT).

In the FPGA, the CLBs can be configured and combined to process tasks, but compared to CPUs, they are not bogged down by extra hardware to slow them down. FPGAs are not great at control-flow-heavy operations but are fantastic for data flow applications. The *bog down* that CPUs see is that FPGAs are inherently parallel in the way they operate (you are simultaneously evaluating many n-input functions in parallel to achieve the same result). Still, they aren't infinite in terms of their performance. There's a steep penalty if your logic functions become too complex and your data buses become too wide (therefore, slowing the clock rate, you can close the design's synthesis).

FPGAs do not *run code* but rather implement logic circuits. FPGAs let you implement application-specific functions directly in hardware, slower than an ASIC would be but faster than executing a single code path on a CPU to do the same thing, potentially. FPGAs can be used to carry out extremely specific tasks and perform them extremely quickly and can also execute tasks in parallel simultaneously. Algorithms such as trading strategies are implemented directly on the FPGA.

The first FPGA was invented in 1985; the chip had a very small capacity, and it was very hard to implement logic on it. Modern FPGAs have multi-million gate counts and can accommodate very complex and large-scale designs. The major vendors are AMD, which manufactured Xilinx, Intel, which designed Altera, and Achronix, among others.

Characteristics of FPGA

In this section, we will discuss the important characteristics of FPGAs, which will help you understand and make it obvious in the next section why HFT firms benefit greatly from using FPGAs.

Programmability

We have already discussed in the previous section that FPGAs contain logic-blocks/CLBs/LUTs connected with configurable switches and flexible fabric. This makes them relatively easily programmable (and reprogrammable) and capable of supporting complex trading algorithms.

Capacity

Modern FPGAs are equipped with millions of CLBs, which yield tremendous capacity. Not only can the algorithms be extremely complex, but they are also capable of scaling tremendously. Capacity comes at the cost of physics, though; a signal needs to propagate across the *die*. Conceptually, processor dies are just the silicon semiconductor material on which the CPU processors reside. As the silicon dies get larger, so do the times for signal propagation. Capacity is huge but not unlimited. In contrast, a CPU has a few points where physics is your enemy; implementing an FPGA requires some knowledge of electrical engineering along with logic design to be successful.

Parallelism

FPGAs, unlike CPUs, do not have a fixed processor architecture – meaning no **operating system** (**OS**) overhead and interrupts, and so on. On FPGAs, the processing paths are parallel, so different functions/operations are not competing for resources but can instead be running in parallel. On a modern FPGA, a single chip can have 10+ code paths running on it simultaneously at different rates.

This parallel architecture on the FPGA is key to it being able to execute buy and sell trades at maximum capacity and speed. One caveat here is that the algorithms or mathematical computations need to be broken down into a set of tasks. Only then can they be processed within different cycles in parallel.

The parallelism also makes FPGAs very resilient and capable of providing a high level of service. Being stable and self-contained, FPGAs make the whole HFT infrastructure function smoothly and makes the infrastructure resilient against changes in non-FPGA hardware and software.

Determinism

As explained in *Chapter 4*, *HFT System Foundations – From Hardware to OS*, when executing instructions on CPUs, there is an element of possible non-determinism (out-of-order processors). Additionally, the OS and event-driven interrupts can lead to many control paths that lead to a lot of randomness. CPUs are great for general purpose tasks that evolve/change over time but not great for guaranteeing performance metrics.

With FPGAs, we can implement hardware algorithms, which leads to a high level of determinism. So, when there are bursts in market activity and networks can be overloaded with data, FPGAs can process and provide market data very quickly and with low variance. An FPGA goes through the same sequence of states each time, providing repeatable and predictable latency/performance.

We talked about FPGA features; we will now talk about how the HFT system can leverage FPGAs.

Diving into FPGA trading systems

FPGA trading systems are the ones that utilize low-latency, high-frequency, and algorithmic trading strategies. These systems need to perform many different tasks and do so within a few nanoseconds. Some of the tasks that such a system would need to perform are described in the following subsections.

Market data

The very first task of an FPGA is to analyze market data from multiple stock exchanges. This involves building the network protocol stack and addressing components such as the Ethernet layer, the **Internet Protocol** (**IP**) layer, the **User Datagram Protocol** (**UDP**) layer, and market data protocols.

Network stacks

Since network **input/output (I/O)** is handled at the kernel and OS layers in an FPGA setup, building the network stack on the FPGA is often the first step in optimizing a trading system. This means handling the Ethernet layer, the IP layer, the UDP layer, and to some extent, the **transmission control protocol (TCP)** layer. There are also opportunities to use hybrid stacks – there's a TCP stack that runs on the host to deal with weird circumstances, while the FPGA can receive TCP market data and decode it until one of these weird states happens (which is rare). The TCP straight in an FPGA is doable but difficult and often a non-elegant solution.

Feed arbitration and replication

Most trading exchanges disseminate market data on multiple channels for redundancy and fairness reasons. FPGA feed handlers that consume market data need to handle A/B feed arbitration (in HFT, it is pretty common to have two channels of communication, A and B, for redundancy when receiving market data) and deal with the redundant feeds. Conversely, trading exchanges or market data providers also need to use similar FPGA technology to process and distribute large volumes of market data updates.

Feed parsers and normalizers

FPGA feed handlers need to process different market data protocols – the **FIX Adapted for STreaming (FAST)** protocol is a very common example. Even the market data update semantics can differ based on the exchange, and FPGA market data parsers and normalizers need to deal with these optimally.

Trading signals

After processing market data received from the exchange, the next step is to calculate different trading signals for the algorithm to find trading opportunities. These trading signals find mispricing in prices and/or orders to see where some profitable trading possibilities exist.

Low-latency execution algorithms

After the trading signals/models are updated based on new market updates, we use the output to exploit fleeting trading opportunities by sending orders as quickly as possible to the market. Algorithms have to be extremely high-performant to beat other orders, that is, get to the exchange before other orders rush for the same opportunity.

Considerations

FPGA trading systems need to be easily customizable and capable of being optimized and tested when handling live updates. Another consideration is to push trading algorithms as close to the **Network Interface Cards** (**NICs**) and minimize system latencies to the maximum possible extent. In this first part, we introduced FPGAs, their characteristics, and how they can be used in HFT systems. We will now talk about the advantages of trading systems built with an FPGA.

Advantages of FPGA trading systems

This section will investigate the advantages that HFT firms get from using FPGAs. In *Chapter 1*, *Fundamentals of a High-Frequency Trading System*, we explained the advantages of using HFT systems. FPGAs help make HFT systems even faster. This section will summarize the main benefits of using FPGAs in trading systems.

Higher profits

HFT algorithms that use FPGAs can beat other participants by being able to execute orders at a price before others. FPGA algorithms can detect and act on opportunities before other participants have a chance to react, and execution at the best prices leads to increased profits right away. The reprogrammable nature of FPGAs means you can change the algorithm's behavior and trading parameters quickly and stay ahead of the competition. The scalability that FPGA trading systems offer leads to being able to execute multiple trades on many instruments simultaneously and leads to even higher revenues. FPGA-based trading systems also allow HFT firms to create safer trading environments, save expenses, and so increase revenue even more.

Security compliance

Over the past several years, trading operations and HFT specifically have come under increased tightening of regulations and risk management. HFT firms have, therefore, been forced to look for new solutions to monitor trading activities and detect/handle potential losses. Traditional CPU-driven systems often have a limitation of being able to view/compute portfolio risks instead of being in real time, so not providing the required level of security. FPGAs allow for near-real-time risk assessment on portfolios and allow firms to meet the stringent risk/regulation requirements that regulatory bodies ask for.

Cheaper maintenance

Relying on FPGAs means HFT businesses can reduce expenses related to the maintenance of computer systems. A single well-designed FPGA can replace a lot of generic CPUs and help bring down company expenses by saving on energy costs, office rentals, and system cooling expenses. Being reprogrammable also means that the device can be modified after installation to meet evolving requirements, which leads to more cost savings related to maintenance.

Disadvantages of FPGA trading systems

We have discussed the advantages that having an FPGA brings to HFT firms; now, this section will look at what disadvantages an FPGA system has.

Hardware cost

FPGA chips are expensive; they can sometimes be significantly more expensive than traditional servers. Traditional servers are also a more cost-effective solution when it comes to running many processes that are not super performance sensitive. FPGAs tend to be hosted inside a normal server anyway, so FPGAs do not replace traditional servers. So, depending on the applications, if the systems are not well thought out and well designed, FPGA chips can lead to many hardware costs.

Development and debugging cost

FPGA chips are much harder to program algorithms for than traditional CPUs. Verilog is generally harder to develop, debug, and troubleshoot algorithms than traditional languages such as C, C++, Java, and so on. The tools and APIs available are much fewer too and quite limited for FPGAs compared to other languages. Debugging FPGA algorithms is also much harder than debugging traditional algorithms due to limited logging abilities and complex decision paths on the chip.

Additionally, there are many capable developers for traditional software development languages, but finding FPGA developers is harder due to less availability and higher costs. There are ongoing efforts to make the development process itself easier and faster. New tools are emerging, such as high-level synthesis tools that convert algorithms to gate-level designs. They have limitations but could support rapid time-to-market or at least prototyping. There are a lot of such tools on the market today, but some popular examples would be **Simulink** (provided by Matlab), **ISE**, **Vivado**, **Vitis**, **ChipScope** (provided by Xilinx), and **Altera Quartus** (provided by Intel; Altera was a company acquired by Intel).

Added trading risk

Generally, FPGA-driven HFT systems and trading algorithms reduce the risk caused by failing software components. But poorly designed or tested FPGAs can have the opposite impact and increase risks. This can be from bugs in the FPGA systems that only trigger under certain market conditions and/or trading parameters, leading to incorrect FPGA behavior. Another factor with FPGA systems is that they are extremely fast in their reactions and order executions, which means that a berserk FPGA system issue can cause significant losses before traditional risk systems can detect the problem and shut them down. In all these cases, firms experience substantial trading losses, regulatory and compliance actions/fines, and can even go bankrupt due to massive losses.

Strategy complexity limits

As mentioned in the *What is FPGA?* section, FPGAs are best suited for designing algorithms that maximize the parallel architecture and deterministic nature of FPGAs. Additionally, building and debugging algorithms for the FPGA is an expensive, time-consuming, and complicated process. Both these factors mean a limit to how complex a trading strategy/algorithm can be built for the FPGA to maximize its benefits. So, implementing a very difficult algorithm with a lot of complex statistical signals, machine learning components, and execution behavior on FPGAs is not realistic/practical.

Final words on FPGAs

The fierce competition for speed in HFT has been an ongoing phenomenon since the year 2000 and is unlikely to end anytime soon. HFT firms will need to continue adopting emerging technological innovations to maintain their edge in the market, and failure to do so might lead to losses and extinction.

FPGAs, which we discussed in this section, are an example of these recently emerged technologies. The parallel architecture and deterministic nature allow FPGAs to deliver the lowest possible latencies in processing market data and order executions. Using FPGAs to accelerate HFT engines to nanoseconds provides many business benefits, such as increased trade volumes and higher profits.

In *Chapter 6, HFT Optimization – Architecture and Operating System*, and *Chapter 7, HFT Optimization – Logging, Performance, and Networking*, we enounced the main guidelines to optimize hardware and software for HFT. We saw in all the other chapters how to apply these optimizations concretely with C++, Java, and Python. The FPGA finishes this book's quest of making trading systems faster. We will now talk about the opposite in terms of performance: HFT for cryptocurrencies.

Exploring HFT with cryptocurrencies

In this section, we will describe the differences between HFT in cryptocurrencies and HFT in traditional assets. There are many other resources on crypto-assets, such as Packt's *Complete Cryptocurrency and Blockchain Course* (video) written by Ravinder Deol, Rob Percival, and Thomas Wiesner (`https://www.packtpub.com/product/data/9781839211096`). We will focus on the HFT in crypto by explaining how transactions work and how the exchange works to build low-latency transactions in this area. Cryptocurrencies have been getting into the trading world since Bitcoin became a major value on the crypto market. More and more companies got attracted by the benefit of trading cryptocurrencies. Like any other assets, hedge funds and trading firms started building HFT systems for digital assets.

What is crypto?

Cryptocurrencies are digital assets that are produced with the use of computer networking software. This computer network is not reliant on any central authority, such as a government or bank, to uphold or maintain it. **Bitcoin** (**BTC**) and other cryptocurrencies use blockchain technology, and it keeps track of who owns something and produces a tamper-proof record of transactions. This is a totally decentralized system.

The term *cryptocurrency* refers to the cryptographic techniques used by developers to combat fraud. These breakthroughs solved a problem that plagued previous attempts to develop totally digital currencies: how to prevent users from replicating their holdings and spending them twice.

Individual units of cryptocurrency are referred to as **coins** or **tokens**. Some are exchange units for goods or services, while others are designed to help computer networks that undertake more complex financial transactions function.

The way to produce Bitcoin is through mining. **Mining** is a time-consuming process. This process involves computers solving difficult puzzles to verify the legitimacy of network transactions. Owners of those computers may be rewarded with newly created Bitcoin. Other cryptocurrencies create and distribute tokens in different methods, with some having a far smaller environmental impact.

How do crypto transactions work?

Even if we can buy crypto assets using decentralized transactions, a centralized exchange is likely the most accessible for new traders. Customers have more trust in centralized exchanges regulating transactions as a third party. These exchanges make money by collecting fees for various services and selling cryptocurrency at market prices.

There are decentralized exchanges for more advanced traders, with cheaper costs than those paid by centralized systems. They are harder to utilize and need more technical expertise, but they may provide some security benefits because no one target for a cyberattack exists. Peer-to-peer transactions are another way to exchange cryptocurrencies. We have defined what digital currencies are, so we will now learn how they are built.

What is a blockchain?

A blockchain is a distributed data ledger. It maintains the transaction history for each crypto unit, showing how asset ownership has changed over time. New blocks are added to the chain's frontend when transactions are recorded in **blocks**. A blockchain file is always kept on several computers throughout a network rather than in a single location. It is often available to all network users. Because there is no one weak spot vulnerable to hacking, human mistakes, or software mistakes, it is both transparent and difficult to modify.

Cryptography (a combination of advanced mathematics and computer science) connects the blocks. Any attempt to alter data disrupts the cryptographic links between blocks, allowing machines on the network to quickly recognize it as fake.

What is cryptocurrency mining?

Cryptocurrency mining refers to checking recent crypto transactions and adding new blocks to the blockchain. Mining computers choose pending transactions from a pool and verify that the sender has enough money to finish the transaction. This is done by comparing the transaction information to the blockchain's transaction history. A second check verifies that the sender used their private key to authorize the cash transfer.

Mining machines assemble legitimate transactions into a new block and try to discover a solution to the complicated process of building the cryptographic link to the previous block. When a machine successfully generates the link, it saves the block to its copy of the blockchain file and broadcasts the change to the rest of the network.

Similarities between traditional asset trading and cryptocurrency trading

We will first look at the main similarities between these two worlds.

What drives the price of cryptocurrencies?

Like the traditional markets, markets for cryptocurrencies are driven by supply and demand. Due to their decentralized nature, they may sound immune to many economic and political issues plaguing traditional currencies. However, we can still observe some correlation between economic metrics and crypto-asset prices.

By comparing the traditional asset, we can notice that the following variables can have a significant influence on their prices:

- The total quantity of coins in circulation and the speed they are released and removed will also impact the price.

- Market capitalization refers to the total worth of all currencies in circulation, as well as how users perceive this value to be changing.

- The way some crypto-assets are perceived in the media and their popularity.

- Integration: Easiness of integrating into existing infrastructure.

- Regulatory events and security issues can impact cryptocurrencies and traditional assets.

All these parameters can also be a part of price movements for regular stocks, bonds, or other derivatives. The factors that are specific to cryptocurrencies are described as follows.

Cost of production

Mining is the process of creating cryptocurrency tokens. The capacity of cryptocurrency to function is thanks to a decentralized network of miners. The protocol creates cryptocurrency tokens and any fees paid to the miners by the trading parties. As mining expenses grow, so must the value of the cryptocurrency. Miners will not mine if the mining money is not worth paying their expenses. Because miners are necessary to operate the blockchain, the price will have to climb as long as demand exists.

Cryptography exchanges

Bitcoin and Ether, two popular cryptocurrencies, are traded on various platforms. The most popular tokens are listed on every exchange. On the other hand, some smaller tokens may only be available on a few exchanges, limiting access to some investors. Some wallet providers will compile quotes for any collection of cryptocurrencies from many exchanges, but they will charge a fee, increasing the cost of investing. In addition, if a cryptocurrency is lightly traded on a tiny exchange, the spread taken by the exchange may be too wide for certain investors. More exchanges listing a cryptocurrency can increase the number of investors ready and able to acquire it, therefore, raising demand. When demand rises, so does the price.

Market participants and competitors

There are dozens of different cryptocurrencies, and new projects and tokens are launched daily. New rivals have a low entrance barrier. However, developing a viable cryptocurrency also involves the creation of a cryptocurrency user network. A useful blockchain application may quickly build a network, particularly if it fixes a defect in a competitor's service. If a new competitor develops traction, it depletes the value of the incumbent, causing the incumbent's price to fall while the new competitor's token's price rises.

Crypto-specific governance

Cryptocurrency networks seldom follow a set of rigid rules. Developers make changes to projects depending on the feedback they receive from the community. Some tokens, known as governance tokens, allow their owners a vote in how a project develops in the future, including how a token is mined and utilized. Stakeholder consensus is required before any modifications to a token's governance can be implemented. Going from a proof-of-work to a proof-of-stake system will render most of the expensive mining equipment in data centers and people's basements obsolete. Cryptocurrency values will surely be affected as a result of this. The long process of updating software to improve protocols, on the other hand, may limit the upside potential of Bitcoin values. It is detrimental to present stakeholders if an update that would unleash value for Bitcoin investors takes months to implement.

Crypto-specific regulations

Cryptocurrencies are securities or commodities. **Securities and Exchange Commission (SEC)** or **Commodity Futures Trading Commission (CFTC)** could eventually regulate the crypto assets. There is no clear way of knowing which one of them will apply rules to this type of trading. However, the regulation will help the trading of these assets. **Exchange-Traded Funds** (**ETFs**) and futures contracts, for example, provide investors wider access to cryptocurrencies, enhancing their value.

Furthermore, regulation may allow investors to take short positions or gamble against the price of cryptocurrencies via futures or options contracts. This should result in more accurate price discovery and less volatility in Bitcoin pricing. Meanwhile, if a government creates rules against crypto, the crypto value will drop significantly.

What type of orders and in what market can we trade cryptocurrencies?

The same basic trading order types are available on most retail trading platforms:

- Market order
- Limit order
- Stop order

Most **decentralized exchanges** (**DEXs**) only provide market orders at the moment, whereas most big, **centralized exchanges** (**CEXs**) offer a full range of orders (market, limit, stop, and others). Additional crypto exchanges are expected to include these capabilities as the crypto trading ecosystem grows. While buying and selling cryptocurrencies on platforms designed for easy user experiences may be quite similar, there are numerous key differences when dealing with these two distinct asset classes.

What is the spread in cryptocurrency trading?

The spread is the difference between an asset's advertised on top of the orderbook for buy and sale prices. When you open a position on a crypto market, we observe two prices, much like many other traditional marketplaces. You trade at the purchase price, which is slightly above the market price, to begin a long position. You trade at the selling price, which is somewhat below the market price, if you wish to initiate a short position.

In crypto trading, what is leverage?

Leverage is a method of acquiring many cryptocurrencies without paying the entire worth of our deal upfront. Instead, we make a tiny down payment called a **margin**. When we terminate a leveraged position, the entire magnitude of the trade determines your profit or loss. This can be similar to trading, except that the leverage in crypto is much higher than traditional asset leverage. Since crypto is very volatile, the risk of loss is very high.

What is the definition of a margin in crypto trading?

In leveraged trading, the margin is a crucial component. It's the term for the initial deposit made to open and maintain a leveraged position. Keep in mind that your margin requirements will vary depending on your broker and the size of your transaction when trading cryptocurrencies on a margin. The margin is expressed as a proportion of the entire position.

Traditional futures contracts versus perpetual futures contracts

Traditional futures contracts have an expiration date that is quite critical when trading to determine the asset value, and the settlement procedure begins when a contract expires. Traditional futures contracts are typically settled every month or quarter, and the contract price converges with the spot price at settlement, and all open positions expire. Crypto-derivative exchanges frequently provide perpetual contracts structured similarly to regular futures contracts.

Perpetual futures contracts have a significant advantage. Traders can retain holdings without an expiration date and do not need to keep track of different delivery months, unlike traditional futures contracts. A trader can keep a short position open indefinitely unless they are liquidated. As a result, perpetual trading contracts and trading pairs on the spot market are extremely similar. Since perpetual futures contracts never settle, exchanges require a system to ensure that futures and index prices regularly converge: a funding rate.

It is possible to short in the future market, but you need to store beta value for the underlying crypto-asset in the spot market. For example, if we want to trade a **BTCUSD (Bitcoin/USD)** pair with a short position, we need to purchase enough BTC and store it in our account before initializing our trading. This pre-purchased BTC action is our beta. Some exchanges offer lending options to encourage trading more but with some interest rates.

Funding rates

Funding rates are payments made to long or short traders depending on the difference between perpetual contract markets and spot prices regularly. Traders will either pay or get funds depending on open positions. Crypto funding rates avoid long-term price disparity in both markets. It is recalculated numerous times during the day, and depending on the exchanges, it can be calculated more often.

The idea behind the funding rate is to measure how expensive it is to open a position in the futures market.

The two basic components of funding rates are the lending rate (the cost to borrow the coin needed to short) and the premium (difference between futures and spot market). The interest rate on some crypto exchanges is fixed at a small percent every day. In the meanwhile, the premium is determined by the difference in price between the perpetual contract and the market price. The perpetual contract and the market prices may differ during periods of extreme volatility. In such cases, the premium rises or falls under the situation. A wide spread means a big premium. A low premium, on the other hand, shows a limited gap between the two prices. Funding rates may have a significant influence on earnings and losses since funding calculations take into account the level of leverage applied. Even in low-volatility markets, a trader who pays for funding may experience losses and be liquidated due to high leverage.

On the other hand, collecting funds may be quite profitable, especially in range-bound markets. As a result, traders may devise trading methods to profit from funding rates, even in low-volatility markets. Funding rates encourage traders to adopt positions that align perpetual contract prices with spot markets.

To come back to the perpetual contract, if the perpetual price is higher than the spot price, whoever has the long position needs to pay the short position holder. On the other hand, if the perpetual price is lower than the spot price, the funding rate becomes negative, and whoever shorts pays the one in a long position. The funding rate can potentially become a cost or a benefit of the margin. This last part concludes the similarities between traditional trading and crypto trading. We will talk about the main differences next.

Main differences between traditional asset trading and cryptocurrency trading

The following components are the most important differences between traditional and crypto trading.

In crypto trading, what is ownership?

Stock shares are securities that reflect a proportion of ownership (or equity) in a firm, known as the issuer. Owners of stocks often get voting rights or a share of the issuer's earnings in the form of dividends. On the other hand, cryptocurrencies differ a lot in terms of how they're utilized and what they're supposed to stand for.

Many digital assets, such as **Ethereum (ETH)**, **Basic Attention Token (BAT)**, and **VeChain Token (VET)**, are utility tokens designed to be utilized inside a blockchain-based ecosystem and do not reflect a legal interest in the company that issued them. Many cryptocurrencies, such as BTC and **stablecoins**, do not have clear use cases connected to actual company activities and are meant to store value. Although these assets are best thought of as digital commodities akin to gold, they do not represent an interest in a company or its activities.

What is market access?

Stock trading is often constrained to established business hours for most investors. Crypto markets never close, allowing anyone to take fresh positions and enter—or quit—the market at any time, regardless of where they live. The crypto markets trade actively during the intersection of the Asian time zone and the USA time zone.

What are the limits on issuance?

Publicly-listed firms that issue stock may choose to issue new shares, subject to the company's internal restrictions and any applicable local legislation. The entire supply of a cryptocurrency, on the other hand, is determined by the issuing organization's internal regulations or the blockchain protocol code it was developed with, rather than by-laws or policies. Furthermore, crypto projects may impose demonstrable and unchangeable hard restrictions on their entire coin supply easily and transparently.

What are the trading pairs?

Unlike equities, which are normally acquired and sold with fiat currencies, cryptocurrencies may be purchased and sold using trading pairs, allowing two cryptocurrencies to be directly traded. As BTC and ETH are two of the most widely traded cryptocurrencies, most trading pairings include one of them. If you wish to trade one cryptocurrency for another, you'll almost certainly need to swap the altcoin you want to trade for something more popular, such as BTC. Then, you may swap that BTC for the cryptocurrency you choose.

Suppose you wish to avoid numerous steps while exchanging one low-market-cap currency for another. In that case, you might choose to use one of the many DEXs that can execute these types of trades utilizing **automated market makers** (**AMMs**). While most stock brokerages provide fiat on- and off-ramps, not all cryptocurrency exchanges allow users to deposit and withdraw fiat. This means that you won't be able to buy crypto-assets using fiat on some exchanges.

When trading crypto, what does liquidity look like?

When trading low-cap coins and tokens or buying and selling on smaller crypto platforms, investors may confront poor liquidity. In stock trading, liquidity concerns can arise, especially when dealing with micro-cap companies or **over-the-counter (OTC)** penny stocks.

Is there any transparency in crypto?

Publicly traded companies must maintain transparency, which is typically achieved through quarterly financial updates, annual reports, regular shareholder meetings, and other official means of informing investors about past performance and expected future earnings. While corporations that raise money through a **Security Token Offering (STO)** may be subject to similar reporting obligations, crypto initiatives are not subject to regulatory scrutiny as publicly traded companies.

Many crypto markets do not compel individual projects to share data regularly, making it difficult for investors and industry analysts to adequately analyze how specific crypto projects are functioning and whether their assets are worth investing in. On the other hand, many crypto projects try to be transparent in terms of community updates and open governance. Transparency is one of the primary concepts of crypto and blockchain, and most high-quality projects strive to adhere to it.

Since this book is about HFT, we will now focus on learning to trade with cryptocurrency exchange.

Trading with cryptocurrency exchange

As we described previously, a **digital currency exchange (DCE)** is another name for a cryptocurrency exchange. It's a website that allows users to convert their money into cryptocurrency and vice versa. The majority of exchanges are primarily focused on helping us swap a cryptocurrency such as BTC into other digital currencies, such as ETH or other crypto-assets.

Although most exchanges operate online, there are a few physical locations. Traditional payment methods and cryptocurrencies can both be exchanged on these exchanges. These alternatives are comparable to currency exchange kiosks seen in international airports, where you can exchange your home currency for the currency of another country.

The following are the most well-known types of cryptocurrency exchanges.

- **CEXs** are comparable to regular stock exchanges in that they are centralized. Traditional stock exchanges are similar to CEXs, and traders are brought together and the exchange acts as a third party. These exchanges often demand a fee to ease transactions between buyers and sellers. Centralization implies *to entrust your money to someone else in the crypto industry*. HFT crypto trading will mainly work with this kind of exchange.

  Examples of CEXs include Binance, Coinbase, and KuCoin.

- **DEXs** aspire to keep faithful to the cryptocurrency industry's pure premise. A DEX does not need an intermediary to store coins, and it's an online marketplace where buyers and sellers meet and conduct business directly. DEXs, in other words, make peer-to-peer trading easier.

  You may exchange crypto-assets directly with other market players on a DEX. Smart contracts and atomic swaps can be used to make transactions. Atomic swaps allow you to trade one cryptocurrency for another without going via a CEX. A smart contract is a piece of code self-executing the term of a contract. It is the foundation of atomic swaps.

  Instead of providing cryptocurrencies to the CEX, we will provide them to an escrow controlled by the network that runs the exchange with the DEX, smart contracts, and atomic swaps. Because transactions can take up to 5 days to clear, the escrow is still in place. As a buyer, your money will be taken out of your account right away, but the funds will not be sent to the seller's account until the crypto transaction has cleared.

  Because of the latency involved in any transactions, performing high-performance trading on this kind of exchange will be difficult.

  Examples of DEXs include UniSwap, PancakeSwap, and SushiSwap.

- **Hybrid cryptocurrency exchanges** are the next-generation cryptocurrency trading platforms. They are a hybrid of CEXs and DEXs. Hybrid exchanges, also known as semi-decentralized exchanges, include on-chain and off-chain parts. Off-chain transactions shift the value of your crypto-asset away from the blockchain. The hybrid approach to cryptocurrency exchanges combines the advantages of both CEXs and DEXs. Hybrids, in particular, aim to combine the functionality and liquidity of a CEX with the anonymity and security of a DEX. Many people believe that such exchanges are the true future of BTC trading.

Hybrid exchanges aim to give institutional users the same speed, simplicity, and liquidity that they expect from regular exchanges. The centralized aspects of a hybrid exchange are linked to a network of decentralized peers. Market participants can access the trading platform as they would on a CEX and then trade with their peers as they would on a DEX. The hybrid then offers blockchain confirmation and records transactions.

Examples of hybrid exchanges include Qurrex and NEXT.

These exchanges cannot be found in a co-location where the trading will happen, and most of the time, they are located in the cloud. In the *How to build a trading system in the cloud* section, we will describe how to build a trading system in the cloud, unsurprisingly. Therefore, the main advantage we have with traditional trading in terms of latency by being in the same location as the exchange will not work for cryptocurrencies.

It is possible to know in which region the exchange (or the matching engine) is located. Therefore, it is possible to have an edge in speed over the other participants.

More recently, some exchanges have decided to have their matching engine in colocation, inviting participants to join them to perform HFT.

Using cryptocurrency market data

The data offered by a crypto exchange is Kline data, Level 1, and Level 2 data. The K line depicts the daily fluctuations in stock prices; it displays the close, open, high, and low prices for the day and illustrates the difference and magnitude between any two values.

The price quoting per IP is unlimited for VIP clients or some major market participants (depending on the volume they trade). But for regular clients, there are some quoting limits for each IP. Some newer exchanges use snapshots on data distribution, but the bigger exchanges use data streaming, creating some arbitrage opportunities.

For HFT, it is important to record any market data. This is because exchanges previously encountered technical issues pretty frequently, and we observe gaps in the historical data. An exchange typically chooses to interpolate data, which can be inefficient on the execution backtest.

Being aware of exchange fees

Transactions are charged in a variety of ways through exchanges. Customers are charged fees, which is how the exchange generates money to continue the business. The most popular technique is when the exchange takes a commission of the money we trade. Most exchanges charge a percentage of less than 1% to remain competitive.

Unlike traditional trading, there are a lot of trading exchanges in crypto trading. It is difficult to have enough liquidity. Because DEXs are less common than CEXs, matching orders with other orders you buy or sell on a DEX may be more challenging. This is a vicious circle since DEX liquidity will stay low as long as they are less popular, and DEXs may stay unpopular as long as liquidity remains low. That is why, for the time being, CEXs are more popular than DEXs in HFT.

Additionally, a CEX will give rebates or lower their commission if traders add liquidities. As in traditional trading, a market-making strategy using a rebate to make money will work in this type of exchange.

In crypto, the transaction fees are 20 to 30 times higher than in traditional markets. In an exchange-based market such as Binance and Huobi, we pay a transaction fee by quote coins (indicating a lot of arbitrage room); in the **non-fungible tokens** (**NFT**) market, we pay a transaction fee called **gas**, which is in ETH.

Some exchanges, such as Binance and Huobi, have their market-making reward program by issuing rebates to qualified market makers who can successfully trade their assigned coins. This can help the rebate earning trading strategy.

Not being capable of selling (or liquidating) an investment promptly and at an acceptable price is likely to happen on any crypto exchange. For any traded asset, liquidity is critical. The **foreign exchange** (**FX**) market is the most liquid in the world, and lack of liquidity may concern any market, including the FX market. If you trade currencies with a small amount of volume, you can conclude your deal since the prices just won't change.

Illiquidity may occur with cryptocurrencies as well. It is one of the issues that contributed to the extreme volatility of BTC and other cryptocurrencies. When liquidity is scarce, there is a greater possibility of price manipulation.

When an **initial coin offering** (**ICO**) occurs on a crypto exchange, the exchange and the company doing its ICO will use market makers to help to sell their digital assets. When the assets are on the exchange, the market maker will help facilitate transactions. A crypto exchange will play a big part in the trading aspect of the exchange by increasing liquidities artificially. Some trading strategies such as spoofing can be used, and the best available prices may not be available.

The likelihood of being filled on the top of the book of a crypto exchange will be much lower than the one on a trading exchange. In HFT, we need to compete against the market maker associated with the exchange, which will make the trading a bit more challenging.

We will now talk about the type of trading strategies working in the cryptocurrency world.

HFT strategies in crypto

In *Chapter 1*, *Fundamentals of a High-Frequency Trading System*, we explained HFT-specific trading strategies. In this section, we will talk about cryptocurrency-specific strategies.

Market making

One of the most tried-and-true HFT tactics is market-making. It entails the continuous and simultaneous quotation of buy and sell orders. Market-making is a financial instrument that adds liquidity to the market and benefits the high-frequency traders engaged. Market makers are traditionally provided by large companies or HFT firms, which is regarded as a positive practice in the financial markets.

Statistical arbitrage

This is the act of betting on the price difference between two exchanges of the same cryptocurrency. The first trader to identify these inconsistencies generally uses the knowledge. To perform statistical arbitrage, you'll need powerful and quick processing machines and up-to-date HFT software. Balancing prices has the overall effect of equilibrating the market.

Smart router trading

High-frequency traders can access liquidity pools simultaneously, choose the optimum order routing destination, and improve order execution. The best bid and offer bids for a certain order are scanned in a pre-defined or real-time market, resulting in the best price.

Maximizing short-term opportunities

Scalping is a word used to describe leveraging short-term possibilities. HFT uses powerful computers with the processing power to execute several orders in a fraction of a second.

Maximizing the trading volume

Traders use automation to their advantage via HFT, also known as high-speed trading. These high-frequency traders can not only execute large numbers of trades, but they also profit from even small price movements.

Building a high-frequency system for crypto trading

Data storage is a priority in all industries, as computer and mobile users have increased. Today's large and small organizations rely on their data, and they spend a lot of money to keep it up to date. It needs solid IT support as well as a storage hub. Not every company can afford the hefty costs of in-house IT equipment and backup support. Cloud computing is a less expensive option. Cloud computing reduces the user's hardware and software requirements.

Like a lot of other domains, crypto started using cloud services heavily. The HFT system we described in the previous chapters can also be used in the cloud.

Types of cloud

We can use the cloud in different ways:

- **Private cloud**: Computing resources are deployed for a single enterprise in a private cloud, where they are managed, owned, and operated by the same company.

- **Community cloud**: Computing resources are supplied for a community and organizations in the community cloud.

- **Public cloud**: This cloud is often used for **business to consumer (B2C)** interactions. The computer resource is owned, managed, and administered by the government, academic institutions, or corporations.

- **Hybrid cloud**: The computer resources are connected by distinct clouds; this deployment strategy is known as a hybrid cloud.

We saw the different types of cloud solutions; we will now talk about the benefits of using the cloud for trading systems.

Benefits of cloud computing

Most of the crypto exchanges adopted cloud services because of the potential for cost savings and the short time-to-market. Cloud computing allows the flexibility to utilize services as needed and only pay for what's needed. We can run IT operations as an outsourced unit without many in-house resources. Additionally, the cost to get engineers is pretty high, and assembling a technical team can be pretty time-consuming.

The main advantages of cloud computing are as follows:

- Users' IT infrastructure and computing expenditures are reduced, resulting in better performance.

- There are fewer maintenance difficulties.

- Updates to the software are available immediately.

- Compatibility across operating systems has been improved.

- Recovery and backup.

- Scalability and performance.

- Increased data security due to increased storage capacity.

The three major cloud computing models are described in the following sections.

Software as a service (SaaS)

SaaS is a software distribution model in which vendors or service providers host programs and make them available to clients through the internet. As foundational technology for **service-oriented architecture** (**SOA**) or web services, SaaS is becoming a more common delivery paradigm. This service is available to people all around the world via the internet. Traditionally, the software had to be purchased in advance and installed on your computer. SaaS consumers, on the other hand, rather than acquiring software, subscribe to it monthly via the internet. Anyone who requires access to a certain piece of software, whether one or two people or thousands of employees in a company, can register as a user. All internet-enabled devices are compatible with SaaS. Accounting, sales, invoicing, and budgeting are just a few of the critical duties that SaaS can help you with.

Platform as a service (PaaS)

PaaS provides a platform and environment for developers to create applications and services. Users can access this service over the internet because it is housed in the cloud. PaaS services are updated regularly, and new features are added. PaaS can help software developers, web developers, and businesses. It serves as a platform for application development. It covers software support and administration, storage, networking, application deployment, testing, collaboration, hosting, and maintenance.

Infrastructure as a service (IaaS)

IaaS is a cloud computing service model. It gives users online access to computer resources in a virtualized environment known as **the cloud**. It offers virtual server space, network connections, bandwidth, load balancers, IP addresses, and other computer infrastructure. The group of hardware resources is formed from a range of servers and networks spread across several data centers. IaaS gains redundancy and dependability as a result of this. IaaS is a comprehensive computing solution. It is one of the options for small organizations wanting to save costs on their IT infrastructure. Maintenance and the purchase of new components such as hard drives, network connections, and external storage devices cost a lot of money every year.

We will now talk about the component managing the **virtual machines (VMs)**: the hypervisor.

Hypervisor

A **hypervisor** is a piece of software, firmware, or hardware that allows the construction and operation of VMs on computers. A host machine is a computer on which a hypervisor runs one or more VMs, and each virtual system is referred to as a **guest machine**. Resources such as CPU, memory, and storage are treated as a pool by the hypervisor, which may be readily reassigned between current guests or new VMs. Because the guest VMs are independent of the host hardware, hypervisors enable the usage of more of a system's available resources and give more IT mobility. The hypervisor is also known as a **virtualization layer** since it allows them to be easily transferred across multiple systems. A single physical server can support several VMs.

Figure 11.1 represents two types of hypervisors:

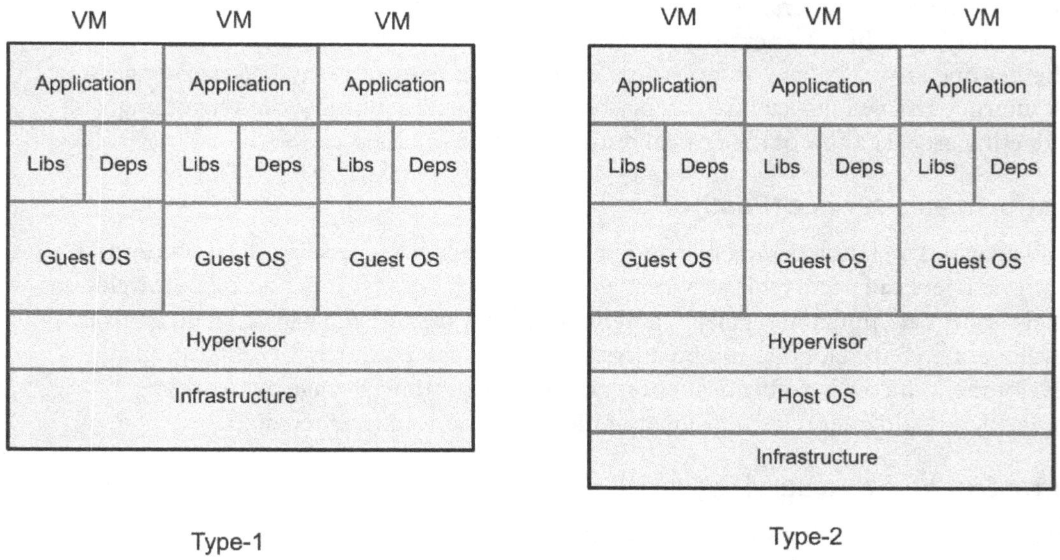

Figure 11.1 – Types of hypervisor

Type-1, native, or bare-metal hypervisors

These hypervisors operate directly on the host's hardware to control the hardware and administer guest operating systems. As a result, they're sometimes referred to as bare-metal hypervisors. This form of hypervisor is most popular in corporate data centers or other server-based environments.

Type-2 or hosted hypervisors

Like other computer applications, these hypervisors run on a standard OS. On the host, a guest operating system runs as a process, and guest operating systems are abstracted from the host operating system by type-2 hypervisors. Individual users who want to run various operating systems on a personal computer should utilize a type 2 hypervisor. The trading system will run on the application level on the type-1 hypervisor. Cloud service providers will provide different hypervisors in different regions and availability zones. The goal will be to have the trading system and the exchange in the same availability zone to perform low latency operations. *Figure 11.2* represents how cloud providers organize their availability zones and regions:

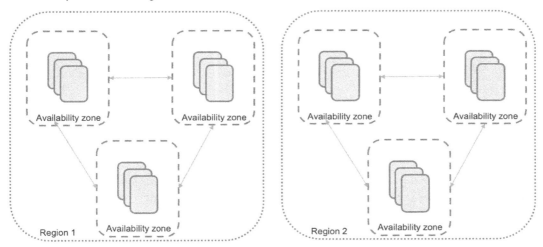

Figure 11.2 – Availability zone and regions

In this part, we reviewed the cloud structure. It is critical for HFT in crypto since you will need to be as close as possible to the availability zone where the crypto exchange is when we do HFT with a CEX.

We will now study how to build a trading system in the cloud.

How to build a trading system in the cloud

There are three major **cloud service providers (CSPs)**: **Amazon Web Services (AWS)**, **Google Cloud Platform (GCP)**, and **Microsoft Azure**.

The choice between providers will depend on the cost and the managed services you are familiar with. It would be difficult to advise one CSP over another one in this section. Their offering is pretty similar in terms of hardware, operating system, and open source software you can use. All of them have professional service teams that can help you to design the trading system. If we could recommend a CSP, we would choose the CSP based on the crypto exchange location you target for your HFT strategies.

Solution 1 – Running our HFT on a CSP

We first need to choose the region where the application will be running. This region should be the closest to the exchange. We will need to create the following components on the CSP of your choice:

- Computing instance
- Type of VM
- Storage instance

A **computing server instance** such as Amazon's **Elastic Compute Cloud (EC2)**, **Google Compute Engine (GCE)**, or Azure VM is required for running applications on the CSP infrastructure. It may be used to create an almost infinite number of VMs.

It is critical to know what **type of VM** you will spin up. Choosing the wrong type of hardware will not give you a performant architecture for HFT. You need to consider the number of cores, the memory, the storage, and of course, the type of network card.

We will need to apply the same rules we used during the previous chapters. Always remember that if you want to have a performant system in HFT, having many cores will help you to get better performance if the system you build works with many processes. Once you have selected the type of hardware, you will need to choose the OS you want to use. All the CSPs will give similar types of operating systems. Because in this book, we focus on the Unix-based OS, we would like to recommend the use of any Linux distribution. CSPs can provide their own OS version, such as Amazon Linux distributions.

The advantage of the cloud is to give you a flexible way of **storing data**. This part is less critical than the computing instance since all the processing will happen in memory. However, we have to collect logs for monitoring and debugging the systems and we need to record all the market data to build models. Amazon S3, Azure Blob storage, and Google cloud storage will provide you the scalability, data availability, and high reliability for your critical data.

Once we choose the hardware features, the OS, and the storage unit, we can use the same code algorithm that we have built in the previous chapters of this book.

Now, we know how to move our software to the cloud on a cloud provider. We can also use the leverage that a CSP offers in terms of software. A CSP provides managed services and open source software to bootstrap quicker to an HFT system. We will now explain how to build a trading system from scratch with managed services.

Solution 2 – Using managed services from a CSP

CSPs provide building blocks to design software. The advantage of using managed services or open source software is to get tested and functioning software. You will just need to connect these building blocks together. We would invite you to contact the CSP for advice in terms of building your solution or to read blogs to see the experience of these CSPs in building trading systems. We would like to suggest one implementation inspired by some work done on the cloud. Let's look at the following figure:

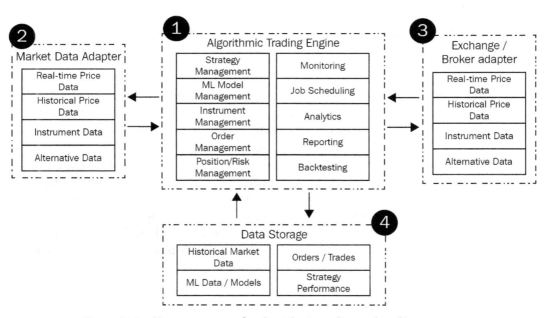

Figure 11.3 – Key components for algorithmic trading and trading systems

Figure 11.3 represents the components we need to build an entire trading system, which completes the information we gave in *Chapter 2, The Critical Components of a Trading System*, where we focused only on the essential path to send an order triggered by market data:

- The system's heart is **Algorithmic Trading Engine**, which allows users to build, test, and run trading strategies utilizing historical and real-time data while also managing relationships with other solution components and offering analytics and reporting capabilities.

- **Market Data Adapter** provides a variety of data types to the engine, including real-time market data, historical pricing data, and more.

- **Exchange/Broker Adapter** handles interactions with the exchange and/or broker, such as placing and rescinding orders and checking the order status.

- **Data Store**, employed by algorithmic trading engines, provides a long-lasting and safe data repository.

CSP offers a diverse set of services that enable the development of a wide range of solutions. The following assessments are proposed for defining the algorithmic trading solution architecture:

- **Trading speed**: When we explained how to build a trading system in *Chapter 2, The Critical Components of a Trading System*, we showed how the speed was important to build an HFT system in the design choice. The managed service selection will be based on the latency speed. You have two types of software on CSP: software processing data in real time and software processing data by batch. Managed services (such as AWS Lambda, Azure Functions Serverless Compute, and Google Firebase Cloud Functions) will be able to provide a quick response to any event (such as market data coming into the system). An event engine capable of calling these functions (such as AWS EventBridge, Azure Event Grid, or Google Eventarc services) will be a good combination. The event engine will call a serverless function to process trading system events.

- **Need for data and analytics**: Designing trading strategy models requires market data to be stored in a very efficient way. We need to be able to run backtesting using this market data. The amount of data can rapidly grow and it is important to have a scalable solution. We already talked about the storage instance in the previous section. We will add on top of this storage unit some services capable of helping you to analyze data; AWS Athena, Azure Synapse Analytics, and Google BigQuery will help to query and use data.

- **Extensibility and flexibility**: An event-driven approach that connects the algorithmic trading engine to market data adapters and external exchanges/brokers over a common API is preferred to decouple all architecture components.

- **Security**: CSPs provide security solutions for anything that is related to identity and authorization. For traditional HFT working in colocation, we don't need to consider security as much as when we have our software in the cloud. That's why we wanted to highlight in this part that the use of security services is important. AWS Identity, Azure Active Directory, or Google Cloud Identity will provide authentication, authorization, encryption, and segregation.

We will now propose a design for a trading system that could be built in a few days on any CSP:

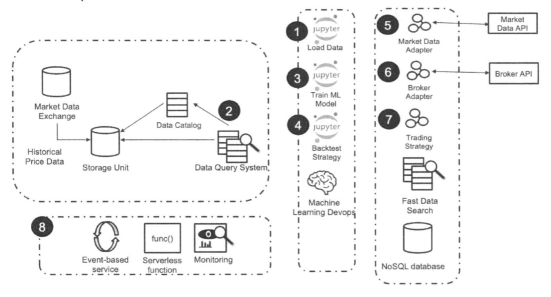

Figure 11.4 – Trading system architecture on a CSP

Figure 11.4 represents a trading system architecture design using the components that we talked about. We simplify the system by using as a user interface just a Python Jupyter notebook. It provides enough flexibility to start processes and build trading strategies:

- The **Load Data** component (**1**) will help get historical data. Market data is obtained through the market data exchange and stored in a storage unit. Any data feed, such as news or other types of trading data sources, might be used depending on the backtesting approach (that is, data already available or produced in-house).

- The **Data Catalog** component (**2**) enables us to have a reference for all the data we have in the system. It will be able to dynamically update data.

- Using the **Jupyter** notebook supplied in this design (**3**), we train the **machine learning** (**ML**) model using the ML DevOps notebook instance (AWS Sagemaker, Azure ML studio, and Google Vertex AI AutoML). This architecture's notebook reads data straight from a data bucket, and the given notebook can be modified or changed as needed.

- After the ML model has been trained (**4**), it is utilized for actual backtesting using data from a data bucket, and it may be deployed after the results fit your criteria.

- The part with the **5**, **6**, and **7** annotations shows taking care of collecting the data in real time from the exchange.

- Seeing annotation **8**, functions such as task scheduling, monitoring, alerting, and logging are necessary after installing the strategy and communicating automatically with **Broker/Market Data**. For example, when **profit and loss** (**PnL**) exceeds preset levels, near-real-time notifications can be created, and alerts can be visual and audible.

This is how we can build an HFT system in the cloud to trade cryptocurrencies. We will now finish this chapter by summarizing what we have learned.

Summary

This chapter was the final chapter of this book. We discussed how to improve the tick-to-trade latency using FPGA. We studied how crypto trading was different from traditional trading. We learned how to build an HFT system in the cloud.

Since this is the end of this book, we would like to take the opportunity to remind you that technology evolves very fast. In this book, we presented the basics of HFT. However, we need to remember that being among the fastest HFT companies costs a lot in terms of money and time. Engineers, hardware, network, and connections are vital parts of HFT. Even if we don't have the quickest architecture, data analysis can always help build robust HFT strategies capable of performing within the limitation of our system. This book drew the basics of creating an HFT system by considering the HFT optimization technique.

We are getting to the end of this journey together. We would like to thank you for reading this book and invite you to contact us if you would like to discuss HFT.

Index

A

active network TAP 108
addressing modes, IPv4 protocol
 broadcast mode 91
 multicast mode 92
 unicast mode 90, 91
Address Space Layout Randomization
  (ASLR) 158
Advanced Encryption Standard
  (AES) algorithm 59
Agrona circular buffer 229
ahead-of-time (AOT) project 214
Altera Quartus 257
Alternate Trading Systems (ATS) 9
Amazon Web Services (AWS) 275
American Standard Code for Information
  Interchange (ASCII) 96
Apache NetBeans
 reference link 211
API
 examining, for communication 29
Application Programming
  Interface (API) mode
 versus Application Binary
  Interface (ABI) mode 244

applications, lock-free data structures
 about 125
 logging and online computation,
  of statistics 126, 127
 order requests, on critical path 126
 market data dissemination,
  on critical path 126
application-specific integrated
  circuits (ASICs) 81, 252
Archipelago Exchange (ArcaEx) 5
array interface 238
asset class 12, 22
associative containers 194
atomicity 169
atomic operations
 properties 170
autoboxing 209
automated market makers (AMMs) 266
Average Access Time (AAT) 130

B

bandwidth 83
bare-metal hypervisors 274
Basic Attention Token (BAT) 266
Basic Input/Output System (BIOS) 156

Bayonet Neill-Concelman (BNC) port 81
Better Alternative Trading
        System (BATS) 8
binding 240
Bitcoin (BTC) 259
blockchain 260
blocks 260
Book Builder 24
Boost.Python library 241, 242
broadcast mode 91
BTCUSD (Bitcoin/USD) pair 264
bus 80

C

C++
    Python, using with 240, 241
    using, in Python 240
C++ 11 memory model
    about 168
    rules 168
C++ 14/17 memory model 166
C++ 20 memory model
    changes 176
C++ HFT libraries
    working, with Python 239
C++ memory model
    principles 172
C++ RTTI mechanism
    performance penalties 184
C++ static analysis 195
C++ STL containers
    deque 193
    list 193
    map 194
    multimap 194
    multiset 194
    set 194

unordered_map 194
unordered_multimap 194
unordered_set 194
vector 193
cable fibers
    about 146
    evolution, to hollow fiber 147
cache 129
cachegrind 155
cache line 63
cache miss 117
caching system
    L0 cache 129
    L1 cache 63, 129
    L2 cache 64, 129
    L3 cache 64, 129
    L4 cache 129
    structure 63
callgrind 155
ccNUMA (cache-coherent NUMA) 60
centralized exchanges (CEXs) 263, 268
Central Limit Order Book (CLOB) 6
central processing unit (CPU) 59, 89, 252
C Foreign Function Interface (CFFI)
    about 244
    using, to accelerate Python
        code 243, 244
Chicago Board Options
        Exchange (CBOE) 100
Chicago Mercantile Exchange
        (CME) 8, 23, 100
chiplets 59
ChipScope 257
chrono 159
circular buffer 227
Clang Static Analyzer 200
class templates 189

cloud
    community cloud 272
    hybrid cloud 272
    private cloud 272
    public cloud 272
cloud computing
    benefits 272
cloud computing, offerings
    Infrastructure as a service (IaaS) 273
    Platform as a service (PaaS) 273
    Software as a service (SaaS) 273
cloud service providers (CSPs) 275
coins 259
command and control 24, 37
Commodity Futures Trading
        Commission (CFTC) 262
communication
    API, examining for 29
community cloud 272
compare-and-swap (CAS) 119
compilers
    about 73
    examples 73, 74
    executable file formats 74
    static, versus dynamic linking 74, 75
Concurrent Collections
    reference link 229
Concurrent Mark Sweep (CMS) 207, 210
constexpr
    using 186
context switches
    about 67, 112
    between threads, and processes 113
    hardware context switches 113
    software context switches 113
context switches, disadvantages for HFT
    default CPU task scheduler
        behavior 116

expensive tasks 117
context switches, features
    about 114
    interrupt handling 114
    multitasking 114
    user and kernel mode switching 115
context switch operation
    steps 115
control flow analysis 196
conversant disruptor
    Agrona circular buffer 229
convoying 122
Coordinated Universal Time (UTC) 109
core logic blocks (CLBs) 252
counters
    cumulative counter 221
    descriptive counter 221
    incremental counter 221
    types 221
Cppcheck 199
CppDepend 199
CPU starvation 114
cryptocurrencies
    about 259
    HFT, exploring 259
    transparency 267
cryptocurrencies, price driving factors
    about 261
    cryptography exchanges 261
    crypto-specific governance 262
    crypto-specific regulations 262
    market participants and competitors 262
    production cost 261
cryptocurrency exchange
    CEXs 268
    DEXs 268
    hybrid exchanges 268, 269
    types 268, 269

cryptocurrency market data
  using 269
cryptocurrency mining 260
cryptocurrency trading
  high-frequency system, building for 272
  leverage 263
  margin 263
  ownership 265
  spread 263
crypto transactions
  working 259
CSP
  HFT, running on 276, 277
  managed services, using from 277-280
ctypes
  using, to accelerate Python
    code 243, 244
curiously recurring template
    pattern (CRTP) 182, 200
custom techniques, for measuring
    performance
  about 156
  Address Space Layout
    Randomization (ASLR) 158
  C++ specific measurement
    routines/libraries 158
  chrono 159
  consistent results, on benchmarks 156
  CPU isolation and affinity 157
  CPU power-saving options 157
  data statistics measurement 158
  gettimeofday 158
  hyper threading 157
  Intel Turbo Boost 156
  Linux process priority 157
  Linux specific measurement
    routines/libraries 158

Tick-To-Trade (TTT)
  measurement 159, 160
Time Stamp Counter (TSC),
    with rdtsc 159
cut-through switching mode
  about 87
  fast-forward switching 87
  fragment-free switching 87
cyclic redundancy checks (CRCs) 79
Cython 242

D

dark pools 9
data analytics
  Python, using 234
database 231
database access 230, 231
data cleaning 234
data crawling 234
data distribution 12
data flow analysis 196
data modeling 234
data visualization 234
deadlock 121
decentralized exchanges (DEXs) 263, 268
dedicated network TAP 106
digital currency exchange (DCE) 267
Direct Edge 8
direct memory access (DMA) 104
disk storage 130
dynamic linking 75
dynamic load library (.dll) 238
dynamic memory allocation
  about 133, 184
  alternatives/solutions 185
  steps 134
dynamic polymorphism 182

E

ECN 24
Eden space 211
efficient market hypothesis (EMH) 15
embedding 240
end-to-end (E2E) byte stream 93
Epoch time 158
Epsilon GC 207
Ethereum (ETH) 266
Ethernet
  about 90
  using, for HFT communication 90
Ethernet TAPs 107
exceptions
  about 186
  benefits 187
  drawbacks 187, 188
exchange fees 269
exchanges
  trading system trade, making 27-29
Exchange-Traded Funds (ETFs) 10, 262
executable and linkable format
    (ELF) file 74
execution order 167
Executors 224
ExecutorService 224
expression templates 191
extending modules 240
exterior networks
  versus interior networks 101
external thread 231

F

failure analysis 196
Fast Ethernet 90
fast-forward switching 87

Federal Bureau of Investigation (FBI) 19
fences 175
fetch-and-add 119
fiber 29
Field Programmable Gate Array (FPGA)
  about 101, 251-253
  capacity 253
  characteristics 253
  conclusion 258
  determinism 254
  latencies, reducing 250
  parallelism 253, 254
  programmability 253
file 231
Financial Industry Regulatory
    Authority (FINRA) 19
Financial Information eXchange
    (FIX) protocol 95, 96
financial protocols
  designing, for HFT exchanges 94, 95
First In First Out (FIFO) 50, 51, 124
FIX Adapted for STreaming (FAST)
    protocol 90, 99, 100, 255
foreign exchange (FX) market 22, 270
FPGA trading systems
  about 254
  considerations 256
  low-latency execution algorithms 255
  market data 254
  trading signals 255
FPGA trading systems, advantages
  about 256
  cheaper maintenance 257
  higher profits 256
  security compliance 256
FPGA trading systems, disadvantages
  about 257
  added trading risk 258

development and debugging cost 257
hardware cost 257
strategy complexity limits 258
fragment-free switching 87
frame-check-sequence (FCS) 87
front-running 19
function templates 188
funding rates 264, 265
FX high-frequency trading system
  building 200, 201

G

G1 GC 207
garbage collection
  algorithms 207
  events, limiting 208
  impact, reducing 207, 208
  stop-the-world (STW) pause 210
Garbage Collection Algorithms
  reference link 207
garbage collector (GC) 205
gas 270
gates 252
Gateways
  about 24, 25
  connecting, to trading exchanges 25
  data collection 25-27
generic programming 189
gettimeofday 158
Global Interpreter Lock (GIL) 237
Global Navigation Satellite
    System (GNSS) 109
Global Positioning System (GPS) 109
GNU Debugger (gdb)
  about 154
  reference link 154

GNU Profiler (gprof)
  reference link 154
Google Cloud Platform (GCP) 275
Google's TensorFlow library 238
Gperftools
  about 155
  reference link 155
GraalVM 214
Grafana dashboard
  reference link 221
graphics processing units (GPUs) 251
Graphite
  reference link 221
guest machine 274

H

hardware context switches 113
head-of-line (HOL) blocking 85
HFT communication
  Ethernet, using for 90
HFT computers
  about 58
  compilers 73
  CPUs 59-61
  I/O devices 65
  operating system (OS) 65
  Random Access Memory (RAM) 62
  shared memory 64
HFT exchanges
  financial protocols, designing for 94, 95
HFT strategies, in crypto
  about 271
  market making 271
  short-term opportunities,
      maximizing 271

smart router trading 271
statistical arbitrage 271
trading volume, maximizing 271
high-frequency system
  building, for crypto trading 272
  networking 78
High-Frequency Trading (HFT)
  about 3, 9-11
  exploring, with cryptocurrencies 259
  features 7
  fierce competition of speed,
    evolution 250, 251
  history 4-6
  network communications,
    between systems 80, 81
  participants 10
  running, on CSP 276, 277
  speed of Python code,
    improving 246, 247
  versus regular trading 7, 8
hollow fiber
  about 146, 147
  evolution, to microwave 147
  working 147, 148
hosted hypervisors 275
hot paths 208
htop
  reference link 222
hub 81
huge pages 70
hybrid cloud 272
hybrid cryptocurrency exchanges 268
hyper-threading
  about 61, 157
  issues 62
  usage 62

hypervisor
  about 274
  type-1 274
  type-2 275

I

illegal activities
  about 19
  front-running 19
  layering 20
  spoofing 19
Illiquidity 270
inboxing 209
information-driven strategies 17
Infrastructure as a service (IaaS) 273
initial coin offering (ICO) 270
inline mode
  versus out-of-line mode 244
input/output (I/O) devices 59
Institute of Electrical and Electronics
    Engineers (IEEE) 802.3 90
Intercontinental Exchange, Inc. (ICE) 7
interest rate 265
interface analysis 196
interior networks
  versus exterior networks 101
internal thread 231
Internet Group Management
    Protocol (IGMP) 92
Internet Protocol (IP) 29, 79
Inter-Process Communication
    (IPC) 144, 221
interrupt descriptor table (IDT) 104
interrupt service routine (ISR) 104
IP version 4 (IPv4)
  about 79
  using, as network layer 90

IP version 6 (IPv6) 79
ISE 257
issuance
    limits 266
ITCH protocol 100

J

Java
    basics 204-206
    compilation chain 205
    heap memory model 206
Java Microbenchmark Harness (JMH) 219
Java microbenchmarks
    issues, for creating 219, 220
Java profiler
    about 222
    reference link 211
Java software
    performance, measuring 219
Java threading
    about 221, 222
    reference link 224
Java util logging 231
Java virtual machine (JVM)
    full C1 compiled code 217
    limited C1 compiled code 216
    optimizing, for better startup
        performance 218
    tiered compilation 214-219
JMH GitHub
    reference link 220
just-in-time (JIT) compilation 214
Just-in-Time (JIT) compiler 237
JVM compilation levels
    C2 compiled code 217
    interpreted code 216
    simple C1 compiled code 216

JVM warm-up
    about 213, 214
    reference link 219

K

kernel bypass
    as alternative 142
    latencies 142, 143
    user space spinning 142
    using 141
    zero copy 142
kernel space
    versus user space 138, 140
key-value pairs 95
kill tolerance 121
Klocwork 199

L

L0 cache 129
L1 cache 129
L2 cache 129
L3 cache 129
L4 cache 129
latency
    about 220, 251
    reducing, with FPGA 250
latency arbitrage 16
layer 1 switching 87
layer 2 switching 88
layer 3 switching 88
layering 20
lending rate 265
leverage 263
libraries
    using, in Python 238, 239

Linux tools, for measuring performance
   about 153
   cachegrind 155
   callgrind 155
   GNU Debugger (gdb) 154
   GNU Profiler (gprof) 154
   Gperftools 155
   LTTng 155
   perf 154
   time 154
   valgrind 155
liquidity 12, 267
liquidity rebates 12
LMAX disruptor
   about 228, 229
   conversant disruptor 229
local area network (LAN) 81
lock contention 120
lock-free data structures
   applications 125
   building 118
   prototype 123
lock overhead 120
locks
   need for 118
logging
   about 150, 230, 231
   infrastructure design 151
   issue 151
   need for 150
London Stock Exchange (LSE) 8
Lookup Tables (LUTs) 252
LTTng
   about 155
   reference link 155

M

main memory 130
managed services
   using, from CSP 277-280
margin 263
market access 266
market data, FPGA trading systems
   about 254
   feed arbitration and replication 255
   feed parsers and normalizers 255
   network stacks 255
market maker 13
market making 13
market-making strategies 14
market taker 13
Mark Sweep Compact (MSC) 210
matching engine 13
matching engine algorithm
   about 46
   First In First Out (FIFO) 50, 51
   pro-rata algorithm 51, 52
Matplotlib 238
Mellanox Messaging Accelerator
      (VMA) APIs 142
memory
   pre-allocating 127
   pre-fetching 127
memory access
   inefficiencies 130, 131
memory allocation 211
memory barrier 119
memory hierarchy 128
memory management unit (MMU) 69
memory-mapped files
   about 143
   advantages 144, 145
   applications 146

disadvantages 145
non-persisted memory-mapped files 144
persisted memory-mapped files 144
types 144
memory model
about 166
need for 167, 168
memory order
Acquire/Release 172
Consume 172
relaxed memory order 172
memory ordering
about 171-173
Relaxed Ordering 174
Release-Acquire Ordering 174
Release-Consume Ordering 174, 175
Sequential Consistency (SC) 173
memory profiling 211, 212
Microsoft Azure 275
microwaves
about 29, 146, 147
advantages 148
disadvantages 149
impact 149
working 148
mining 259
momentum ignition trading technique 17
motivation, for removing
      runtime decisions
about 177
compiler optimizations 177
CPU and architecture
      optimizations 177
multicast mode 92
Multiple Producer Multiple
      Consumer (MPMC) 123-125
Multiple Producers Single
      Consumer (MPSC) 125

N

National Association of Securities
      Dealers Automated Quotations
      (NASDAQ) 5, 7
National Best Bid and Offer (NBBO) 16
network
monitoring 105
network address translation (NAT) 88, 89
networking
fundamentals 29, 30
networking, HFT systems 78
Network Interface Card
      (NIC) 61, 78, 141, 256
network layer
IPv4, using as 90
network TAP
about 107
active network TAP 108
passive network TAP 107
New York Stock Exchange
      (NYSE) 7, 22, 42
non-fungible tokens (NFT) 270
non-persisted memory-mapped files 144
non-uniform memory access
      (NUMA) 60, 64, 130, 224
Numerical Python (NumPy) 238

O

Open Systems Interconnection
      (OSI) model
about 30, 78
application layer 79
data link layer 79
network layer 79
physical layer 79
presentation layer 79

session layer 79
transport layer 79
operating system, for HFT system
about 65
CPU resource management 67, 68
functionalities 66
interruption management 72
kernel space 66, 67
memory management 68
paged memory 69, 70
page tables 69, 70
process scheduling 67, 68
system calls 70
threading 71
user space 66, 67
order book
best price scenario 47, 48
multiple orders, with same price 50
no match scenario 49
partial fill scenario 48
order book management
about 30, 31
amendment/modification operation 32
cancelation operation 32
considerations 32-34
insertion operation 32
order management system (OMS) 36
Order Manager 24
OUCH protocol 100
out-of-line mode
versus inline mode 244
over-the-counter (OTC) 267

P

packet capture
working 106

packet life
comprehending, in send/receive
(TX/RX) path 104, 105
packets
about 83
analysis 106
life cycle 102-104
pandas 238
parallel program
execution, scenario 226
parallel/throughput collector 207
Parasoft 199
parity checks 79
parser 82
participants, High-Frequency
Trading (HFT)
about 10
requisites 10, 11
passive network TAP 107
PCI eXtended (PCI-X) 80
perf
about 154
reference link 154
performance measurement
about 152
custom techniques, using 156
Linux tools, using 153
motivation 152, 153
performance measuring tools
characteristics 153
performance mental model 112
performance penalties, virtual functions
about 179
branch prediction 179
cache evictions and
performance 180-182
compiler optimizations 179

curiously recurring template
    pattern (CRTP) 182
prefetching 179
Run Time Type Identification
    (RTTI) 183
Peripheral Component Interconnect
    Express (PCIe) 59, 65, 80
Peripheral Component
    Interconnect (PCI) 80
perpetual futures contracts
    versus traditional futures contracts 264
persisted memory-mapped files 144
Philadelphia Stock Exchange (PHLX) 42
physical address space 69
physical layer switch 87
pinging 18
Platform as a service (PaaS) 273
portable executable (PE) file 74
pre-allocation-based alternatives, to
    dynamic memory allocation
    about 134
    memory, limiting to stack 135
    memory pools 135
Precision Time Protocol (PTP) 109
pre-emption tolerance 121
pre-fetching based alternatives,
    to boost performance
    about 131
    appropriate containers 132
    cache-friendly algorithms 132
    cache-friendly data structures 132
    implicit structure, exploiting of data 132
    spatial locality 132
    temporal locality 131
    unpredictable branches, avoiding 133
    virtual functions, avoiding 133
primitive types 210, 211
priority inheritance 122

priority inversion 122
private cloud 272
problems and inefficiencies, locks
    about 119
    application programming 120
    async signal safety 121
    convoying 122
    kill tolerance 121
    pre-emption tolerance 121
    priority inversion 122
    skill requirements, debugging 120
procedure linkage table (PLT) 75
process 67
Process Control Block (PCB) 115
processor registers 129
process scheduling
    cooperative multitasking 68
    preemptive multitasking 68
process switching latency 113
Profiler
    reference link 211
Program Counter (PC) 115
program order 167
pro-rata algorithm
    about 51, 52
    using, with other algorithms 52
protocol 89
protocols, for FIX communication
    about 96
    CME market data protocol 100
    FAST protocol 99, 100
    ITCH/OUCH protocol 100
    orders 98, 99
    price changes 96-98
public cloud 272
pulse-per-second (PPS) signals 109
PVS Studio 200

Python
    about 234
    C++ HFT libraries, working with 239
    C++, using 240
    libraries, using 238, 239
    reasons, for slow execution 236, 237
    trading strategy, building 235, 236
    using, for data analytics 234
    using, with C++ 240, 241
Python code
    accelerating, with CFFI 243, 244
    accelerating, with ctypes 243, 244
    speed, improving in HFT 246, 247
Python module
    building 246
Python virtual machine (PVM) 237

Q

quants (quantitative traders) 239
queues 227

R

Random Access Memory (RAM)
    about 62
    caches 62
    cache structure 63
ReadyNow!®
    about 213
    reference link 213
real-time performance
    measuring 220, 221
rebate strategies 18
receive (RX) buffer 104
Registered Jack-45 (RJ-45) port 81
Relaxed Ordering 174
Release-Acquire Ordering 174

Release-Consume Ordering 174, 175
Resource Acquisition Is
        Initialization (RAII) 187
retail trading platforms
    basic trading order types 263
revolutions per minute (RPM) 220
ring buffer 227
router 81
runtime decisions
    removing 176
runtime performance penalty
    about 184
    cache performance 185
    heap fragmentation 185
    heap tracking overhead 185
Run Time Type Identification
        (RTTI) 178, 183

S

scalping 15, 271
scheduler 67, 223
Scikit-learn 239
Scrapy 239
Securities and Exchange Commission
        (SEC) 6, 19, 262
Securities Information Processor (SIP) 16
Security Token Offering (STO) 267
Sequential Consistency (SC) 168-173
Serial GC 207
service-oriented architecture (SOA) 273
shared memory models
    non-uniform memory
        access (NUMA) 64
    uniform memory access (UMA) 64
shared memory systems 64
Shared Object (.so) 238

Shenandoah collector
  reference link 207
signal handlers 121
Simple Binary Encoding (SBE) 100
Simplified Wrapper and Interface
    Generator (SWIG)
  about 244, 245
  interface file, writing 245
Simulink 257
simultaneous multithreading 61
Single Producer Single Consumer
    (SPSC) 123-125
socket buffer 104
soft interrupt request (soft-IRQ) 104
Software as a service (SaaS) 273
software context switches 113
software layer
  network data, reading 105
  network data, writing 105
source code order 167
spoofing 19
spread 263
stablecoins 266
Stack Pointer register (SP) 115
Standard Template Library (STL)
  about 132, 189, 193
  performance, at runtime 194
static analysis
  about 195
  benefits 197, 198
  control flow analysis 196
  cosmetic 196
  data flow analysis 196
  design 196
  drawbacks 198, 199
  error checking 196
  failure analysis 196
  formal 196

interface analysis 196
  need for 195, 196
  predictive 196
  steps 197
  tools 199, 200
static linking 74
static polymorphism 182
statistical arbitrage 15, 16
statistics
  about 150
  infrastructure design 151
  issue 151
  need for 150
  online/live statistics computation 150
statistics collector 220
std::atomic 169, 170
std::lock_guard 169
stockbroker 46
stock exchange (exchange)
  architecture 44, 45
  features 43
  listings 43
  market data 43
  market participants 43
  matching engine 43, 46, 47
  order book 46, 47
  post-trade 43
  regulation 44
  working 46
stock shares 265
stop-the-world (STW) pause 210
store-and-forward mode 87
strategy making decisions,
    on when to trade
  about 34
  order management system (OMS) 36
Stratum 0 109
Stratum 1 109

Stratum 2 109
switch 81
switched port analyzer (SPAN) 106
switches
  forward/filter decisions 82
  packet forwarding, configuring 82
  working 82, 83
switching modes
  about 86
  cut-through switching mode 87
  store-and-forward mode 87
switch queuing 85
synchronization mechanisms
  about 119
  compare-and-swap (CAS) 119
  fetch-and-add 119
  memory barriers 119
  test-and-set 119
Syslog 231

T

Taskset
  reference link 225
Task State Segments (TSSs) 113
techniques, for avoiding/minimizing
    context switches
  threads, pinning to CPU cores 117
templates
  about 188
  class templates 189
  function templates 188
  performance 192
  variadic templates 189
templates, advantages
  compile-time polymorphism 190
  compile-time substitution 190
  development cost 190

generic programming 189
lines of code (LOC) 190
template metaprogramming 191
time 190
templates, disadvantages
  about 191
  better than C macros, and
      void pointers 190
  code bloat 192
  compiler support 191
  difficult to understand 192
  header only 191
  increased compilation times 191
  tough to debug 192
template specialization 189
test access point (TAP) 106
test-and-set 119
thread map 224, 225
thread pool
  using, with threads 222, 223
threads 221, 222
thread switching latency 113
throughput 83
tick-by-tick data 12
tick-to-order period 36
tick-to-trade period 36
Tick-To-Trade (TTT)
  about 156, 159-161
  end-to-end measurement 159
tiered compilation 219
tiered compilation, JVM 214-218
time distribution 108
time, Linux tools
  about 154
  reference link 154
timeslice 68
Time Stamp Counter (TSC) 159
time-synchronization services 109

tokens 259
Tokyo Stock Exchange (TSE) 8
tools, static analysis
  Clang Static Analyzer 200
  Cppcheck 199
  CppDepend 199
  Klocwork 199
  Parasoft 199
  PVS Studio 200
total store ordering (TSO) 168
trading
  modern era 6
  post-1930s era 5
trading API documents, examples
  reference link 29
trading as a service (TaaS)
    business model 44
trading exchange
  about 5
  architecting, for handling
    large scale orders 42
  history 42
  Gateways, connecting to 25
trading floor 5
trading pairs 266
trading strategy
  about 23
  building, in Python 235, 236
  execution part 35
  signal component 35
trading system
  about 22
  architecture 24
  building, in cloud 275
  command and control 37, 38
  critical components 36
  functional components 27

non-critical components 37
  services 38
trading system trade
  making, with exchanges 27-29
trading techniques 23
traditional futures contracts
  versus perpetual futures contracts 264
translation lookaside buffer (TLB) 70, 113
Transmission Control Protocol (TCP)
  about 29, 30, 79, 141
  for transport layer 92, 93
Turbo Boost 156

U

UDP for Orders (UFO) 93
unicast mode 90, 91
uniform memory access (UMA) 64
unique identifier (UID) 104
User Datagram Protocol (UDP)
  about 29, 30, 79, 141, 221
  for transport layer 92, 93
user space
  versus kernel space 139, 140

V

valgrind
  about 155
  URL 155
variadic templates 189
VeChain Token (VET) 266
venues 24
virtual address space 69
virtual dynamic shared object (vDSO) 71
virtual functions
  about 178
  working 178

virtualization layer 274
virtual memory space 113
virtual table 178
visibility 170, 171
Visual VM
  URL 211
Vitis 257
Vivado 257

W

wide area network (WAN) 90
wire 29
WireDirect/TCP Offload Engine
    (TOE) APIs 142

Z

Z GC
  reference link 207

`Packt.com`

Subscribe to our online digital library for full access to over 7,000 books and videos, as well as industry leading tools to help you plan your personal development and advance your career. For more information, please visit our website.

Why subscribe?

- Spend less time learning and more time coding with practical eBooks and Videos from over 4,000 industry professionals

- Improve your learning with Skill Plans built especially for you

- Get a free eBook or video every month

- Fully searchable for easy access to vital information

- Copy and paste, print, and bookmark content

Did you know that Packt offers eBook versions of every book published, with PDF and ePub files available? You can upgrade to the eBook version at `packt.com` and as a print book customer, you are entitled to a discount on the eBook copy. Get in touch with us at `customercare@packtpub.com` for more details.

At `www.packt.com`, you can also read a collection of free technical articles, sign up for a range of free newsletters, and receive exclusive discounts and offers on Packt books and eBooks.

Other Books You May Enjoy

If you enjoyed this book, you may be interested in these other books by Packt:

Learn Algorithmic Trading

Sebastien Donadio and Sourav Ghosh

ISBN: 9781789348347

- Understand the components of modern algorithmic trading systems and strategies

- Apply machine learning in algorithmic trading signals and strategies using Python

- Build, visualize and analyze trading strategies based on mean reversion, trend, economic releases and more

- Quantify and build a risk management system for Python trading strategies

- Build a backtester to run simulated trading strategies for improving the performance of your trading bot

- Deploy and incorporate trading strategies in the live market to maintain and improve profitability

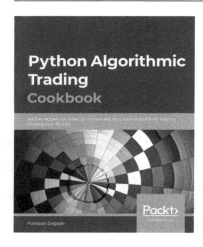

Python Algorithmic Trading Cookbook

Pushpak Dagade

ISBN: 9781838989354

- Use Python to set up connectivity with brokers

- Handle and manipulate time series data using Python

- Fetch a list of exchanges, segments, financial instruments, and historical data to interact with the real market

- Understand, fetch, and calculate various types of candles and use them to compute and plot diverse types of technical indicators

- Develop and improve the performance of algorithmic trading strategies

- Perform backtesting and paper trading on algorithmic trading strategies

- Implement real trading in the live hours of stock markets

Packt is searching for authors like you

If you're interested in becoming an author for Packt, please visit authors. packtpub.com and apply today. We have worked with thousands of developers and tech professionals, just like you, to help them share their insight with the global tech community. You can make a general application, apply for a specific hot topic that we are recruiting an author for, or submit your own idea.

Share Your Thoughts

Now you've finished *Developing High-Frequency Trading Systems*, we'd love to hear your thoughts! Scan the QR code below to go straight to the Amazon review page for this book and share your feedback or leave a review on the site that you purchased it from.

https://packt.link/r/1-803-24281-7

Your review is important to us and the tech community and will help us make sure we're delivering excellent quality content.